Competing Discourses: Perspective and Ideology in Language

Real Language Series

General Editors:
Jennifer Coates, Roehampton Institute, London,
Jenny Cheshire, Universities of Fribourg and Neuchâtel,
and
Euan Reid, Institute of Education, University of London.

Titles in the series:

Competing Discourses:
Perspective and Ideology in Language

David Lee

Senior Lecturer in English
University of Queensland

LONGMAN
London and New York

Longman Group UK Limited,
Longman House, Burnt Mill, Harlow,
Essex CM20 2JE, England
and Associated Companies throughout the world.

*Published in the United States of America
by Longman Publishing, New York*

First published 1992

British Library Cataloguing-in-Publication Data
Lee, David Alan
     Competing discourses: Perspective and ideology in
     language. – (Real language series)
     I. Title   II. Series
     306.4

     ISBN 0–582–07850–4 ppr
     ISBN 0–582–07849–0 csd

Library of Congress Cataloging in Publication Data
Lee, David (David A.)
     Competing discourses : language and ideology / David Lee.
        p.   cm. -- (Real language series)
     Includes bibliographical references and index.
     ISBN 0–582–07849–0 (cased). -- ISBN 0–582–07850–4 (paper)
     1. Language and languages.   2. Discourse analysis.   3. Ideology.
     I. Title.   II. Series
     P106.L335   1991
     401'.41--dc20   91–12999
                                                                   CIP

Set 7R in Sabon

Produced by Longman Singapore Publishers (Pte) Ltd
Printed in Singapore

To Sheila, Vicky, Debbie and Cathy

Contents

Preface

The nature of the relationship between language, perspective and ideology is a question that has long aroused the interest of a wide audience – not only linguists but philosophers, anthropologists, sociologists, psychologists, semioticians, communication theorists and literary theorists. In modern linguistics, the question has had something of a chequered history. The topic was implicit in the Saussurean concept of the linguistic sign, as we shall see in the discussion of Saussure in Chapter 2, but did not receive serious attention from linguists, with the exception of Whorf and Sapir, until relatively recently. This stems largely from the need felt by many linguists to establish the subject as an autonomous discipline and the consequent focus on the development of the theoretical apparatus oriented to the description and explanation of language structure as opposed to language function. There has of course been a continuing tradition within the field concerned with the social functions of language. However, the apparently spectacular successes of the structuralists, particularly those achieved by generative grammar, have tended to overshadow approaches to the subject that were more concerned with the role of language in social processes. Moreover, the emphasis on structure has led to the notion of a linguistic code that existed and could be studied somewhat independently of its social context.

The recent resurgence of interest in the social function of language is due to a widespread feeling that language is such an integral part of the social process that to abstract away from this is to distort the subject matter of linguistic enquiry. Recent developments in sociolinguistics have shown, however, that there are many ways of approaching the question. One of the most influential methodologies (pioneered by William Labov) has focused on variation in the phonological, morphological and syntactic components of the linguistic system, correlating sociolinguistic patterns defined in quantitative terms with such components of social identity as social class, context, gender, region, age, ethnicity and so on. Other strands of work in the field – particularly in the ethnography of communication – postulate a rather different kind of relationship between language and society. Instead of seeing language as a mirror of autonomous social structures, this approach takes linguistic practices to be the primary medium through which social processes operate. Social and institutional diversity is established and perpetuated through diversity in linguistic usage, different 'ways of speaking'. This view is essentially the one to which the argument of this book is directed.

The first two chapters have an introductory role. Chapter 1 is concerned with those general properties of language that are relevant to the basic argument and Chapter 2 with historical sources and current perspectives on crucial issues, particularly concerning the nature of conceptual categories. The third chapter addresses two literary texts, focusing particularly on William Golding's novel *The Inheritors*. This work provides a striking example of the thesis that a particular language does not encode a unitary, homogeneous conceptual orientation, as some interpreters of Whorf have suggested. The text is constructed on a way of using English that mediates a quite idiosyncratic world-view – one that diverges quite significantly from our familiar modes of perception. Thus the chapter introduces the notion of 'discourse' as a 'way of speaking' (in the sense in which this term is used in the ethnography of communication). Discourse is defined here simultaneously in both formal terms (its lexical and grammatical characteristics) and in semantic terms – as a cluster of types of meaning that are systematic reflexes of a specific way of making sense of the world.

Chapter 4 highlights the crucial role of metaphor in the process of classification, and develops the thesis that language is essentially a heterogeneous phenomenon. Metaphor is not a process that is confined to the literary language but has a vital part in the everyday production of meaning. It also plays an important role in providing alternative ways of integrating experiences into our conceptual frameworks and in enabling language to adapt to an ever-changing world. The following chapters develop the notion of discourse by showing how particular ideologies operate through specific linguistic practices. Chapter 5 is concerned with European perspectives on Africa, illustrated in newspaper reports, and Chapter 6 with discursive practices involved in the construction of gender.

The following two chapters develop the concept of discursive interaction. Chapter 7 engages in the close analysis of a literary text (the first chapter of Jane Austen's *Emma*) and a non-literary text – a letter from a university Head of Department to the members of his department. In the first case we focus on the linguistic reflexes of the tension between contrasting perspectives on the central character, primarily involving that area of meaning usually called 'modality'. The second example illustrates the interaction between conflicting discourses deriving from social and institutional tensions in the local context – an interaction that also operates mainly through modality. Chapter 8 considers a number of texts (again both literary and non-literary) in which ideological or social tensions and contrasts work themselves out through linguistic variation. Chapter 9 draws the various strands of the argument together.

One of the aims of the book is to move across a number of traditional divisions – between spoken and written texts, between 'high' and 'low' genres, between 'language' and 'literature', and between different traditions within linguistics itself (in particular between variation theory and the ethnography of communication). The concept of discourse crosses all these boundaries.

Textual exemplification plays a central role. The argument is constructed through the analysis of a wide variety of texts: conversations, literary materials, newspaper reports, editorials, official memoranda and television commercials. It is in textual structure that we see in operation all the processes of negotiation and contestation that are central to the ongoing production and development of meaning.

The general argument owes a great deal to Gunther Kress. The research which he pioneered into language and ideology in the 1970s together with a group of colleagues (particularly Bob Hodge) at the University of East Anglia and which he has developed since his return to Australia in 1976 has been a constant source of stimulation. I wish to express my gratitude to the editors of this series – Jenny Cheshire, Jennifer Coates (to whom I owe the title) and Euan Reid for their generous help and advice. I am also most grateful to Anne Freadman and Anna Shnukal for their detailed comments on an earlier version and to Helen Tiffin for bringing my attention to the relevance of post-colonial literature to the general themes of this book. Needless to say, none of these scholars bears any responsibility for its shortcomings. On a personal level, I owe a great deal to my wife, Sheila, and to my daughters Vicky, Debbie and Cathy. They have shown enormous patience and I dedicate the book to them wholeheartedly.

David Lee
University of Queensland
July, 1991

Acknowledgements

We are grateful to the following for permission to reproduce copyright material and tradenames:

Barilla G. e R. Filli for the tradename 'Barilla' & text material; Adlink International Ltd for an extract from editorial material in 'Daily News' Tanzania 3.6.75; Elida Gibbs Ltd for the tradenames 'Impulse' & 'Incognito' both (c) Unilever plc; King's College, Cambridge & The Society of Authors as the literary representatives of the E.M. Forster Estate for an extract from *A Passage to India*; Henkel KGaA for the tradename 'dato'; Kodak Ltd for the tradename 'Kodak'; L'Oreal for the tradenames 'Dedicace' & 'Aquavital'; Mars G.B. Ltd for the tradename 'Whiskas'; Master Foods for the tradename 'Dolmio'; Mobil Oil Co Ltd for the tradename 'Mobil'; Mouton de Gruyter, a division of Walter de Gruyter & Co for the article by David Lee in *Multilingua* 10,3 1991 on which ch.8 part 2 'Variety, discourse, ideology' is based; The Nestle Group for the registered tradenames 'Ambiance', 'Nescafe' & 'Findus'; Proctor & Gamble Ltd for the tradenames 'Ariel', 'Arielette' & 'Topexan'; Showbox Photoservice for the tradename 'Showbox' & text material; Times Newspapers Ltd for extracts from articles in *The Times* 2.6.75 & 3.6.75. © Times Newspapers Ltd 1975

1 *Classification and Selection*

Classification

The main aim of this first chapter is to identify some of the most important properties of human language that enable it to function as a mediator of world-view. We will focus in particular on the role of classification and selection in linguistic encoding and decoding. The imposition of structure on our raw experiences through these processes is closely bound up with questions of perspective. The thesis that coding creates reality rather than simply reporting it will be illustrated in discussion of two short texts, one literary, one non-literary, which provide an illustration of the operation of ideological factors in interpretation.

One of the main reasons why language is so closely bound up with world-view has to do with the classificatory function of language. Language can be seen as a tool for the classification of our experience of the world in many different ways and at many different levels. At a very basic level, individual words are clearly classificatory devices. In order to be able to use appropriately the English word *dog*, for example, the child acquiring English has to identify a very disparate range of phenomena, including poodles, Dalmatians, Alsatians, as all belonging in some sense to a single category. The task is far from straightforward, since in some ways the linguistic categories appear rather arbitrary. In many respects, an Alsatian resembles a wolf much more closely than it resembles a poodle, for example. Some insight into the problematic nature of the task of discovering the precise nature of the fit between language and the world is provided by the process of 'overextension' in child language development. This term refers to the process whereby young children use words such as *dog, apple, ball, moon, fish, cow, ketchup* and so on to refer to a much wider range of phenomena than do adults. For example, one child used the word *cow* not only for a picture of a cow but also for a horse, a reindeer, a zebra, a camel, a buffalo, an elephant, a polar bear, a kangaroo, a gorilla and some ants! Another used *apple* not only for an apple but also for a banana, a lemon, a strawberry, a cherry, an orange, a pear, a tomato, an onion, a red ball, an artichoke, a round biscuit, a ball lamp, a ball of soap, a solid oval and a teapot (Thomson and Chapman 1977: 364–5).[1]

Nouns are not the only words that classify the phenomena of experience. Consider, for example, a verb like *climb*, which is used to denote a wide variety of situations. When you climb a ladder, you perform quite different actions from those involved in climbing a rope and there is very little in common between these situations and those of a plane climbing into the sky or a spider climbing across a web. *Climb* can also be used to refer to downward movement (*She climbed down the rock face*). It might even denote a situation in which there is no movement at all, as when I use a sentence such as *See how the ivy climbs up to that window* to describe what is in effect a static situation.

Many adjectives illustrate the same point. The meaning of *strong* varies considerably across expressions such as *a strong horse, a strong cup of tea* and *a strong possibility*. There is nothing about the notion of physical strength that necessarily links it to the notion of 'degree of concentration' as this applies to a cup of tea or to the meaning 'highly probable' as expressed by the phrase *a strong possibility*. This is not to say that the meanings in question are unrelated (a question to which we will return in Chapter 4, where we discuss the role of metaphor in ordinary language). But the fact that a single word can be used to cover this particular range of meanings would seem odd to speakers of many other languages.

The point that language imposes a classificatory scheme on the observed phenomena of experience is illustrated not only by lexical entities but also by grammatical elements. Consider, for example, the difference in English between the present perfect construction and the simple past tense. When we wish to refer to an event that occurred in some period of past time, the grammar of English forces us to choose between a present perfect form such as *John has found the money* and a simple past such as *John found the money*. We tend to use the former if the event in question relates to the present situation in some way (hence the tendency to use it for very recent events), whereas the latter is used if the event is thought of as being unconnected with the present. Since (with minor exceptions) one of these forms has to be used for events in past time, we can say that the grammar of English **forces** speakers to divide events in past time into two categories – those that impinge on the present and those that do not. Not all languages do this, even those that have a similar formal contrast. German, for example, has both a perfect tense and a simple past tense, but they are not used in the same way – hence the considerable difficulties experienced by German learners in the appropriate use of these forms in English. It is not that native speakers of German find difficulty in distinguishing between the two kinds of event in past time. It is simply that their acquired habits of language usage have not accustomed them to encode this distinction linguistically.

The notion of language as a classificatory instrument also applies at a more general level than that of individual lexemes and grammatical elements. For example, there is a sense in which the grammatical systems of all human languages are constructed around two very basic types of conceptual unit – physical objects and actions. It seems not unreasonable, therefore, to suggest that these two general categories constitute the basic building blocks of our world-view. It should be emphasised, however, that this claim is not based on the simplistic idea that the grammatical categories of 'noun' and 'verb' can be equated in a straightforward way with the semantic categories of 'physical object' and 'action'.

The nature of the relationship between the level of meaning and the level of grammar is one that is crucial for our general argument and we will return to it on a number of occasions. At this point it is useful to establish an important methodological principle. When we consider the nature of the relationship between grammatical and semantic categories, we need to make an initial distinction between two levels of grammatical analysis – the language-particular level and the language-general level (Huddleston 1984: 74–6). At the language-particular level, the category of nouns includes not only those words denoting physical objects such as *stone, table, house, tree* but also many words denoting actions and events (*arrival, destruction, disappearance, collision*) as well as others denoting more abstract concepts (*joy, charm, weakness, truth*). The characteristics that identify all of these words as nouns in English concern their grammatical properties rather than their meaning.

For example, the fact that they all inflect for plurality, the fact that they take determinatives (such as *the*, *a*, *this*, *each*) and adjectives as dependents and the fact that the type of phrase which they head fills a particular set of clause functions such as Subject and Object (for full discussion see Huddleston 1984: ch. 6).[2]

The language-general level is concerned with the naming of grammatical classes, once these have been established for each language on the basis of language-particular criteria. It is at this level that the semantic categories of 'physical object' and 'action' make an important contribution to the definition of metatheoretical terms such as 'noun' and 'verb'. The important point here is that the grammatical systems of human languages are organised in such a way that the vast majority of words denoting physical objects in any language are typically to be found in one class (defined by a distinctive set of language-particular grammatical properties) and the vast majority of words denoting actions are to be found in another (defined by a different set). It is in this sense that we can say that grammatical systems are organised around the semantic categories of physical object and action.

Even at the language-particular level there is a sense in which the nouns that denote physical objects, such as *chair* and *table* in English, are more central members of the noun category than nouns which denote other types of concept such as *arrival* (an event) or *willingness* (an attribute). In the first place *chair* and *table* each consist of a single morpheme. *Arrival* and *willingness*, on the other hand, are morphologically complex, both of them being 'derived' by the morphological process of suffixation from the simple stems *arrive* and *willing*.[3] The second point is that all English words that denote concrete objects belong in this particular word-class, whereas this is not true of those that denote actions or events (most are verbs), nor of those that denote attributes (mostly adjectives). A third point concerning *willingness* is that it does not inflect for plurality and this applies to many other nouns denoting abstract concepts (*aggressiveness*, *determination*, *readiness*, *likelihood*). In other words, membership of the noun category is not an all-or-nothing matter but a gradient phenomenon. *Chair* and *table* are central or prototypical members of the category; *arrival* is slightly less prototypical because of its morphological character and its semantic properties; *willingness* is a peripheral member of the category. Whereas all these words are nouns, some are more 'nouny' than others. The claim that category membership is a gradient phenomenon is important, in that it applies not only to grammatical categories but also to semantic ones. We will develop this point as the book proceeds.

The fact that certain members of the noun category in English denote entities and concepts that are not physical objects raises a question relating to world-view. Consider concepts such as *storm, wave, lightning, wind*. In many languages the words denoting these concepts behave like verbs (Whorf 1971d: 215). Thus, in these languages there are structures such as *It is storming in the West, The sea is waving violently today, It is winding strongly outside*. These structures are impossible in English because the grammar of English treats the corresponding words as nouns. We therefore express the corresponding meanings by constructing sentences around Noun Phrases – *There's **a storm** in the West, **The waves** are rough today, There is **a strong wind** outside*. The obvious question is whether the fact that the grammar treats these words as nouns causes speakers of English to think of the corresponding concepts as objects. A small piece of evidence suggesting that this is so is the fact that many beginning linguistics students fail to see any problem in these examples for the traditional definition of nouns as words that refer to 'people, places or things'.

One point about words such as *storm, wave, wind* and so on is that the corresponding concepts do resemble physical objects in certain ways. Waves, for example, have certain characteristics of shape, size and weight that relate them to physical objects, so that their inclusion in the noun class in English does have some semantic motivation. In other respects, however, they are much more like events. One would suspect that speakers of those languages in which these concepts are treated as verbs are much more sensitive to their event-like characteristics than to their object-like characteristics. It is also worth noting in this connection that, whereas grammatical categories tend to be relatively clear-cut, semantic categories are often much more problematic. There is no doubt that the word *lightning*, for example, is a noun in English but it is much less clear that the phenomenon in question is a 'thing'. This discrepancy between the status of grammatical and semantic categories is fundamental to the argument of this book, since one of our main themes has to do with the nature of the fit between language and the world.

A related question arises in English with respect to a grammatical process known as 'nominalisation'. We noted above a distinction between 'basic' nouns such as *chair, stone, table* on the one hand and *arrival, destruction, disappearance* on the other, such that the latter are seen as being in some sense 'derived' from words that are basically verbs. There is an analogue to this situation in the domain of syntax. Thus, consider a sentence such as *Max commented on the dessert*, which clearly denotes an event. The grammar of English makes available an alternative grammatical structure for referring to this event: *Max's comment on the dessert*, a structure that is generally referred to as a 'nominalised' form of the sentence (or clause) *Max commented on the dessert*. The nominalised form is generally used when speakers wish to express complex propositions containing embedded propositions. Thus, if I wish to refer to the event 'Max commented on the dessert' and say of this event that it surprised me, one way of expressing this complex proposition is to use the nominalised form (*Max's comment on the dessert surprised me*).

Again, the general question is whether a nominalised form leads us to conceptualise the event in question as a kind of thing – i.e. whether the grammatical process of nominalisation is associated with the semantic process of 'reification'.[4] This view is far from implausible. In the case of the example cited, when somebody makes 'a comment' by uttering certain words, it is very easy to conceptualise the proposition in question as a kind of object which they have produced. There are all kinds of ways in English of talking about speech acts that support this view: *your announcement, my remark, John's speech, their suggestion, his advice* and so on. In other words, English speakers have a general conceptual framework relating to speech acts, such that they are naturally conceptualised as a kind of object.

The situation is in fact even more general than this, since the process of reification can apply not only to speech acts but to most actions. Thus if John kicks a goal, it is possible to refer to this event as *John's goal*, as if it too were a kind of object. We can also apply the same kind of attributes to many actions that we apply to objects – *a long kick, a high catch, a heavy fall, a light punch, a narrow escape*.

One important area of meaning that is encoded in the grammars of all languages is the notion of agentivity and the related notion of causality. These concepts belong to the area of relational meaning rather than referential meaning (Lee 1986: 8–10). Thus in (1) below the words *dog*, *chased* and *bird* are referential elements, designating specific elements of the situation, objects or action, whereas the notion of agentivity applies to the **relation** between 'dog' and 'chase'.

(1)   *The dog chased the bird*

The notion of agent is typically encoded in English by word order. The concept of 'patient' is also a relational meaning, involving 'bird' and 'chase' in (1), and it too is normally expressed in English by word order. Many languages encode these meanings inflectionally. Examples (2) and (3) illustrate this point in Latin.

(2)   *Necavit Caesarem Brutus* ('Brutus killed Caesar')
(3)   *Necavit Caesar Brutum* ('Caesar killed Brutus')

The different roles of the two main participants, Caesar and Brutus, are marked not by word order but by different inflectional markers on the words that refer to them.

Again, the fact that the notion of agentivity is encoded universally indicates that the concept is fundamental to the human world-view.[5] Thus, not only are categories such as physical object and action the fundamental building blocks of the human world-view but so are the relational concepts that bind them together. (In Chapter 3 we will consider a world-view in which the notion of agentivity differs markedly from our own.) Note, however, that the question of whether a particular situation is encoded as an agentive or as a non-agentive event is often a matter of perspective and interpretation, rather than an 'objective' property of the situation (Kress and Hodge 1979: 19–20, Kress 1985: 34). Suppose, for example, that I pick up a vase and it drops out of my fingers, smashing on the ground. An observer might report the event in agentive terms, using a form of words that suggests I did something to the vase (*You dropped the vase*), whereas I might report it non-agentively (*The vase fell out of my hands*). There are clearly differences of interpretation here concerning the extent of my responsibility for the event. Similarly, although *Bill sold the car to Jack* and *Jack bought the car from Bill* may report what is at some level the 'same' event, there are differences in terms of how the speaker sees the situation, relating to the question of which participant is perceived as the main instigator or agent of the transaction.

Some ways of reporting an event create a certain degree of vagueness or ambiguity about whether the event is being reported in agentive or non-agentive terms. Thus, if I say *The vase was broken*, it is unclear whether I am reporting an event that I believe to have been caused by some unknown agent, or whether I am reporting a state of affairs. This ambiguity arises from the fact that past participle forms of verbs such as *broken* have grammatical properties that relate them to adjectives. And, as we noted above, whereas verbs typically denote actions, adjectives typically denote states. In semantic terms, the ambiguity is connected with the fact that actions give rise to states of affairs, so that in many cases, the boundary between the action and the ensuing state may be far from clear. These issues bear on the process of categorisation in the sense that the decision to treat an event as agentive or non-agentive, as an action or as a state, is a classificatory question. In analysing a number of texts in this and subsequent chapters, we will argue that decisions of this kind are often connected with very general considerations relating to speaker- or addressee-perspective.

Selectivity

Given that language is an instrument for the assignment of the phenomena of human experience to conceptual categories, it is clearly not simply a mirror that reflects reality. Rather, its function is to impose structure on our perceptions of the world. Language is also highly selective and in this sense, too, the process of linguistic encoding involves a significant degree of abstraction away from 'reality'.

> A sentence is not a verbal snapshot or movie of an event. In framing an utterance, you have to abstract away from everything you know, or can picture, about a situation, and present a schematic version which conveys the essentials. In terms of grammatical marking, there is not enough time in the speech situation for any language to allow for the marking of everything which could possibly be significant to the message. Probably there is not enough interest, either.

Language *evokes* ideas; it does not represent them. Linguistic expression is thus *not* a natural map of consciousness or thought. It is a highly selective and conventionally schematic map. At the heart of language use is the tacit assumption that most of the message can be left unsaid, because of mutual understanding (and probably also mutual impatience). The subset of semantic notions which is formally marked in a particular language serves more to guide the listener to the appropriate segments and categories of analysis than to fully represent the underlying notions. The task facing the child learner is to determine which particular subset of notions receives formal marking in his or her language, and to discover the means for projecting these notions onto utterances. (Slobin 1982: 131–2)

In illustration of this point let us consider one of Slobin's examples, elaborating on it somewhat. Consider a child who, seeing her father kick a ball, says *Daddy kicked the ball*. This utterance encodes only a tiny part of the event as perceived by the speaker. It does not encode, for example, any information about how long before the time of utterance the action took place – it may have happened just a few seconds before or several hours or days ago. Nor does it encode information about the shape of the ball (whether it was a soccer or rugby ball, for example). In some languages both of these items of information are encoded obligatorily. Many East African languages have two distinct past tenses – one for events in the recent past, the other for events in the more distant past. And in the Amerindian language Navaho there is a system for subclassifying nouns according to the shape (and other attributes) of the object which the noun denotes.

If I ask you in Navaho to hand me an object, I must use the appropriate verb stem depending on the nature of the object. If it is a long flexible object such as a piece of string, I must say *saléh*; if it is a long rigid object such as a stick, I must say *santíih*; if it is a flat flexible material such as paper or cloth, I must say *sanilcóós* and so on. (Carroll and Casagrande 1958: 27)

It is interesting to note that for many native speakers, subtle grammatical distinctions of this kind operate below the level of conscious awareness.

Although most Navaho-speaking children . . . used these forms unerringly, they were unable to tell why they used a particular form with any particular object. Even though a child could not name an object, or may not have seen one like it before, in most cases he used the correct verb form according to the nature of the object. (Carroll and Casagrande 1958: 27)

We will return to this point in Chapter 2 when we discuss further examples of such 'covert' (or subconscious) grammatical categories.

Another characteristic of the situation not encoded in the example is the question as to whether the event was actually seen by the speaker or whether the statement is based on another's report. Again, the distinction between these two situations is built into the grammatical system of some languages such as Turkish, in that the use of one form of the verb indicates that the statement is based on speaker observation, whereas the use of a contrasting form indicates that the basis is hearsay (Slobin 1982: 135). Since the system forces the speaker to make a choice between the two contrasting forms, the question of the evidential status of the utterance cannot be ignored in Turkish, though this information is not relevant to grammatical encoding in English.

This is only the tip of the iceberg, however. Most aspects of a situation are not normally encoded in an utterance in **any** language. The utterance *Daddy kicked the ball* does not express any information about the colour of 'Daddy's' eyes, what kind of clothes he was wearing, how tall he was, whether he kicked the ball with his left or right foot, what colour the ball was and so on, even though all of these features (and many more) were real properties of the situation. The speaker judges, however, that most of this information is of no interest. The information **could**, of course, be encoded, if the speaker judged it to be significant. But no matter how much was said, the situation could never be described exhaustively. Clearly there is ample scope for factors relating to ideology or perspective to influence the selections made on a particular occasion. The lexical and grammatical systems of languages play some role here in encouraging (and in some cases **forcing**) speakers to select certain features for encoding and to pay less attention to others.

Processes of selection apply not only to the identification of elements for encoding but also to the way in which these are presented. All languages provide mechanisms for highlighting certain elements and backgrounding others, for example. In English some of these mechanisms are illustrated in the following examples.

   (4) *The dog chased the bird*
   (5) *It was the dog that chased the bird*
   (6) *It was the bird that the dog chased*
   (7) *What the dog did to the bird was chase it*
   (8) *What the dog did was chase the bird*
   (9) *What happened to the bird was that the dog chased it*
  (10) *The bird was chased by the dog*
  (11) *It was the bird that was chased by the dog*
  (12) *It was the dog that the bird was chased by*

Grammatically these possibilities are usually described in the same kind of terms that were used above to describe nominalised structures. That is, we make a distinction between a basic structure such as (4) and the non-basic structures (5)–(12). The latter are described as being 'derived' from the basic structure by a number of grammatical processes. (5) and (6), for example, are derived from (4) by a grammatical process called 'Cleft' (Huddleston 1984: 17). The Cleft rule picks out one of the non-verbal elements in the basic structure (*the dog* or *the bird* in (4)) and incorporates it into a main clause of the form *It was X that/which* . . . , attaching the remainder of the original structure to this 'new' structure as a subordinate clause. Other variants of the Cleft process are available for selecting out the verbal element, giving examples (7)–(9). A third process, Passivisation, can also apply to the basic structure, deriving (10). One important advantage of this approach is that we do not then need to postulate additional processes in order to deal with (11) and (12). These are accounted for by the interaction between Passivisation and Cleft.

The function of processes such as Cleft and Passivisation is to enable the speaker to place certain elements in focus and others in the background. The existence of processes of this kind in English (and of related processes in other languages) points to an important aspect of interpersonal communication in general. The processes of selection and arrangement that are involved in encoding are strongly influenced by speaker judgements concerning what we might call the 'knowledge base' of the addressee (Moore and Carling 1982: 11). Thus, if the speaker assumes that the addressee already knows that the dog chased something and the new information is that this was the bird, then it would be more natural to use (6) than (5). On the other hand, (5) would be the more appropriate response if the new information was that the animal responsible for chasing the bird was the dog rather than, say, the cat. In the spoken language the choice of intonational emphasis (whether we say *The dog chased the **bird***, or *The **dog** chased the bird*, for example) is governed by factors of this kind.

This is a crucial point of very general significance. Every utterance that we produce is shaped by our evaluation of the position from which addressees view the situation as well as by our own perspective. In other words, our utterances are designed to interact with the knowledge, presuppositions, attitudes, prejudices of our audience, as we perceive them. Even more significantly, we often use linguistic processes to **construct** a viewpoint for addressees and **assign** them to it. Thus, if I say *What annoys me about what you've just said* . . . , the information that I am annoyed may in fact be new information as far as my addressee is concerned but the form of my utterance suggests that the information is in some sense 'given'. This is a rhetorical device which can be extremely effective in putting my addressee on the defensive. In a quite subtle way it conveys the message 'Surely you knew that this would annoy me' and therefore functions not only as a statement but also as a reproach.

There are many other grammatical devices that can be used to achieve the same sort of effect. One such involves the use of a definite rather than an indefinite Noun Phrase. If I announce in the middle of a meeting *The problem with Ken's argument* . . . , my use of the definite article suggests that everybody present already knows that there is a problem. These devices owe their rhetorical effect to the fact that it is often much more persuasive to **assume** that one's audience holds a particular view than to attempt to persuade them into it by explicit argument.

There is one further point that we need to make about selectivity here. Some of the crucial factors affecting the choice of forms of encoding have to do with social factors, which may be highly relevant to issues concerned with perspective or ideology. At the very highest level, the question of which language is to be chosen as the medium of encoding is often a function of factors of this kind. A few years ago, I had occasion to consult a solicitor in the North Wales town of Bangor, where I was living. At one point during the consultation, the solicitor needed to telephone my bank manager. The conversation opened and was carried on for some minutes in Welsh. When it became necessary to engage me in the conversation, the solicitor made the suggestion that the conversation might switch into English (I am not a Welsh speaker). There were clearly a number of reasons for the initial use of Welsh in this case, some of which could be said to be ideological in an informal sense. The main factor operating here was clearly the general feeling among Welsh speakers that language is a crucial marker of personal and national identity and that Welsh people have the right to use the language as the normal medium of personal interaction in their daily lives. In this context the use of Welsh functions as a symbol of community solidarity, English as a marker of distance. Examples of this kind, where the selection of encoding medium is crucially bound up with social meaning, could be illustrated from many communities around the world (Fasold 1984: ch. 6, Wardhaugh 1986: ch. 4).

At a slightly lower level, the same point also applies to the choice of language variety. In German-speaking Switzerland, for example, local varieties of Swiss German function as an important marker of Swiss identity in opposition to that of the Federal Republic of Germany. Although the standard variety of High German is in widespread use in Switzerland, particularly in formal contexts, the use of this variety can be quite alienating. These attitudes have a long history. Already in 1914 the Swiss poet Carl Spitteler was regarded with some irony by his fellow-Swiss, since he constantly exhorted them to be less pro-German in their attitudes yet consistently used High German whilst doing so (Steinberg 1976: 105). We will illustrate these points in more detail in Chapter 8.

Processes of socially governed selectivity are also found within a particular variety. Many languages have different stylistic levels, the choice between them being governed by formality of context.

In Javanese it is nearly impossible to say anything without indicating the social relationship between the speaker and the listener in terms of status and familiarity . . . A number of words (and some affixes) are made to carry in addition to their normal linguistic meaning what might be called a 'status meaning'; i.e., when used in actual conversation they convey not only their fixed denotative meaning 'house', 'body', 'eat', 'walk', 'you', 'passive voice' but also a connotative meaning concerning the status of (and/or degree of familiarity between) the speaker and the listener. As a result, several words may denote the same normal linguistic meaning but differ in the status connotation they convey. Thus, for 'house' we have three forms (*omah*, *grija*, and *dalem*), each connotating a progressively higher status of the listener with respect to the speaker. Some normal linguistic meanings are even more finely divided (*kowe*, *sampejan*, *pandjenengan*, *pandjenengan dalem*, for ascending values of 'you'), others less (*di-* and *dipun-*) for the passive voice. (Geertz 1960: 248)

In English there are particular ways of speaking associated with particular social contexts – the kind of language used in a sermon, for example, is normally quite different from that employed by the after-dinner speaker. At a still more delicate level, there are linguistic choices that correlate with very specific features of context, for example the opposition between *tu* and *vous* in French, which relates to the nature of the speaker-addressee relationship. Again it is important to emphasise that in all these ways language does not simply **reflect** the nature of the social situation in which it is embedded. In many respects language **constitutes** that situation. For example, if I were a French speaker, I might use *vous* in order to distance myself from someone with whom I had previously used *tu* – after a quarrel, perhaps. In this case language would be one of the mechanisms functioning to **create** and **perpetuate** an estranged relationship rather than simply reflecting it.

Texts

Blainey: *A Land Half Won*

Let us now examine two short texts, illustrating some of the main points made in this introductory discussion. The first is an extract from a book by the Australian academic historian Geoffrey Blainey, cited in Kress 1989: 459.

Blainey is the author of a number of studies of Aboriginal history and therefore speaks from a position of some authority within the Australian establishment. In recent years, he has moved into the arena of public political debate with a number of controversial statements on issues related to immigration and multiculturalism. He has argued in particular that tighter controls should be imposed on what he calls 'Asian immigration'.

Blainey's text needs to be read in the light of an opposition between the terms *settlement* and *invasion* as ways of referring to the European incursion into Australia that began towards the end of the eighteenth century. It has been customary in general Australian discourses for this incursion to be referred to as *European settlement*. This is obviously in harmony with an ideology which sees the process in terms of Europeans arriving in a land that was essentially wild, uncultivated and unproductive.[6] There is an interesting ambiguity in the word *settle* in this context. On the one hand there are meanings associated primarily with the notion of habitation. The term *European settlement* suggests that the land was for all practical purposes uninhabited when the First Fleet made landfall, so that the arrival of the Europeans converted the land into a place that was 'settled' in the sense of 'inhabited'. On the other hand, there are also meanings associated with peacefulness and stability. To refer to the European migration as *settlement* implies that the process brought peace to Australia.

These meanings are of course quite unacceptable to Aboriginal people (and indeed to many white Australians). In recent times, the expression *European invasion* has emerged as a rival to *European settlement*. Whether speakers use *settlement* or *invasion* now provides some indication of their political viewpoint. In the following text, however, Blainey attempts to undermine the opposition between these terms by referring to the incursions of Aboriginal peoples into the territories of their neighbours in both pre- and post-colonial times as *invasions*.

In central Australia . . . the Pitjantjatjara were driven by drought to expand into the territory of a neighbour. Several of these invasions might be partly explained by a domino theory: the coastal invasion of the whites initially pushing over one black domino which in turn pushed down other dominoes. But it would be sensible to believe that dominoes were also rising and falling occasionally during the centuries of black history. We should be wary of whitewash-

ing the white invasion. We should also be wary of the idea that Aus-
tralia knew no black invasions. (Blainey 1980: 88–9)

In setting up the concept of 'black invasions', Blainey is attempting here to challenge one aspect of the perspective expressed by the concept of 'European invasion of Australia'. Essentially the issue is a classificatory one. The basic question is whether Aboriginal incursions into neighbours' territories are to be perceived as the same kind of phenomenon as the general European incursion into Australia. Clearly if this mode of classification is accepted, the uniqueness of the European incursion in Australian history is undermined. It then takes its place as just one of a long series of 'invasions', perpetrated by both blacks and whites, and thereby tends to lose the status that it has in the eyes of many Australians as a major crime against the Aboriginal peoples.

The text illustrates a number of points made above. First, it highlights the role of language as a classificatory instrument. It shows quite clearly that categories are not objective, ready-made, inherent properties of the external world but are subject to processes of perception and interpretation. It also shows that terms can be used in an attempt to impose a classificatory scheme on the reader not by argument but through the more insidious process of naming and reference. Blainey simply takes it for granted that it is legitimate to describe the movements of the Pitjantjatjara as *these invasions*. We also see that meaning is not an inherent property of words but is strongly influenced by contexts of use. The fact that *invasion* and *settlement* are oppositional terms in ways of speaking about the European presence in Australia is probably surprising to readers unfamiliar with Australian discourses.

This point has important implications for the process of language change. Blainey's text confronts an established discursive practice whereby the term *invasion* is commonly used to draw attention to the violent and unlawful nature of a specific event in Australian history. Blainey challenges this interpretation by extending the range of the term to encompass other events. In redefining its referential scope in this way, he is challenging the classificatory system on which the established discursive practice is based. As this book proceeds, we will encounter many such cases where the problematic nature of the 'fit' between language and the world opens up the possibility for conceptual challenges of this kind and ultimately for significant changes in the area of referential and connotational meaning.[7]

Forster: *A Passage to India*

For a rather different kind of illustration of the themes introduced above, we turn now to an extract from E. M. Forster's novel *A Passage to India*. Again it is necessary to know something of the ideological position of the main participants in the text here and of the general context. The novel is set in India under British colonial rule. Ronny is a British administrator, extremely conservative in attitudes. Adela is his fiancée, newly arrived from England, wishing to 'get to know' India and the Indians, well-meaning but naive. When this conversation takes place, Adela is paying a visit to the local school with Mrs Moore, Ronny's mother. The (British) Headmaster, Fielding, has just taken Mrs Moore to look at the school buildings, while Adela has stayed behind, talking to two Indians, Dr Aziz and Professor Godbole. Ronny enters in search of the two women and is clearly shocked to find Adela engaged in informal chat with Aziz and Godbole.[8]

Ronny:	*What's happened to Fielding? Where's my mother?*
Adela:	*Good evening.*
Ronny:	*I want you and mother at once. There's to be polo.*
Adela:	*I thought there was to be no polo.*
Ronny:	*Everything's altered. Some soldier men have come in. Come along and I'll tell you about it . . .*
Godbole:	*Your mother will return shortly, sir. There's but little to see at our poor college.*
Aziz:	*Come along up and join us, Mr Heaslop; sit down till your mother turns up . . .*
Ronny:	*Don't trouble to come mother. We're just starting. I say, old man, do excuse me, but I think perhaps you oughtn't to have left Miss Quested alone.*
Fielding:	*I'm sorry, what's up?*
Ronny:	*Well . . . I'm the sun-dried bureaucrat, no doubt; still I don't like to see an English girl left smoking with two Indians.*
Fielding:	*She stopped, as she smokes, by her own wish, old man.*
Ronny:	*Yes, that's all right in England.*
Fielding:	*I really don't see the harm.*

Ronny:	If you can't see, you can't see . . . Can't you see that fellow's a bounder?
Fielding:	He isn't a bounder. His nerves are on edge, that's all.
Ronny:	What should have upset his precious nerves?
Fielding:	I don't know. He was all right when I left.
Ronny:	Well, it's nothing I've said. I never even spoke to him.
Fielding:	Oh well, come along now and take your ladies away. The catastrophe is over.
Ronny:	Fielding . . . don't think I'm taking it badly, or anything of that sort . . . I suppose you won't come on to the polo with us. We should all be delighted.
Fielding:	I'm afraid I can't, thanks all the same. I'm awfully sorry you feel I've been remiss. I didn't mean to be.
Mrs Moore:	Goodbye, Mr Fielding, and thank you so much . . . What lovely college buildings! (Forster 1936: 75–6)

Our main interest in this text concerns those processes of negotiation in play that involve classification and selection. Consider, for example, Ronny's categorisation of Fielding's actions as 'leaving Adela alone' and 'leaving an English girl smoking with two Indians'. The term *leave*, like *settle* discussed above, carries interesting ambiguities. There is no doubt that Fielding 'left' Adela in the sense that he (with Mrs Moore) moved away physically from a place where he, Adela and the others had all been together. In other words, the core meaning of 'X left Y' simply involves a change of state from a situation in which X and Y are in physical proximity to one in which they are not, as a result of the movement of X. There are, however, also meanings connected with abandonment, deriving from circumstances often associated with the basic situation. X's moving away may be against the wishes of Y and may leave Y vulnerable. So the question of whether the present situation does in fact belong to the category of 'X left Y' situations is problematic. In the basic sense, it clearly does. But Ronny's rebuke is based on the secondary meanings concerned with abandonment, meanings which emerge in interaction with the notion that Adela was 'alone' when she was with Aziz and Godbole and with the assignment of Adela to the category of 'English girl', with its connotations of vulnerability.

Part of what is at stake here is the question of agentivity. By claiming that Fielding 'left' Adela, Ronny is identifying the situation as one created solely by Fielding as agent. However, the assignment of agency here is quite problematic, since Adela had decided not to walk around the college at Mrs Moore's suggestion. Fielding points this out. On the other hand, it is not at all clear that this absolves Fielding from responsibility. Ronny's view is that Fielding should not have allowed Adela to remain, so that the 'blame' for the ensuing situation is in fact entirely his. These contrasting constructions of agency and responsibility derive from different interpretations of local cultural norms (*That's all right in England*).

There are also ideological differences between Aziz and Godbole, which have quite specific linguistic reflexes. The question has to do with how the various participants interpret the nature of the interpersonal relationships here. Godbole constructs the relationship between himself and Ronny in terms of a power differential, addressing Ronny as *sir* and expressing self-deprecatory meanings (*There's but little to see at our poor college*). Aziz on the other hand adopts a more egalitarian approach, addressing Ronny as *Mr Heaslop*, inviting him to perform certain actions, using imperative structures to do so (*Come along up, Join us, Sit down*) and also employing informal expressions such as *turn up* in contrast to Godbole's more formal register. Again it is important to note that the role of these linguistic behaviours is not to reflect objective properties of the situation but to **construct** it in a particular way. Faced with a particular set of phenomena, individuals differ significantly from each other in terms of how they integrate these phenomena into existing classificatory schemas through their discursive practices.

Selectivity also plays an important part in the interactive processes at work here. The most obvious example of this is Ronny's reference to Adela's smoking. Ronny might have referred to the situation in terms of Adela's having been 'left chatting', 'left talking', 'left sitting' or simply 'left'. His selective reference to 'smoking' is clearly connected with the fact that smoking is an index of intimacy. In focusing on this particular feature of the situation, Ronny is exploiting general attitudes of disapproval of women indulging in such emancipated behaviours. To have said that he did not like Adela's being left with two Indians would have been too explicit an acknowledgment of the racist basis of his attitudes. The reference to her smoking gives his objection a veneer of social acceptability and at the same time it 'mystifies' the nature of his objection by making it slightly unclear whether his principal objection is to the fact that she was left, or to the fact that she was smoking, or to both.[9]

The final point here concerns the way in which conflicting social pressures work themselves out through linguistic processes. The basic problem for Ronny is that he feels the need to rebuke Fielding but at the same time to preserve solidarity with him as a fellow member of the British community. This conflict manifests itself in the process of 'modalisation' – a term designating those ways in which speakers attempt to make their utterances more acceptable to addressees by incorporating linguistic expressions into their utterances which express tentativeness or politeness.[10] The most obvious manifestation of this process here is the presence of such forms as *I say*, *old man*, *do excuse me*, *I think* and *perhaps* in Ronny's initial rebuke. Each of these expressions performs a slightly different kind of modalising function. *I say* announces the imminent occurrence of some kind of speech act, its function deriving from the fact that its very presence signals some hesitation in producing the speech act in question. *Old man*, by contrast, is concerned with the social relations between the participants to the speech act, signalling the 'in-group' status of speaker and addressee. *Excuse me* has a mitigatory role with respect to the addressee's anticipated reaction to the utterance – its 'perlocutionary effect' (Austin 1962: 101). *I think* and *perhaps* are functionally identical in that they qualify the propositional content of the rebuke. Ronny's *I'm the sun-dried bureaucrat, no doubt* also has a modalising function, as does the whole of the closing sequence in which Ronny invites Fielding to the polo – clearly an attempted remedial move (Owen 1983).

Conclusion

In this chapter we have made a preliminary approach to the question of the relationship between classification, selection and perspective in linguistic processes. The observation that classification is fundamental to the encoding of our experiences undermines the traditional view that language is simply a container into which we pour the meanings that exist independently of and prior to language. On the contrary, it seems that our native language plays at least some part in the structuring of our experience. A child who encounters a new token of a familiar category is likely to attempt to interact with it in familiar ways. This may not always be a wise strategy (some dogs are more amenable to being patted than others!) but it is one that is difficult to resist and is indeed an integral part of the process of creating meaning. Our ability to construct and survive in a complex environment depends on the fact that linguistic categories generally allow us to make successful predictions about how the world is likely to behave.

Similar points can be made about selectivity. There are many respects in which the lexical structures and grammatical processes in our native language draw our attention to certain recurring features in situations. In learning a language we learn to perceive situations in particular ways that are compatible with and can be 'mapped onto' the formal structures that occur in our language. The diversity exhibited by the lexical and grammatical systems of human languages suggests that there must be considerable diversity in the way that speakers of different languages construct their worlds.

There is one qualification that needs to be placed on the arguments outlined above. It is quite easy to leap from these observations to the conclusion that a language **imposes** a distinctive, homogeneous perceptual framework on its speakers. This argument is based on the view that a language is a monolithic system rather than a heterogeneous form of human behaviour. Language is, in fact, such a complex phenomenon that there is some degree of plausibility in both perspectives. It is necessary to insist on the importance of the latter view, however. Our brief discussion of the textual materials cited here supports the argument that there are different ways of using the resources of a particular language that mediate different modes of interpretation. For all kinds of reasons connected with the complexities inherent in our social structures, individuals view their social world from different positions and construct their interpretations through different linguistic practices. Since the processes of categorisation and selection are often problematic, they may function as the site of contestation, where participants attempt to impose their own modes of interpretation on others or negotiate a way through the social tensions that inevitably arise from difference.

We will be developing these themes throughout the book. In the next chapter, we consider some of the historical sources for these ideas, leading to a review of recent work on the nature of categories.

Notes

1. The phenomenon of overextension is not a particularly easy one to interpret. In examples of the kind cited here, the child may have a concept very close to the adult concept for 'cow', 'apple', etc. and simply be saying that some other object is like a cow or an apple rather than that it is one. There seems little doubt, however, that at least some cases of overextension result from the child's uncertainty concerning the referential range of the word. For further discussion see Lee 1986: 32–4.

2. Following Huddleston (1984: 304) I use the term 'determinative' rather than the more usual 'determiner' as the name for the class containing words such as *the*, *a*, *this*, *each*, reserving the latter term for the function filled by this class (and by other classes).

3. For a general discussion of morphological processes see Huddleston 1984: 21–33.

4. Throughout the text I use the term 'reification' for a process that Fowler and Kress (1979a: 208) refer to as 'objectification'. See also Kress 1986: 406.

5. The relatively early emergence of the concept of agentivity in the child's communicative system supports this view. Lee (1986: 38–40) discusses evidence suggesting that the concept is established during the first year of life.

6. Similarly Wax and Wax (1971: 131–2) refer to the 'wilderness ideology' of the European invaders of the American continent, the function of which was to 'rationalize their seizing and occupying of Indian lands'. Wax and Wax note the close connection between this wilderness ideology and the 'vacuum ideology' which fails to see any value in the cultures of aboriginal peoples.

7. Chomsky 1986: 276–86 raises similar issues in his discussion of the application (or non-application) of the term *invasion* to the Russian incursion into Afghanistan and the American incursion into South Vietnam.

8. The following 'conversation' is extracted from the narrative text of the novel (Forster 1936: 75–6).

9. For discussion of the concept of 'mystification' see Fowler and Kress 1979a: 38.

10. The process of modalisation will be examined in some detail in Chapter 7. Modalisation has a particularly important role to play in utterances (such as Ronny's rebuke) that are a potential threat to the addressee's 'negative face' (Brown and Levinson 1978).

2 *Grammar, categories and world-view*

Saussure

The idea that language plays an important role in structuring our experience of the world can be traced back to a scholar often referred to as the 'father' of modern linguistics – Ferdinand de Saussure. There are two strands of Saussure's argument that converge on this question. The first is the idea that language is in some sense prior to and instrumental in the structuring of thought.

> Psychologically our thought – apart from its expression in words – is only a shapeless and indistinct mass. Philosophers and linguists have always agreed in recognizing that without the help of signs we would be unable to make a clear-cut, consistent distinction between two ideas. Without language, thought is a vague, uncharted nebula. There are no pre-existing ideas and nothing is distinct before the appearance of language ... Thought, chaotic by nature, has to become ordered in its decomposition. (Saussure 1974: 112)

For Saussure, then, language creates the structure of thought and it does so by segmenting reality into conceptual chunks. Our emphasis in the previous chapter on the importance of categorisation in conceptual processes clearly relates directly to this argument.

The second strand of Saussure's thought that bears on this question is the idea that different languages 'carve up' reality in different ways. Each language assigns to a particular lexical or grammatical category a range of phenomena that do not correspond to any lexical or grammatical category in another language. Saussure argued that the incommensurability between what appear to be corresponding terms in different languages derives from the fact that each term belongs to a different system and the 'value' of a particular element is determined by the full set of relationships within the system.

> Language is a system of interdependent terms in which the value of each term results solely from the simultaneous presence of the others. A few examples will show clearly that this is true. Modern French *mouton* can have the same signification as English *sheep* but not the same value, and this for several reasons, particularly because in speaking of a piece of meat ready to be served on the table, English uses *mutton* and not *sheep*. The difference in value between *sheep* and *mouton* is due to the fact that *sheep* has beside it a second term while the French word does not. (Saussure 1974: 115)

It is, of course, a well-known fact that languages differ significantly in terms of how they structure particular conceptual fields, some languages having a much richer set of terms than do others in certain areas. This means that there may be no equivalents in one language to distinctions that are made in another. The difference between a maternal and a paternal uncle is not lexicalised in English, for example, since it is a relatively unimportant distinction in our culture. In those societies where the distinction is crucial, however, it is usually marked by different words (Trudgill 1974: 27–8). Such incommensurabilities usually involve not only aspects of referential meaning but also connotational meaning. An English word such as *cosy* has rather different overtones from the French word *confortable* and the connotations of the closest German word *gemütlich* are different again. These are of course some of the factors that make translation from one language to another such a problematic exercise.

These two strands – the idea that language structures thought and the idea that different languages dissect reality in different ways – appear to converge on the suggestion that to acquire a particular language is to acquire a particular way of perceiving the world. This idea is not, however, one that was explored in detail by Saussure. In part this may be due to the fact that it is by no means a straightforward matter to move from the level of linguistic 'value' to that of cognition. To take Saussure's own example, it would clearly be absurd to suggest that speakers of French do not make any cognitive differentiation between a live sheep and the animal's meat, just as it would be absurd to suggest that speakers of English do not differentiate between the two corresponding meanings of the word *lamb*. To recognise this point, however, is to reject the idea that the 'value' of a particular term in Saussure's sense can be directly equated with a particular cognitive construct. The fact that the English word *sheep* has a different value from the French word *mouton* does not have any obvious implications for the cognitive systems of speakers of the two languages in this area. On the other hand, to argue that linguistic value has no relevance whatever to the process of cognition would be inconsistent with Saussure's claim that language structures thought. This conceptual difficulty in Saussure's argument may be one of the reasons why he did not pursue the question of the relationship between language and cognition.[1] This issue is not one that we will attempt to resolve at this juncture. In order to address it, a sophisticated theory of categories is needed of the kind that has begun to emerge only in very recent work (Lakoff 1987). We will consider Lakoff's theory in the fourth section of this chapter.

There are a number of other difficulties with Saussure's position. Part of the problem with his argument is that it suggests that each term within a linguistic system designates a well-defined semantic area, clearly demarcated from other equally discrete areas. In fact, however, the semantic relationships between words are so complex that Saussure's metaphor of language dissecting reality into component parts becomes highly misleading. A few minutes browsing through Roget's *Thesaurus* is sufficient to demonstrate the problematic nature of the semantic distinctions between sets of related words. How easy would it be to obtain agreement in any group of speakers of English concerning the subtle semantic differentiation between such words as *sullen, moody, ill-tempered, morose, crusty, surly* and *sulky* or between *cheerful, happy, glad, blithe, bright, breezy, vivacious, jaunty, sprightly* and *spry* (to mention but a few)? The idea that language structures our world into sharply differentiated categories seems particularly problematic in such cases.

Another (related) difficulty with Saussure's argument is that it is based on a view of the relationship between meaning and form that has been thrown into question by much recent work. The view seems to be that meaning is a property of individual components of the linguistic system – the lexical or grammatical terms. On this view the meaning of a particular linguistic structure is seen as deriving from the summation of the meanings of the forms of which the structure is composed.[2] An alternative view, much closer to that of current work in the field and one which will be developed as the book proceeds, is that meaning is a product of the interaction between linguistic forms and the minds of language users. Social factors as well as cognitive factors play an important part in this interaction. Moreover, since language users find themselves in situations that are constantly in flux, language is under continual pressure to produce new meanings with existing forms. This is essentially the reason why the conceptual categories that correspond to linguistic forms are characterised by the kind of indeterminacies noted in the preceding chapter. Fuzziness is in some sense an essential property of a finite system that has to cope with a constant flow of new situations.

For the moment we can accept Saussure's general argument that the process of categorisation is crucially involved in the process of language acquisition, and that different languages tend to produce different schemas of categorisation. On the other hand, we do not accept the argument that it is necessary to conceptualise language as a static, self-contained system in order to validate this view. The preliminary evidence examined in the previous chapter suggests that it will be necessary to deal with language in use in order to fully explore the relationship between categorisation and conceptualisation.

Whorf

The idea that language is intimately involved in the way that we perceive the world was taken up in a rather different context by the American linguist Benjamin Lee Whorf. Whorf's particular field of interest was that of Amerindian languages. He was struck – as were many of his contemporaries in linguistics – by the very marked differences between the lexicogrammatical systems of these languages and those of the more familiar Indo-European group. Observation of these differences led him to the view that the American Indians must have quite different perceptions of the world from Europeans.

The point can best be illustrated with one of Whorf's own examples. Consider the following pair of sentences from Shawnee.

(1) *Kwaškwi-tepe-n-a*
(2) *Kwaškwi-ho-to*

In the first sentence, *kwaškwi* has no direct equivalent in English, but designates a situation in which there is pressure applied in one direction, encountering a certain resistance; *tepe* means 'head'; the morpheme *-n* indicates the involvement of the hand in some action and *-a* is a morpheme which expresses the idea that there was action by an agent on a patient – it is a transitivity marker. The position of the various elements in the structure is also relevant – the position occupied by *tepe* expresses the idea of location, for example. Putting all this information together, we can say that the first of these sentences in Shawnee means that the speaker (*ni*) is involved as agent acting upon a patient (*-a*), using the hand (*-n*), in causing force to be applied at the head (of the patient), encountering some resistance. Whorf (1971c: 235) glosses the sentence as 'I push his head back'.

The second sentence is also constructed around the word *kwaškwi* but in this case the locative position is occupied not by *tepe* but by *ho* which means 'water surface'. The final position is occupied not by the transitivity marker *-a* but by the morpheme *-to*, an instrumental marker. This sentence means that the speaker is involved with an instrument in a situation where there is a force encountering a resistance at the surface of water. Whorf glosses it as 'I drop my paddle in the water (and it bobs back)'.

It is possible that there is a certain fancifulness about Whorf's examples here but they are useful to make an important general point about his views. Whorf has often been interpreted as maintaining the view that 'language structures reality' but in fact his discussion of these and other examples makes it clear that his position is rather more subtle than this. With respect to (1) and (2) Whorf seeks to make the point that, although the Shawnee sentences are very similar to each other, particularly in the way that they are structured around the central concept designated by the word *kwaškwi*, the corresponding English sentences – *I push his head back* and *I drop my paddle* – are quite different from each other. For Whorf, this contrast indicates that Shawnee speakers conceptualise these situations differently from the way in which English speakers conceptualise them. Speakers of Shawnee see the two situations as being very closely related to each other; speakers of English do not. The more general point is that Whorf wishes to approach the question of possible differences of world-view not in terms of how a particular individual sees a single situation but in terms of the **connections** that individuals perceive between observed phenomena. The underlying suggestion is that speakers establish networks of correspondences across situations but that there will be different network patterns for speakers of different languages. One way of describing the different ways in which the two languages treat the relevant situations here is to note that there is an English word – *push* – that is available to talk about situations in which an agent is involved in causing a situation characterised by a 'force-applied-resistance-encountered' component. Thus, for speakers of English 'agent-cause-force-applied-resistance-encountered' is a single conceptual element. Shawnee, however, encodes the elements of this complex conceptual unit onto two distinct linguistic units (*kwaškwi* for the 'force applied resistance encountered' component and *-a* for the agentivity component). This means that, if we consider two types of situation – those involving a 'force-applied-resistance-encountered' component **with** an agent and those involving the same component **without** an agent – then the two types of situation are encoded similarly in Shawnee but differently in English. For Whorf these differences relating to linguistic encoding have conceptual implications.

Whorf's observations about the kind of cross-language data illustrated above led him to add an important qualification to the commonsense view that, if two sentences are similar to each other in some language, this is because they designate similar situations. The problem that Whorf sees with this position is that the concept of 'similar situations' is not a given. Certain situations are perceived as similar by speakers of Language A, as dissimilar by speakers of Language B. This emphasis on the idea that our perception of relationships across phenomena in the 'real world' is a function of the (linguistic) position from which we contemplate those phenomena led to the characterisation of Whorf's ideas as 'linguistic relativity'. The parallels with Einstein's theory are obvious. Whorf (1971c: 235) expresses his position in the following terms:

> The point of view of linguistic relativity changes Mr. Everyman's dictum. Instead of saying 'Sentences are unlike because they tell about unlike facts', he now reasons 'Facts are unlike to speakers whose language background provides for unlike formulation of them'.

A further concept imported into this discussion by Whorf (1971b: 88–9) is that of a 'cryptotype'. This notion is based on a distinction between overt grammatical categories and covert ones (cryptotypes).

> An overt category is a category having a formal mark . . . which is present (with only infrequent exceptions) in every sentence containing a member of that category . . . A covert category is marked, whether morphemically or by sentence patterns, only in certain types of sentence and not in every sentence in which a word or element belonging to the category occurs. The class membership of the word is not apparent until there is a question of using it in one of these special types of sentence and then we find that the word belongs to a class requiring some sort of distinctive treatment . . . This distinctive treatment we may call the 'reactance' of the category.

The notion of an overt grammatical category is illustrated by the phenomenon of gender in a language such as French, since the fact that a word is masculine or feminine is marked by the form of the dependents (determiners or modifiers) in nearly every sentence in which a noun occurs. Similarly the category of definiteness in the Noun Phrase in English is an overt category, since almost every NP carries a marker of definiteness or indefiniteness in the form of determinatives such as *the, my, this, both,* etc. (definite) or *a, some, any,* etc. (indefinite). By contrast, Whorf (1971e: 71) argues that verbs such as *fold, tie, wrap, cover, fasten* and many others constitute a covert category (cryptotype) in English. The set does not include such verbs as *lift, snatch, hold, drop.* The property that characterises the class in question is the fact that they can all take the prefix *un-.* That is, whereas *John untied the knot* is a well-formed structure in English, **John unlifted the parcel* is not. (Following general practice, the asterisk is used to identify structures that are ungrammatical or unacceptable in some sense.) However, this is clearly not a property that shows up in the general use of *fold, tie, wrap, cover,* etc., so that the fact that these verbs constitute a category is well below the level of conscious awareness of native speakers.

Whorf argues that grammatical categories – especially covert grammatical categories – are often significant in a number of ways. For one thing, they are not arbitrary from the point of view of semantics. Verbs such as *fold, tie, wrap, cover*, as well as sharing the grammatical property of taking the *un-* prefix, are also distinguished from other verbs in that they denote a particular set of process types – attaching objects to surfaces, covering objects or enclosing objects. Whorf suggests that, if a new word such as *flimmick* came into the language, and if it was possible to use it in the form *unflimmick*, then those speakers of English who did not know what it meant would nevertheless 'know' in some intuitive sense that it too must be a surface-attaching, covering or enclosing verb.

Whorf's point seems to be that processes of this kind constitute a specially important category for speakers of English – that there is something in our cultural history or in the way that we perceive the world that has led to the fact that verbs denoting these types of process are characterised by a special grammatical (in this case morphological) property. Other examples make this point a little clearer. Another cryptotype in English operating within the class of nouns consists of words such as *deer, caribou, salmon, mackerel* (Whorf 1971b: 96). The grammatical property that characterises words belonging to this subset of nouns is that their plural forms are not marked with a *-s* suffix.

(3)   *There were many caribou/ *caribous on the plain*
(4)   *We caught a few salmon/ *salmons this morning*

Again the words in question do not constitute an arbitrary set. They have in common the fact that they all denote animals (or fish) that have a special importance in our cultural history in that they all belong to the category 'game'. By contrast words like *cat* and *dog* denote domesticated animals and these have plural forms that are constructed in the regular way with an *-s* suffix.

A rather more interesting example comes from the Amerindian language Hopi. Whorf (1971a: 104) argues that there are at least three cryptotypes within the Hopi verb system. The sub-classes in question consist of those verbs which correspond to the English verbs below:

Class A: *sleep, laugh, eat, die, bend*
Class B: *run, flee, come, go, open, close*
Class C: *fall, tumble, spill, spin, jump, whirl*

The grammatical property which distinguishes the three sub-classes has to do with the way in which the idea is expressed in Hopi that the relevant process is in its 'beginning' stage. Like many other Amerindian languages Hopi has a number of special forms termed 'inceptive' (or 'inchoative') markers. In other words, if a speaker wishes to express the idea that someone is falling asleep, then an inceptive marker is attached to the verb *sleep* – 'he sleep-begin'. In Hopi there are three different forms of the inceptive marker: *-va*, *-ni* and *-to* and it is precisely this variation that under-lies the distinction between the three sub-classes indicated above, since *-va* is used with the class A verbs, *-ni* with the class B verbs and *-to* with the class C verbs. This is a covert grammatical dis-tinction rather than an overt one, since it is only in one particular structure – the inceptive – that any grammatical distinction be-tween the verbs in question shows up.

What is particularly interesting about this situation is the seman-tic rationale that appears to underlie these cryptotypes and the way in which this illuminates Whorf's general thesis about the re-lationship between linguistic structure and world-view. From the point of view of a speaker of English, the sub-classes appear to be entirely arbitrary. For a speaker of Hopi, however, the class of processes within each cryptotype seem as natural as does the idea that game animals and fish constitute a natural semantic class for speakers of English. As far as the first class is concerned, Whorf (1971e: 72) writes:

> Hopi regards the subject of these verbs as working into and through
> the action by a process of dynamic adjustment. The subject pro-
> gressively adjusts himself into the action, and throughout the action
> is maintaining this adjustment either to develop or to stabilize and
> continue the effect.

By contrast the second class of processes are those where the sub-ject 'is classed as instantly assuming a full-fledged new status, not as dynamically working into and through a process'. But it is the third cryptotype that has a particular interest.

> This cryptotype implies that the subject is seized and assimilated by
> a field of influence, carried away by it, as it were; and it consists of
> gravitational and moving inertia phenomena; 'falling, tumbling,

spilling, jumping, whirling,' and also, strange though it seems to us, 'going out' and 'going in.' According to the logic of Hopi linguistics, a person about to enter a house or go outdoors launches off and yields himself to a new influence like one who falls or leaps. (Whorf 1971e: 73)

If Whorf's analysis is correct, this all suggests a very different way of viewing the world from the way in which we see it. Particularly interesting is the membership of 'whirling' in the same set of processes as 'jumping' and 'falling'. To speakers of English 'whirling' is a process that individuals initiate deliberately and continue under their own volition. Whorf's discussion suggests (although he does not make it explicit in quite these terms) that the Hopi see 'whirling' as a kind of force that exists in the world independently of human beings and that manifests itself in certain types of situation in the same sort of way that (in our view) gravitational forces manifest themselves in certain conditions. Individuals then abandon themselves to the whirling force in exactly the same sort of way that one abandons oneself to the force of gravity when one leaps off a cliff. This interpretation of whirling situations is almost certainly much more than a straightforward cognitive difference between members of an English-speaking culture and the Hopi. It may well be connected with the spiritual significance of whirling and the trance-like states that are associated with it in Hopi culture.

One criticism that can be made of Whorf's position as indicated in the foregoing discussion has to do with the sharp distinction that he draws between overt and covert grammatical categories. There is no intrinsic reason why cryptotypes should be any more significant for world-view than overt categories, nor indeed for the view that there is a sharp dividing line between the two category types. Part of the reason why Whorf took this position may have had to do with the view prevalent in linguistics at the time that most grammatical categories – particularly overt ones – were arbitrary. That is, there was a strong tradition in American structural linguistics that the grammatical systems of the world's languages were patterned independently of semantics. Martin Joos (1966: 96) expressed this view most clearly when he claimed that 'languages could differ from each other without limit and in unpredictable ways'. It may be, then, that Whorf was content to accept this view for overt categories but wished to argue against the view that it applied to all types.

More recent work has shown, however, that although the relationship between formal grammatical categories and semantics in particular languages is extremely complex, it is simply not the case that grammatical categories are constructed in total independence of semantics. Rather, most grammatical categories are structured around some semantic core. The most obvious case, as we noted in the previous chapter, is that of nouns – a grammatical category structured around the concept of 'concrete, physical object' – but the point has quite general application. As noted above (page 4), semantic categories play an important part in the definition of many grammatical categories at the language-general level. The fact that grammar is pervaded with semantics undermines to some extent Whorf's suggestion that overt grammatical categories are less revealing in this context than covert categories.

Dixon: Dyirbal

An example of the relevance of an overt grammatical category for world-view comes from Robert Dixon's work on the Australian Aboriginal language Dyirbal (Dixon 1972). Dyirbal has a noun sub-classificatory system which parallels in many ways the gender systems of languages such as French and German. Essentially a language can be said to have a gender system if two conditions are met. The first condition is that the nouns fall into different classes in terms of specific grammatical properties, typically if the form of noun dependents varies according to the noun sub-class. For example, in French and German, the forms of the definite article and adjective vary according to the class of the head noun. (There is no similar process in English.) The second condition that has to be met is that there should be some correlation between the system of noun sub-classification and the biological category of sex. French is said to have a gender system because in general the words denoting male entities belong to a different grammatical class from those denoting female entities. This is not to say, of course, that all the nouns that belong in the masculine set denote male entities – simply that there is a semantic core to the grammatical category system related to biological sex.

Dyirbal has four grammatical sub-classes of noun. The grammatical basis of the sub-classification has to do in part with variation in the form of noun dependents such as *bala, yala* and *ngala*.[3] These are similar to articles in French or German, except that they carry certain extra meanings not associated with articles in European languages. For example, *bala* has a similar meaning to the English demonstrative *that* but it also encodes the information that the referent of the noun is visible to the speaker. *Yala* means 'here and visible' and *ngala* means 'not visible but audible' (Dixon 1972: 45).

The noun marker *bala* has four forms, depending on the subclass of noun that governs it, as illustrated in the following Noun Phrases:

(5)   Class A: *Bayi yara*   'that man'
      Class B: *Balan djugumbil*   'that woman'
      Class C: *Balam bungdjan*   'that walnut'
      Class D: *Bala djina*   'that foot'

In general terms most of the words that denote male entities belong with *yara* in class A, taking the form *bayi*; most of those that denote female entities belong in class B with *djugumbil*; class C contains most of the words denoting edible substances; class D is a residual class.

There are a number of interesting points about this situation. Most of the gender systems of European languages contain either two classes (masculine and feminine) or three (masculine, feminine and neuter). In both cases we see a strong orientation towards the biological category of sex, with the neuter class in the three-class system available as a residual category. As far as Dyirbal is concerned, although it seems appropriate to regard it as a gender system, the existence of a special class oriented towards the semantic category of edible substances means that it is not a prototypical example of such a system. In the context of gender systems in the languages of the world as a whole, the Dyirbal system is unusual or 'marked'.

The marked nature of the Dyirbal system is surely not a coincidence. It must derive at some level from the fact that for many thousands of years Australian Aborigines have lived in one of the most hostile climates in the world, in which the distinction between edible and non-edible objects has been crucial to their survi-

val. The close relationship between the people and their environment and the delicate adjustment of their lives to that environment
has come to be encoded into the grammar of their language. For
Aborigines, the land is not a resource to be exploited and possessed in the European sense of personal, private ownership.
Rather, the land is built into the fabric of their culture and personal identity. Thus in Dyirbal a certain crucial property of the environment has a central status in the grammatical system along
with such important concepts as male and female. We can see this
as another manifestation of Whorf's argument that linguistic categories may be culturally significant.

One neo-Whorfian argument with which it seems impossible at
first sight to reconcile the Dyirbal example is the idea that language structures reality ('linguistic determinism'). It would clearly
be absurd to argue that it is because the Dyirbal language has a
certain kind of word-class system that the Dyirbal people had the
kind of relationship to and perspective on their environment indicated above. Causation evidently operates in the opposite direction
here ('cognitive determinism' or 'social determinism'). On the
other hand, if we consider the situation from the point of view of
the child learning Dyirbal, we see how the language-acquisition
process can sensitise the child to the distinction between edible and
non-edible objects. The formal patterns in the language operate at
a very deep level to structure the child's perceptions and behaviours. We can thus see the distinction between linguistic determinism and social determinism as not necessarily involving
mutually incompatible positions. The view that one adopts on this
question will depend to a large extent on whether one takes an historical perspective, considering how linguistic systems change and
evolve through time under the influence of changing social and en-
vironmental factors, or whether one is concerned with the way in
which the structure of the system at some particular time impinges
on and interacts with the development of the child.

The Dyirbal gender system is interesting in another respect in
the context of this discussion. We have noted that most of the
words that denote male human beings belong in class A and that
most of those which denote females belong in class B. This observation is not enough to explain the system as a whole, however.
Dixon (1972: 308) notes that certain more general principles are at
work here. For example, class A nouns include not only most

words denoting males but also most words denoting animates (excluding specifically female animates). In addition to words for females, class B nouns include words denoting such natural phenomena as water, fire and light, as well as words connected with fighting. Having noted these points, however, Dixon observes that there appear at first sight to be many apparent exceptions to these tendencies. Although the words for most types of fish are in class A because of the animacy criterion, some are in class B. The words for most birds are in class B rather than the expected class A. Since the moon is a natural phenomenon, one would expect the word *moon* to be in class B, whereas it is in fact in class A. Although most of the words for various types of spear are in class B, because of their association with fighting, the words for certain multi-pronged spears are in class A.

Dixon suggests that most of these apparent exceptions to the general rules governing class membership can be accounted for if we invoke two additional rules:

1. If some noun has characteristic X (on the basis of which its class membership would be expected to be decided) but is, through belief or myth, connected with characteristic Y, then generally it will belong to the class corresponding to Y and not that corresponding to X.
2. If a subset of nouns has some particular important property that the rest of the set do not have, then the members of the subset may be assigned to a different class from the rest of the set, to 'mark' this property; the important property is most often 'harmfulness'. (Dixon 1972: 308)

The fact that *moon* is in class A rather than the expected class B, with most other natural phenomena, is accounted for by the first rule, since the moon in Dyirbal mythology is believed to be the husband of the sun. It is therefore quite appropriate for the word *moon* to be in the masculine category. The same rule accounts for the fact that the words for most birds are in class B (feminine), since birds are believed to be the spirits of dead human females. Three kinds of willy wagtail, however, are mythical men and the words which designate them are in class A. The second rule accounts both for the fact that the words for *stone-fish* and *gar-fish*, because these creatures are particularly harmful, are in class B rather than the expected class A and for the fact that the words for two types of stinging tree and a stinging nettle vine are in class B, whereas the words for most trees with no edible parts are in class D.

Again, then, we see here a clear example of the relationship between world-view and linguistic structure, operating on several levels. At a relatively mundane level, it is interesting to note the grammatical marking of special properties such as 'harmfulness' – a characteristic of the language which can be seen to have practical survival value for its speakers in a difficult environment. At a more general level, this interaction between linguistic structure and environment can be seen as a reflex of the Aborigine's special relationship with the land. At a yet higher level Dixon has documented here a particularly subtle way in which mythology and belief impinge on linguistic structure.

Lakoff

Dixon's discussion of the Dyirbal system has been taken up and elaborated in an important recent study of the nature of categories by George Lakoff (1987). Lakoff's discussion encompasses an extensive range of issues. We will be able to consider here only those general points that are relevant to our immediate concerns. We will focus in particular on the argument concerning the implications of the Dyirbal system for a general theory of the role of categories in human cognition.

Lakoff's argument is directed against what he calls the classical or 'Objectivist' theory of categories, which he believes to be fundamental to our most deep-seated philosophical assumptions.

> To appreciate the philosophical importance of the classical theory of categorization, we must first consider the worldview in which it is embedded – a metaphysical view of reality that is taken as being so obviously true as to be beyond question.
>
> OBJECTIVIST METAPHYSICS: All of reality consists of entities, which have fixed properties and relations holding among them at any instant.
>
> Objectivist metaphysics is often found in the company of another metaphysical assumption, essentialism.

ESSENTIALISM: Among the properties that things have, some are essential; that is, they are those properties that make the thing what it is, and without which it would not be that *kind* of thing. Other properties are accidental – that is, they are properties that things happen to have, not properties that capture the essence of the thing.
The classical theory of categories relates properties of entities to categories containing those entities.

CLASSICAL CATEGORIZATION: All the entities that have a given property or collection of properties in common form a category. Such properties are necessary and sufficient to *define* the category. (Lakoff 1987: 160–1)

The fact that the relevant properties are held in this view to be inherent to the members of a particular category means that categories have objective existence, independently of human perception. On this view, human beings arrive at a true understanding of the world when they construct cognitive models which correspond to or accurately represent the structure of external reality.

OBJECTIVIST KNOWLEDGE: Knowledge consists in correctly conceptualizing and categorizing those things in the world and grasping the objective connections among those things and those categories. (Lakoff 1987: 163)

Lakoff argues that these views are incompatible with recent discoveries concerning the nature of categories. His argument derives principally (but not exclusively) from work in linguistics. Let us take the Dyirbal system as a case in point.

Lakoff begins by noting that the two rules invoked by Dixon to explain the apparent irregularities in the Dyirbal word classification system can be replaced by a more general principle. Dixon had identified associations in mythology and special properties, particularly harmfulness, as factors that might override the normal factors (such as animacy) in the classification of a particular word. Lakoff proposes that these rules be subsumed under a general 'domain of experience' principle, expressed as follows:

If there is a basic domain of experience associated with *A*, then it is natural for entities in that domain to be in the same category as *A*. (Lakoff 1987: 93)

Lakoff suggests that danger and mythology are two domains of experience that are relevant to classification for speakers of Dyirbal. Although these domains are highly 'motivated' by the nature of Dyirbal culture, there is no way in which they can be said to be 'determined' by that culture. We cannot predict for any particular language which domains of experience will turn out to be relevant to classificatory patterns and we cannot therefore hope to provide principles that account for the system in a purely automatic way. Fishing, for example, is a domain of experience that appears to be relevant to grammatical categorisation in Dyirbal. Not only are all the words for fish in category A (with the exception of dangerous species such as the 'stone-fish' and 'gar-fish') but so are fishing implements such as fishing spears and fishing line (whereas the words for spears used in fighting are in category B). However, the word for *water* is not in category A, so that the way in which water is related to fish (domain of habitation) proves to have no relevance to this grammatical system. Other domains that turn out to be relevant include: eating, fighting, fire, mythology, danger. As far as eating is concerned, it is interesting to note that the words for fruit trees, unlike the words for most trees, belong in class C (edibles) but that if one is referring specifically to the wood of such a tree (for example, in reference to firewood or making an implement), then the noun marker for the residual category D (*bala*) is used (Lakoff 1987: 94). The culture-specific nature of these principles of categorisation is clearly incompatible with the traditional view that categories are objective, culture-independent phenomena. Part of what is involved in learning a language is discovering which domains of experience are relevant to categorisation and how they are constructed.

A particularly important feature of human cognitive categories is that they are characterised by a distinction between 'central' (or 'prototypical') members and 'non-central' members. The importance of this observation was first highlighted by Eleanor Rosch (for a useful summary of her work, see Clark and Clark 1977: 464–70, 526–31). In a series of experiments using a variety of techniques, Rosch showed that many categories are structured around certain 'cognitive reference points', that subjects judge certain members of categories as being more typical members than others. For example, robins and sparrows are more representative of the category 'bird' than are chickens, penguins and ostriches, and desk chairs are more representative of the category 'chair' than are rocking chairs, barber chairs, beanbag chairs or electric chairs (Lakoff 1987: 41). In Chapter 1 we noted a similar distinction between central and non-central members in English nouns. The distinction has both grammatical and semantic aspects. Nouns such as *willingness, determination, likelihood* are non-central members of the noun class on account of the fact that they have certain grammatical properties that distinguish them from prototypical nouns. They do not naturally occur in the plural form, for example, and they are morphologically complex. They also differ semantically from prototypical nouns in that they denote attributes or abstract concepts rather than physical objects. Some other grammatical categories in English exhibit the same distinction between central and non-central members. The verb *beware* is a particularly clear example of a non-central member of the verb class, since it lacks many inflectional forms characteristic of verbs in general (note the ungrammaticality of *They bewared of the dog*, *They are bewaring of the dog*, *They have always bewared of the dog*) and unlike prototypical verbs it does not denote an activity.

In Dyirbal the structure of the major word classes illustrates the same point. As we have seen, the Dyirbal classification system, like that of many other languages around the world, is based in part on biological sex. The concept of maleness is the cognitive reference point for category A *(bayi)* and femaleness has the same status for category B *(balan)*. Words denoting other concepts are members of one or other of these categories by virtue of the fact that there is some property that connects them in Dyirbal culture with these central concepts.

One piece of evidence relevant to this claim comes from a study by Schmidt (1985) of what happens when the language begins to die. Dixon's study was conducted in 1963. In recent years younger people in the Dyirbal community have grown up speaking mainly English, learning only a simplified version of Dyirbal. In the speech of these younger people, the traditional word-class system is breaking down. Class A still contains the words for human males and class B those for females but for some younger speakers all other words are placed in class C, which has simply become a residual class. So, what appears to happen in language death is that the culturally-based concepts that bind the members of the category together begin to atrophy. As the strands connecting central to non-central members wither, the complexity of the internal structure of the category disappears and the class contracts to its central core (Lakoff 1987: 96–8).

The notion of centrality is closely associated with the notion of 'chaining'. In Dyirbal this is demonstrated most clearly in category B (*balan*). The central members of this category are words denoting human females. The word for the sun is a (non-central) member by virtue of its mythological association with women. The word for sunburn is in this class because it belongs to the same domain of experience as the sun and the word for a hairy-mary grub is also in the class because it produces similar sensations to those produced by sunburn. Thus, we see a chain of connections which places the word for hairy-mary grub in the same category as words for women, even though there is no feature linking these concepts directly. The importance of chaining is that it provides an explanation for the fact that categories are to some extent open. New concepts can be assigned to existing categories on the basis of perceived similarities to any of the members of the chain. It is this ability of linguistic categories to incorporate new phenomena that accounts at least in part for the ability of individual languages to adapt to new situations. It also accounts for the fact that familiar phenomena can be reinterpreted in terms of new associative networks. Geoffrey Blainey's attempted incorporation of Aboriginal incursions into the category of 'invasions' in the text discussed in Chapter 1 (p. 15) illustrates such a case. Although the population movements to which Blainey refers are clearly not prototypical members of the category of 'invasions', there are certain features which they share with other members of the category to provide some motivation for Blainey's attempt to tie them in.

The traditional Dyirbal system thus provides a perfect example of the kind of properties that characterise human conceptual categories: centrality versus non-centrality, chaining, lack of common properties, openness, culture-specific experiential domains, motivation. These characteristics are interrelated. Centrality connects with chaining, lack of common properties, openness. Lakoff uses the term 'radial structure' to characterise categories of this kind. Radially structured categories consist of a central core with non-central members standing in some kind of relationship to the core by virtue of such principles as the domain-of-experience principle. Since there are a variety of dimensions through which non-central members may relate to the central area, it will normally be the case that there is no single feature or set of features shared by all members of the category. This violates one of the central principles of the Objectivist paradigm. Lakoff does not claim that all categories are radially structured but he does argue that this is an important and widespread principle of organisation, particularly in respect of linguistic categories and the conceptual categories associated with them.

The Dyirbal category system illustrates a relatively high-level linguistic category in the sense that the concept applies at the level of major lexical classes. The same kind of structuring can be observed at lower levels of the linguistic system – at the level of individual words, for example. Consider once more the English word *climb*. In the previous chapter, we noted that this word can be used to denote a variety of situations. Consider the following expanded list:

(6) *She climbed the hill*
(7) *She climbed the rock face*
(8) *She climbed the ladder*
(9) *The aircraft climbed into the sky*
(10) *See how that creeper climbs up to the window*
(11) *The spider climbed gingerly across the web*
(12) *She climbed down the rock face*
(13) *In the recent confrontation with the American President, the Russian Premier was forced to climb down*

The range of activities designated by the word *climb* here can be seen to constitute a somewhat disparate set of situations, which the conventions of English usage define as a category. This too is a radially structured category. It possesses such characteristics as: centrality versus non-centrality, chaining, lack of common properties, openness, culture-specific experiential domains, motivation. Examples such as (6), (7) and (8), for example, which denote the concept of upward motion in physical space resulting from walking-like movements, seem to be the central members. The other examples relate to this central core area in different ways. Sentences (9) and (10) relate to the core in that they denote upward motion but they lack the notion of walking-like movements (and in the case of (10) the movement involved is not so much a feature of the present situation as of a process in the past that has given rise to it). Sentences (11) and (12), on the other hand, relate to the central core by virtue of the fact that they denote motion in physical space involving walking-like movements but there is no meaning of upward direction. Thus, contrary to the Objectivist theory of categories, there is no feature shared by examples (9)–(12). They are members of the category 'climb' only because they each possess one – but only one – of the cluster of features that characterise the central area.

The relevance of the concept of experiential domains is illustrated by example (13), though in a slightly different way from its role in the Dyirbal system. The fact that we can use the expression *climb down* in order to refer to the process of making a concession in negotiations derives from an interaction between two metaphors that are pervasive in the everyday use of English. One of these metaphors is 'argument is war'; the other is 'power is up' (Lakoff and Johnson 1980). We will be devoting more detailed discussion to these metaphors and to the general significance of metaphorical processes in Chapter 4. As far as this example is concerned, let us simply note at this stage that speakers of English think of the process of negotiation as a battle between opposing forces. We also think of the 'victor' in a battle as occupying a higher position in physical space than the 'loser'. Since the aim of the battle/negotiation is to attempt to impose one's will on the other participant, concession ('bowing' to the will of the opponent in some respect) is linked to the notion of defeat. And since defeat is loss of power, defeat and concession are 'down'. There are probably further subtleties here. The fact that concession is expressed in terms of 'climbing down' rather than simply 'moving down' or 'walking down' may have something to do with the fact that it is a somewhat delicate operation and is therefore metaphorically linked to the process of climbing down a rock face. Be that as it may, the main point here is that one domain of experience (negotiation) is being constructed in terms of a quite different domain (battle) through the metaphor 'power is up'. These processes mediate a very specific ideology and thus shed light on how speakers of English have learned to construct their world. The example indicates the potential of metaphor (a highly culture-specific phenomenon) to become involved in the construction of the radial networks that constitute the categories of our experience.

There is one further point that we should make about the examples here. It would clearly be an oversimplification to suggest that English forces its speakers to assign the range of phenomena identified in examples (6)–(13) to a single category. The point here is that in most, if not all, cases, there are alternative ways of talking about the particular situations: *She walked up the hill, She struggled up the hill, She sauntered up the hill, she moved up the ladder, She made her way up the ladder, The aircraft rose into the sky, The aircraft soared into the sky, The spider crawled across the web* and so on. Of course, some of these alternatives construct rather different meanings, in some cases more specific meanings, from those in the original sentences. However, we have already made the point (pages 8–14) that a linguistic expression can never encode all the features of a situation, no matter how explicit the speaker may wish to be. It is never, therefore, simply a question of choosing a form of words that 'corresponds' in some straightforward sense to a particular situation. Rather, languages provide their speakers with a range of options (in many respects an open-ended range) for talking about particular situations. In this sense there is considerable flexibility with respect to how particular situations can be constructed, how they are to be inscribed into existing classificatory schemas. This is not to say that there may not be quite strong pressures on the language user in particular contexts to construct a situation in a particular way, pressures that derive not only from the nature of the linguistic units that the language makes available but from general conventions of usage. We will be taking up these issues in more detail in subsequent chapters.

Conclusion

This chapter started out from Saussure's argument that a language constitutes a system of interrelated terms, such that the 'value' of any linguistic term derives from its relationship to all the other terms in the system. This is a fundamental principle of the structural approach to language. The major consequence of this argument is that the terms in one system are not commensurable with those in another, that different languages 'carve up' reality in different ways. Although there are certain difficulties with the details of Saussure's argument (the problem of drawing conclusions about human conceptual systems on the basis of the notion of 'linguistic value', the degree of idealisation involved in the idea that a language is an autonomous static system, the problematic implications of the metaphor of 'segmentation'), the fundamental point is crucial to the principle of linguistic relativism. The fact that our native language operates with a set of terms that stand in a highly structured set of relationships to each other is clearly vital to our understanding of the process by which our experience of the world is constructed and encoded.

Whorf took Saussure's arguments a step further through his analysis of Amerindian languages. He was able to provide detailed evidence showing how the existence of specific linguistic forms (*kwaškwi* in Shawnee, for example) can function as conceptual units, around which the interpretation of everyday situations is constructed. Since linguistic units play such a structuring role in a wide variety of situations, they act as a bonding mechanism that tie a range of situations together for speakers of the language in question. In other languages, however, the existence of a quite different set of conceptual units leads inevitably to the construction of quite different classificatory networks. It is perhaps useful to note that this observation depends on the idea advanced in the previous chapter that language is a highly selective tool in the encoding of our perceptions. If language encoded **every** aspect of an objectively defined situation, then there would inevitably be total commensurability between encodings in different languages. It is the highly selective nature of the encoding process that allows scope for situations to be constructed in quite different terms in different languages.

Whorf also provided detailed evidence for the connection that Saussure had postulated between grammatical and conceptual categories. In particular he showed how many grammatical categories that seem quite arbitrary to outside observers turn out to be highly motivated, once an understanding of the relevant culture is brought to bear. This idea, advocated by Whorf at a time when the dominant view in linguistics was that grammatical systems were entirely arbitrary and unmotivated, has gained wide acceptance as a result of subsequent work in sociolinguistics.

Recent work has developed considerably our understanding of the relationship between linguistic structure and world-view. Dixon's study of Dyirbal has shown that Whorf's insistence on the need to focus on **covert** categories was somewhat misplaced – that equally revealing insights can be derived from a careful analysis of **overt** categories. This point was enthusiastically taken up by Lakoff. He argues that the Dyirbal word-class system is not only highly significant for the light that it throws on Dyirbal culture but that it constitutes a perfect example of an important type of human conceptual category. The major word classes of Dyirbal are radially structured. They have a central semantic core and less central members connected to the core by chaining. The nature of these structures poses major problems for the traditional theory of categories in a number of ways. The radial structure means that there may be no criterial defining features shared by all members of the category. Strands in the structure may be constituted in terms of particular domains of experience that are highly culture-specific, an observation which seriously undermines the notion of objectively given categories. This claim is further borne out by an analysis of other categories such as the English word *climb*, showing that the strands of the radial structure may even be constructed in terms of the notoriously culture-specific phenomenon of metaphor.

Lakoff's theory of categories provides the outline of a solution to the problem with Saussure's argument concerning the relationship between linguistic value and cognition. Citing examples such as *sheep* and *mouton* in English and French, Saussure had noted that terms in different languages may have the same signification but not the same 'value', from which he drew the problematic conclusion that different languages construct different conceptual systems. The problem with this argument is that it suggests that the process of acquiring a particular vocabulary involves the acquisition of a particular set of internally homogeneous, discrete concepts, each of which is paired in a relatively straightforward way with a particular vocabulary item. Lakoff has shown that in fact conceptual 'units' are characterised by complex internal structure (including differentiation between central and peripheral areas, radial connections, chaining) and that these conceptual networks may connect, interweave and overlap with other networks in intricate ways. There seems little doubt that language does have an important role to play in the construction of these networks, but that Saussure's metaphor of segmentation is misleading in suggesting that our conceptual schemas are much more rigidly and discretely structured than is in fact the case.

Concepts such as 'the world-view of the Shawnee', 'the Dyirbal culture', 'the ideology of speakers of English' have figured prominently in this chapter. Although they undoubtedly have a certain validity at a very general level of analysis, they have the drawback of constructing the notion of a relatively homogeneous language tied to a relatively homogeneous culture or world-view. This is a position which we will modify considerably as the book proceeds. Over the next few chapters, we will move to a more 'delicate' level of analysis in an exploration of the way in which different perspectives, different ideologies interact within a particular language and a particular culture. The next chapter constitutes a transitional phase in this move. It will deal essentially with two relatively homogeneous perspectives and in this respect it connects with the themes with which we have been concerned above. However, the perspectives in question, although mediated through English, are quite unfamiliar, even alien. Thus it will emerge that a language does not 'impose' a particular world-view on its speakers (as some interpreters of Whorf have suggested) but that there is in fact ample scope for the mediation of quite different modes of perception within a single linguistic 'system'.

Notes

1. The difficulties inherent in inferring the existence of conceptual distinctions on the basis of the notion of linguistic value have been demonstrated experimentally by Eleanor Rosch (1973). She showed, for example, that primary colour categories are real for the Dani people of Papua New Guinea, even though Dani has only two words for major colours (see Lakoff 1987: 40–1 for discussion). Other experiments have produced similar findings for three-year-old children (Heider 1971).

2. For a classic illustration of this approach see Katz and Fodor (1964).

3. Strictly speaking these forms are parts of noun markers, rather than full markers and should therefore be represented as *bala-*, *yala-*, *ngala-* (Dixon 1972: 45).

3 Language and world-view: Golding and Faulkner

Introduction

We have noted in earlier discussion an opposition between two different views of language. On one view a language is a kind of object which its native speakers 'acquire' in the first few years of life – a process which causes them to construct a particular way of seeing the world that is strongly influenced by the 'structures' of their native tongue. On the other view language is an aspect of human behaviour rather than an object. Even within a particular culture human behaviour is notoriously heterogeneous and since language is an extremely important medium of social interaction and social differentiation, it too must be a highly heterogeneous phenomenon.

How have these quite different perspectives arisen? The first tradition is associated with those linguists who have seen as their main aim the description of phonological and grammatical systems. It arises from the fact that in general terms the phonological and syntactic resources of a particular language are fully shared by nearly all those who use the system, even when those speakers are scattered over enormous geographical distances and over widely divergent cultures. To take a very obvious case, if we compare standard British English with standard Australian English, then the phonological and grammatical systems of the two varieties exhibit remarkable similarities, even though they are spoken at opposite ends of the earth. This leads to the view that there is a single relatively homogeneous object called 'English' which has slightly different forms or manifestations in the different regions in which it is spoken. Some linguists adopt the position that it is the task of the linguist to take this underlying, somewhat abstract phenomenon as the major object of study, as the following well-known quotation demonstrates:

> Linguistic theory is concerned primarily with an ideal speaker-listener, in a completely homogeneous speech-community, who knows its language perfectly and is unaffected by such grammatically irrelevant conditions as memory limitations, distractions, shifts of attention and interest and errors (random or characteristic) in applying his knowledge of the language in actual performance. (Chomsky 1965: 3)

This perspective seems to be the commonsense view, since almost all our everyday ways of talking about language encapsulate it. The very fact that we have labels such as 'English', 'Italian', 'Swahili' suggests strongly that there are object-like entities to which these labels refer. Moreover we often use such labels to assign attributes to the 'objects' in question: 'Italian is a beautiful language', 'Chinese has more speakers than any other language', 'French is descended from Latin' and so on.

The contrasting view that language is a heterogeneous phenomenon derives from a long tradition of study of language in society. It has been articulated particularly clearly by the Russian linguist Mikhail Bakhtin.

> Language is ... unitary only as an abstract grammatical system of normative forms, taken in isolation from the concrete, ideological conceptualizations that fill it, and in isolation from the uninterrupted process of historical becoming that is a characteristic of all living language. Actual social life and historical becoming create within an abstractly unitary national language a multitude of concrete worlds, a multitude of bounded verbal-ideological and social belief systems; within these various systems ... are elements of language filled with various semantic and axiological content and each with its own different sound. (Bakhtin 1981: 288)

This perspective on language tends to be associated with those linguists who have taken as their major focus of interest the functional aspect of language use. When we consider the enormous complexity of social structures within which a particular language operates, the discrepancies between individuals in terms of their access to the range of social functions, the power differences that characterise individuals in both the general social context and in specific situations, as well as the fact that all of these contexts are associated with different ways of speaking, one is inevitably led to focus on the heterogeneity of the phenomenon. It is this theme that we will be developing as the book proceeds. Following current practice, we will apply the term 'discourses' (a term derived from Foucault) to the many different ways of speaking that are associated with different social contexts, different speaking positions.[1] There is a sense in which no single individual 'knows English' in that nobody has access to or control over the vast range of discourses in which 'English' is used.

One further preliminary point needs to be made here. The idea that a language is a relatively homogeneous object has led most linguists to treat literary language as marginal. On this view the 'real' language is the language of the 'ordinary person' involved in 'normal, everyday communication'. Literature is seen as a highly specialised use of language, highly restricted in terms of its producers and consumers. The opposing view, however, in problematising the concept of 'ordinary language usage', also calls into question the distinction between literary and non-literary language. Once we see that so-called 'ordinary language usage' comprises a vast range of different discourses, then these heterogeneous practices merge in complex ways into the area of literary language. Bakhtin in fact identifies one of the central characteristics of the novel as the site of competing discourses, most of which overlap with discourses encountered in non-literary contexts.

> The novel can be defined as a diversity of social speech types (sometimes even diversity of languages) and a diversity of individual voices, artistically organized. The internal stratification of any single national language into social dialects, characteristic group behaviour, professional jargons, generic languages, languages of generations and age groups, tendentious languages, languages of the authorities, of various circles and of passing fashions, languages that serve the specific sociopolitical purposes of the day, even of the hour (each day has its own slogan, its own vocabulary, its own emphases) – this internal stratification present in every language at any given moment of its historical existence is the indispensable prerequisite for the novel as a genre. (Bakhtin 1981: 262–3)

Thus, the dichotomy implied by terms such as 'literary' and 'non-literary' language is entirely misleading within a functional perspective on language.

The aim of this chapter is to make an initial attack on the view that a particular language correlates with a single ideology. The texts to be discussed here are both drawn from the domain of literature and therefore each represent a world-view that has been created imaginatively. They both demonstrate in a quite striking manner the fact that it is possible for a particular language like English to be used in such a way that it mediates a distinctive world-view, one that contrasts markedly with the normal modes of perception of most speakers of English. In spite of significant differences in subject matter, the texts are closely related to each other by virtue of the fact that they share a particular set of linguistic characteristics. These features, which appear somewhat disparate at first sight, prove in fact to constitute a unitary phenomenon as mediators of a specific world-view. The fact that the same features appear in two works which are in other ways strikingly different from each other constitutes strong evidence for the connections that we will attempt to establish here between language and perception. One important point that will emerge is that, although certain aspects of the **structure** of a particular language may be oriented to a particular world-view, it is equally important to consider linguistic **usage** here. These texts illustrate the point that it is the selective and idiosyncratic application of the resources of a language that plays the major role in the mediation of perspective.

Golding: *The Inheritors*

The first text to be examined is William Golding's novel *The Inheritors*. The plot of *The Inheritors* derives from an anthropological fact – the discovery of Neanderthal remains in 1856 and the issues arising from this and other related finds.[2] One of the questions raised by these discoveries is whether the Neanderthalers were ancestors of *homo sapiens* or whether they constituted a closely related but separate branch of primates; a branch which died out possibly as a result of competition from the co-existing line of *homo sapiens. The Inheritors* starts essentially from this latter premise. The central character of the novel, Lok, is a member of a small group of Neanderthalers. When the novel opens, the 'people' (as the group is known) are in the process of moving from their winter quarters near the sea to their summer quarters in the mountains. It is in the course of this migration that they come into contact with an invading group of *homo sapiens* – a contact that leads in the course of the novel to the extinction of Lok and his people.

Although the people are technologically less 'advanced' than their rivals, they have qualities of innocence and spirituality which the others lack. They have a strong religious sense, connected with the glaciers ('ice goddesses') in the mountains. They see nature as an extension of themselves rather than as something to be used. Their relationships with each other are close, warm and free of the rivalries and jealousies that characterise the invading group. Part of this is connected with the way in which they communicate. As well as possessing language, they have something akin to a telepathic gift, which occasionally allows them to share 'pictures' with each other. Sometimes these pictures can be evoked by language, but it is not always successful in this way – particularly in the case of Lok, who is not the most intelligent member of the group. Lok is an innocent. Part of the irony of the novel is the curiosity and excitement that he feels at the first indications of the presence of 'the new people'.

For the major part of the novel, situations and events are perceived through the eyes of Lok, and mediated through his language (his system of meanings). One of the most telling illustrations of this point involves an event which occurs after one of the people's children, Liku, has been abducted by the invaders. Lok is following Liku's cries, when he comes to a river and catches a glimpse of one of the 'others' on the far side. What happens then is expressed in the following terms.

(1) *The bushes twitched again. Lok steadied by the tree and gazed. A head and a chest faced him, half hidden. There were white bone things behind the leaves and hair. The man had white bone things above his eyes and under the mouth so that his face was longer than a face should be. The man turned sideways in the bushes and looked at Lok along his shoulder. A stick rose upright and there was a lump of bone in the middle. Lok peered at the stick and the lump of bone and the small eyes in the bone things over the face. Suddenly Lok understood that the man was holding the stick out to him but neither he nor Lok could reach across the river. He would have laughed if it were not for the echo of the screaming in his*

> *head. The stick began to grow shorter at both ends. Then it*
> *shot out to full length again.*
> *The dead tree by his ear acquired a voice.*
> *'Clop!'*
> *His ears twitched and he turned to the tree. By his face there*
> *had grown a twig. A twig that smelt of other and of goose and*
> *of the bitter berries that Lok's stomach told him he must not*
> *eat.* (Golding 1961: 106)

The differences between Lok's perception of the world and ours
show up in this passage at a number of levels. At the lexical level,
words such as *stick* for 'bow' and *twig* for 'arrow' reflect the fact
that Lok does not fashion tools out of natural objects – he is content to operate in nature rather than upon it – and he does not
therefore have two distinct lexical sets, one for manufactured objects and one for the corresponding natural objects. This also
shows up elsewhere – the dug-outs used by the new people are
referred to as *logs*.

At the syntactic level, the passage is characterised by the use of
intransitive rather than transitive structures. Thus, the intransitive
expressions *A stick rose upright, The stick ... grew shorter at
both ends, Then it shot out to full length again* correspond to our
transitive structures *He raised the bow, He drew the bow, He re-
leased the bow*. These grammatical differences represent a specific
mode of perception. For us the meaning expressed by *A stick rose
upright* is in conflict with our understanding of how entities in the
world normally behave, so that when we experience sense impressions similar to those experienced here by Lok, our cognitive orientation causes us to construct an interpretation of the experience in
terms of an agent acting upon an object. For Lok, however, given
his general understanding of nature and the place of people and
objects within it, the corresponding sense data require no such
interpretation (Halliday 1971: 350).

The central irony here stems from a particular mode of interpretation operating at a higher level. Lok assumes that the man's ges-
ture is essentially a friendly one (*Lok understood that the man was
holding the stick out to him*). He recognises the absurdity of this
interpretation but is unable to formulate an alternative.

The passage cited above is not an isolated case. There are many
systematic differences between the meanings expressed by Lok and

those that characterise our own world-view. The examples below, mostly from the early part of the book, illustrate cases in which natural objects can move or otherwise act of their own accord.

(2) *The bush went away* (p. 11)
(3) *The log has gone away* (p. 12)
(4) *As if the log had crawled off on business of its own* (p. 14)
(5) *The bushes waded out* (p. 107)
(6) *The logs sidled right into the bank* (p. 139)

One way of describing these cases is to say that the 'selectional re-strictions' that operate in normal language, such that certain verbs of movement require animate subjects, do not apply. Another (and perhaps better) description might be to say that natural objects are characterised as animates in Lok's grammar and in his world-view.

It is interesting to note that natural objects are not the only en-tities that enjoy greater autonomy in Lok's world than they do in ours. This is also true of parts of the body.

(7) *Lok's feet were clever. They saw. They threw him round the displayed roots of the beeches* (p. 11)
(8) *His nose examined this stuff and did not like it* (p. 106)
(9) *His feet would not enter it* (p. 189)
(10) *His ears took over the business of living. They discounted the noise of the people and concentrated on the moorhens* (p. 195)

The pervasive animacy that characterises Lok's world imposes on him a more restricted sense of self, so that the parts of his own body are assigned to the external world of 'non-self' rather than the internal world of 'self'. This blurring of Lok into the natural world connects with the kind of relationship with nature estab-lished by the lexical and syntactic patterns discussed above.

Another linguistic feature which serves as an indicator of Lok's world-view is the use of progressive aspect. This is particularly no-ticeable in the following passage.

(11) *There came a screaming from the figures by the hollow log and a loud bang from the jam. The tree began to move for-ward and the logs were lumbering about like the legs of a giant. The crumplefaced woman was struggling with Tuami on*

the rock by the hollow log; she burst free and came running
towards Lok. There was movement everywhere, screaming,
demoniac activity; the old man was coming across the tum-
bling logs. He threw something at Fa. Hunters were holding
the hollow log against the terrace and the head of the tree with
all its weight of branches and wet leaves was drawing along
them. The fat woman was lying in the log, the crumpled
woman was in it with Tanakil, the old man was tumbling into
the back. The boughs crashed and drew along the rock with
an agonized squealing. Fa was sitting by the water holding her
head. The branches took her. She was moving with them out
into the water and the hollow log was free of the rock and was
drawing away. (p. 216)

The striking feature of this passage is the heavy use of progressive
forms such as *The logs were lumbering about, The crumplefaced*
woman was struggling with Tuami, The old man was coming
across the tumbling logs, Hunters were holding the hollow log,
The head of the tree ... was drawing along them, The fat woman
was lying in the log, The old man was tumbling into the back, Fa
was sitting by the water holding her head, She was moving with
them out into the water, [The log] was drawing away. In normal
usage, a series of progressives of this kind typically denotes a number of events or situations which are 'in progress' simultaneously:
The sun was shining, the birds were singing, Lord Emsworth was
happily pottering in the garden. In this case, however, it is clear
that many of the events were not simultaneous. Rather, we have a
sequence of happenings. This is particularly clear in the case of
'the old man' – he came across the logs, threw something at Fa,
jumped into the dug-out with 'the crumpled woman' and pushed it
out into the river (note the sequence of non-progressive forms in
constructing this interpretation). And the situation of Fa sitting by
the water holding her head is succeeded by her moving out into the
water (after being taken by the branches). Yet both event sequen-
ces are depicted by progressives.

The main effect of the progressives here is clearly to create a
sense of confusion, since this is precisely how Lok experiences the
situation. A number of distinct sensory experiences impinge on
him but they all coalesce into a single blurred impression of con-
fused activity. Just as he failed to make connections between the
sense impressions associated with the bow and arrow, so he fails

here to see the way in which these experiences are connected. The use of progressives is only one way in which this kind of effect is achieved. The structure of the text also contributes to it – the sentences reporting percepts associated with the old man, for example, are separated from each other by sentences reporting other perceptual experiences.

The effect created by the progressive forms derives from the fact that the general function of this grammatical form is to focus on a particular sub-part of an event or situation (Huddleston 1984: 153). When we say *It was raining when I arrived home yesterday*, no information is given about the time when the rain started or about when it stopped. Rather, attention is focused on a very small part of that whole event – the part that coincided with the moment of my arrival home. There is a sense in which we could say that *It was raining* serves to 'freeze' the action at a particular moment in time, to create a static situation out of a dynamic process. This is illustrated by the fact that we can capture the concept 'he was falling off his horse' with a single still photograph but the process represented by 'he fell off his horse' can only be captured with a **sequence** of still photographs, or by a movie, since perception of the latter involves a series of sense experiences and an understanding of the relationships between them.

The stative character of the progressive is connected with the fact that there are a whole range of phenomena that Lok sees in stative rather than dynamic terms. Consider such examples as the following:

(12) *Then there were feelings between them* (p. 14)
(13) *Mal is not old but clinging to his mother's back. There is more water not only here but along the trail where we come. A man is wise. He makes men take a tree that has fallen* (p. 15)
(14) *Fa looked again at the island. Then suddenly she was writhing herself round the corner and was gone* (p. 99)
(15) *Suddenly Lok understood that the man was holding the stick out to him* (p. 106)
(16) *All at once it seemed to him that his head was new* (p. 191)

In these examples events that could be reported in dynamic terms (*They began to share feelings, A man had an idea, Fa disappeared, Lok realised*, and so on) are reported in stative terms

(*Then there were feelings*, *A man is wise*, *[Fa] was gone*, *Lok understood*). The underlying assumption about the nature of the world conveyed by these stative expressions is that situations suddenly come into existence with a certain degree of spontaneity – they do not necessarily arise out of earlier, preparatory circumstances. At one moment, Fa is looking at the island; then she is suddenly in the process of 'writhing herself' round the corner, a state of affairs which, even though unprepared for, apparently occasions Lok no surprise. And even here, the use of the progressive has the effect of separating out this process from the subsequent situation of Fa's absence. The general characteristic of Lok's world, then, is that events which for us are linked by a chain of causation are for him autonomous. Sensory experiences succeed each other without being tied together by strands of agentivity and causation that we call 'making sense' of the world.

The final linguistic feature characterising the language of *The Inheritors* that is worth mentioning here is conjunction. Examples (17)–(19) constitute a small sample of sentences from the novel consisting of conjoined clauses.

(17) *A stick rose upright and there was a lump of bone in the middle* (p. 106)
(18) *He rushed to the edge of the water and came back* (p. 107)
(19) *The tree began to move forward and the legs were lumbering about* (p. 216)

The striking feature of these examples is that the word *and* which conjoins the two clauses here is an additive element rather than a purposive one. It contrasts with the meaning of *and* that occurs in such sentences as *I got up and went to the window*, where *and* functions not only to express the idea that the second event followed the first in time but also suggests that the first event happened **in order that** the second event might happen. The two are therefore tied together by the notion of causativity. The absence of this causative link in Lok's perception of the world shows up very clearly again in these examples.

The general point emerging from this discussion is that the language of *The Inheritors* is characterised by a set of features which appear on the surface to be unrelated to each other but which clearly serve a single function. They all serve to mediate the world-view of the central character. There are various facets of Lok's perception of the world, each of which finds its expression in one or more features of the language. Certain grammatical structures assigning qualities of animacy and agency to natural objects arise from Lok's perception of himself as another kind of natural object, not essentially different or distinct from logs, bushes, trees and the like. This lack of distinctiveness is also expressed by the semantics of body parts and by transitivity patterns. The fact that Lok operates **within** rather than **upon** nature is related to his relatively weak grasp of the notion of causality, for it is essentially this that prevents him from making tools. This aspect of Lok's world-view is also mediated by the transitivity patterns as well as by those involving progressive aspect, stative constructions and conjunction.

Faulkner: *The Sound and the Fury*

The claim that there are connections between the rather disparate textual features indicated in the preceding discussion can be confirmed if the same set of features is found elsewhere. Since the unifying link is the fact that they mediate a particular world-view, it seems natural to look for supporting evidence in a text characterised by the same kind of contrasts that are implicitly present in *The Inheritors*. Such a text is William Faulkner's novel *The Sound and the Fury*. Although there are many important differences between the two novels, there are sufficient common threads for a linguistic comparison to be worthwhile. In *The Sound and the Fury*, as in *The Inheritors*, the events in the early part of the novel are seen through the eyes of a character whose world-view contrasts sharply with our own, so that both novels pose the reader with the problem of making sense of the narrative. Like Lok, Benjy – the central character of the first part of *The Sound and the Fury* – is cognitively 'retarded'. He too lives in a world of uncoordinated sensory experiences, a world in which the notion of causality is absent, or at least restricted. As in *The Inheritors*, however, this deficiency is compensated for by an innocence, a freshness and intensity of experience which throw into sharp relief the lack of these qualities in the other characters.

These parallels show up very clearly in a comparison of the linguistic features of the two novels. Consider the following sentences from *The Sound and the Fury*:

(20) *Then the barn wasn't there and we had to wait until it came back* (Faulkner 1964: 26)

(21) *Then he fell into the flowers and I ran into the box. But when I tried to climb onto it, it jumped away and hit me on the back of the head* (p. 42)

(22) *The room went away but I didn't hush and the room came back* (p. 46)

(23) *I tried to pick up the flowers. Luster picked them up and he went away* (p. 55)

(24) *I looked at the fire. A long piece of wire came across my shoulder. It went to the door and then the fire went away* (p. 58)

These sentences parallel those in *The Inheritors* in which words denoting natural objects function as the subject of verbs of motion. Certainly there are differences between the perceptions of Lok and Benjy. Benjy lives in a world of man-made objects and his vocabulary reflects this. Words such as *barn, box, room, wire, door* could not have occurred in *The Inheritors*. Apart from this, however, the parallels are striking. All of these objects are endowed with the same kind of animacy that is attributed to natural objects in *The Inheritors*.

This also shows up in the way that Benjy conceptualises the parts of his own body.

(25) *My throat made a sound. It made the sound again and I stopped trying to get up and it made the sound again* (p. 42)

(26) *Dilsey reached back and hit Luster on the head. My voice was going louder every time ... My voice went louder then and my hand tried to go back to my mouth* (p. 59)

(27) *I squatted there, holding the slipper. I couldn't see it but my hands saw it* (p. 70)

As with Lok, the pervasive animacy of Benjy's world is associated with a way of interpreting the status of his own body that creates a distinctive, more restricted sense of self.

The transitivity structures that play such an important role in mediating Lok's world-view are also echoed in *The Sound and the Fury*.

(28) *I could see them hitting ... They took the flag out and they*

were hitting ... 'Here, caddie!' He hit ... They were hitting
little across the pasture (p. 11)

(29) *I tried to pick up the flowers. Luster picked them up and they*
went away (p. 55)

(30) *He leaned down and puffed his face. The candles went away*
(p. 57)

(31) *A long piece of wire came across my shoulder. It went to the*
door and then the fire went away (p. 58)

(32) *Father went to the door and looked at us again. Then the dark*
came back, and he stood black in the door and then the door
turned black again (p. 72)

In one case here, we have an example of a grammatical departure
from 'normal' usage, with the normally transitive verb *hit* being
used intransitively. More interesting, however, are intransitive
structures such as *went away* in (30). Examples of this kind highlight the fact that even such a mundane expression as *blow out* (as
in *He blew out the candles*) encapsulates a particular view of the
world. It is in fact just one member of a very large set of such expressions (*cut down, carry in, take out, prise apart, drive insane,*
make angry) which have in common the fact that they tie together
in a single linguistic structure both the nature of a particular process (*blow, cut, carry*) and the end result of the process. In other
words, their use is inextricably bound up with the notion of causality. In examples such as (30) the causal link that binds the process to the result has been teased apart: *He ... puffed his face.*
The candles went away. This results in the 'replacement' of the
fully transitive expression *blow out* with two separate structures,
the first one a transitive structure with Luster operating on a part
of his own body, the second an intransitive one in which an inani-
mate object functions as the subject of a verb of motion.

The significant role played both by stativity and progressive aspect in the mediation of world-view in *The Inheritors* is replicated
in *The Sound and the Fury*.

(33) *Quentin held my arm and we went toward the barn. Then the*
barn wasn't there and we had to wait until it came back (p.
26)

(34) *I wasn't crying but the ground wasn't still and then I was*
crying (p. 26)

(35) *Luster had some spools and he and Quentin fought and Quentin*

> had the spools. Luster cried and Frony came and gave Luster a
> tricar to play with and then I had the spools (p. 34)

(36) She went away. There wasn't anything in the door. Then
Caddy was in it (p. 46)

(37) And then her head came into my lap and she was crying, holding me and I began to cry (p. 57)

(38) Dilsey reached back and hit Luster on the head. My voice was
going loud every time (p. 59)

(39) Caddy put the spoon into my mouth easy. There was a black
spot on the inside of the bowl ... It got down below the
mark. Then the bowl was empty. It went away. 'He's hungry
tonight', Caddy said. The bowl come back and I couldn't see
the spot. Then I could. 'He's starved tonight', Caddy said (p.
69)

Again, it is very clear that there are important differences between
Benjy's perception of everyday events and our own. Purposive and
causal factors in particular are missing, so that the elements which
create a conceptual unit out of a series of experiences are absent
from the encoding here. The result is a description in terms of a
succession of apparently unrelated static situations. This is true
even when Benjy himself creates a particular situation, as in
example (39) where he is the one who causes the spot on the side
of the bowl to appear.

Finally, it is noticeable that conjunction plays the same kind of
role in Benjy's perception of events as it does in Lok's.

(40) They took the flag out and they were hitting (p. 11)

(41) My throat made a sound. It made the sound again and I
stopped trying to get up and it made the sound again and I
began to cry (p. 42)

(42) Luster picked up the flowers and they went away (p. 55)

(43) A long piece of wire came across my shoulder. It went to the
door and then the fire went away (p. 58)

In the discussion of The Inheritors it was noted that there were
certain events in which the existence of a causal chain was evident
to the reader but not understood by the perceiver. This was particularly clear in the incident of the bow and arrow and in the activities of the old man in the scene described in extract (11) above
(page 55). In these cases, events that were causally related were re-

ported merely in terms of temporal sequence. The same is clearly true of these examples of conjunction. The causal link between the appearance of the wire and the disappearance of the fire is clear to the reader, as is the intent behind the removal of the flag, but these connections remain hidden from Benjy. Again, even when he himself is the causer of the event, as in example (41) the notion of human agency is essentially absent.

Conclusion

We started out in this chapter from the observation that there are different ways of conceptualising language itself – as a homogeneous object tied to a single ideology or as a set of heterogeneous behaviours mediating a multiplicity of perspectives. Golding and Faulkner have demonstrated quite conclusively that there is no barrier in principle to the creation of new ways of using English that invoke unfamiliar perspectives.

Of particular interest here is the fact that the features characterising the language of Lok and Benjy constitute a somewhat disparate set, ranging over selection restrictions between subjects and verbs, transitivity choices, aspectual choices, stativity and conjunction. In other words, Lok and Benjy have a particular 'way of speaking' about the various aspects of their experience – about objects, about their own body-parts, about the actions of others – that is quite systematic and coherent (though it may have certain limitations from our point of view). Of course these are artificial texts, constructed for a specific literary purpose. However, we will see similar situations in subsequent chapters where non-literary texts can also be seen to exhibit particular ways of speaking that are characterisable in terms of functionally related clusters of grammatical and semantic features.

We have already applied the term 'discourse' to particular ways of speaking about phenomena that derive from a particular perspective – the habit of White Australians of referring to 'European settlement', for example. We can now develop this concept by identifying Lok's way of speaking about the world (or Benjy's) as a specific 'discourse', where this term is interpreted in such a way as to identify a particular cluster of semantic and grammatical characteristics that mediate a particular perspective. In the case of Lok and Benjy the features in question are particularly salient because of the distinctive characteristics of their ideology. What has to be demonstrated now is how the concept of discourse applies to the more subtle processes of interaction between social and linguistic factors in non-literary language.

Notes

1. See, for example, Foucault 1971, 1972.
2. The novel is prefaced by an extract from H. G. Wells's *Outline of History* referring to the Neanderthalers.

4 *Metaphor*

Introduction

Towards the end of *The Inheritors* Lok is desperately trying to understand the terrible things that have happened to him and his people. The 'new people' seem to him possessed of the same kind of magical powers as those he attributes to his god, Oa. Suddenly he experiences a remarkable insight:

> Lok discovered "Like". He had used likeness all his life without being aware of it. Fungi on a tree were ears, the word was the same but acquired a distinction by circumstances that could never apply to the sensitive things on the side of his head. Now, in a convulsion of the understanding Lok found himself using likeness as a tool as surely as ever he had used a stone to hack at sticks or meat. Likeness could grasp the white-faced hunters with a hand, could put them into the world where they were thinkable and not a random and unrelated irruption.
>
> He was picturing the hunters who went out with bent sticks in skill and malice.
>
> "The people are like a famished wolf in the hollow of a tree."
>
> He thought of the fat woman defending the new one from the old man, thought of her laughter, of men working at a single load and grinning at each other.
>
> "The people are like honey trickling from a crevice in the rock."
>
> He thought of Tanakil playing, her clever fingers, her laughter, and her stick.
>
> "The people are like honey in the round stones, the new honey that smells of dead things and fire."
>
> They had emptied the gap of its people with little more than a turn of their hands.
>
> "They are like the river and the fall, they are a people of the fall; nothing stands against them."

1992

> He thought of their patience, of the broad man Tuami creating a
> stag out of the coloured earth.
> "They are like Oa."

In this extraordinary passage there are strong echoes of Whorf's
argument that our world is structured through the relationships
that we establish between different situations, through our perceptions of similarity. It is this network of relationships that constitutes the fabric of our cognitive system, that makes our world
'thinkable'. Moreover, these perceptions of similarity operate
through language. Lok suddenly realises that the word he uses for
'fungi' is the same as the one he uses for 'ears' and, more import-
antly, that this is not an accidental fact. This observation points to
the main theme of this chapter – the crucial role of metaphor not
only in language but in the way in which we understand our
world.

   Until quite recently, metaphor was thought of by most people as
a process that was marginal to the everyday use of language, as a
phenomenon that was confined to special domains such as that of
literary language. As a consequence of the marginalisation of the
literary language referred to in Chapter 3, metaphor was also mar-
ginalised, or even ignored by linguists. It was also thought of as a
linguistic rather than as a **conceptual** phenomenon. Lakoff and
Johnson (1980: 3) make these points in the following terms:

> Metaphor is for most people a device of the poetic imagination and
> the rhetorical flourish – a matter of extraordinary rather than ordi-
> nary language. Moreover, metaphor is typically viewed as charac-
> teristic of language alone, a matter of words rather than thought or
> action. For this reason, most people think they can get along per-
> fectly well without metaphor. We have found, on the contrary, that
> metaphor is pervasive in everyday life, not just in language but in
> thought and action. Our ordinary conceptual system, in terms of
> which we both think and act, is fundamentally metaphorical in
> nature.

Metaphor plays an important role in language at a number of different levels. It is relevant to the level of word meaning and it is
also relevant to the more general level of discourse. We will deal
with each of these points in turn.

Metaphor and word meaning

As an illustration of the claim that metaphor plays a fundamental role in ordinary, everyday language, let us consider some aspects of the meaning and distribution of a very basic element in the English lexicon – the word *give*. Consider, in particular, the following examples.

(1) *Jo gave Kim a book*
(2) *Jo gave Kim a push*
(3) *Jo gave Kim a hearing test*
(4) *Jo gave Kim an opportunity to speak*
(5) *Jo gave Kim some good advice*
(6) *Jo gave Kim a lot of help*
(7) *Jo gave Kim a strange look*

Give appears to cover an extensive semantic range here. The traditional approach (as exemplified by the practice of generations of lexicographers) is to treat situations of this kind as cases of polysemy or multiple meaning. The assumption is that a number of different meanings can be assigned to the word in question according to the various contexts in which it occurs. Thus, whereas the meaning of *give* in (1) includes the notion of transfer of possession, this is clearly not applicable in (2) or (3) where Kim clearly does not come to possess a push in (2) or a hearing test in (3). The meaning of *give* in these examples seems akin rather to that of 'administer'. In (4), (5) and (6), however, neither of these meanings seems satisfactory. There is clearly no transfer of possession of an object and there is no direct application of a process by an agent to a patient of the kind suggested by the meaning of 'administer'. For these examples, a meaning like 'provide' or 'supply' seems more appropriate. Again, however, when we come to (7) none of the meanings so far established seems to fit too well. 'Jo's look' is not something that Kim comes to 'possess', nor is it something that is 'administered' or 'supplied' to him. A fourth meaning like 'transmit' seems to be required here.

There are clearly serious problems with the approach outlined above. One difficulty is that each new context in which the word *give* appears seems to force us to construct a new meaning – the approach does not provide satisfactory predictions or generalisations. A second problem is that the model does not explain why the same word *give* can be used for each of these various situations. Although the different meanings are clearly related to each other in some sense, the decision to treat them as separate dictionary entries fails to capture these intuitive relationships.

We can provide a more satisfactory explanation for these patterns by invoking the concept of metaphor in conjunction with a method of representing lexical meanings currently in use in Cognitive Grammar (Langacker 1987). Let us suppose that the basic meaning of *give* can be schematically represented somewhat as follows:

(8)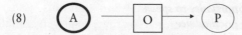

This diagram simply represents the idea that the central meaning of *give* involves the transfer of some object (O) from an agent (A) to a patient (P). (The heavy circle around 'A' represents the fact that *give* involves focus on the source of the transfer, in contrast to *receive* which involves focus on the 'target'.) The interpretation of (1) with respect to this diagram is straightforward: 'Jo' maps onto the 'A' element, 'the book' onto the 'O' element and 'Kim' onto the 'P' element. The mapping of most of the other sentences onto this structure is slightly more indirect, since it involves the metaphorical process of 'reification' (p. 6). This is particularly clear in (2) and (3), where the final Noun Phrase (*a push*, *a hearing test*) represents an event rather than a physical object. However, reification (operating through the grammatical process of 'nominalisation') enables us to conceptualise events as objects, so that (2) and (3) can be mapped without any real difficulty onto (8). This way of constructing the relationship between (1), (2) and (3) allows us to see *give* as having the same meaning in each sentence, the apparent differences between them being accounted for by reification. The absence of the notion of possession in (2) and (3) follows from the semantic character of the Noun Phrase which maps onto 'O'. A similar account can be given of examples (3)–(6), in which the entity denoted by the final Noun Phrase also denotes an abstract concept rather than a physical object.

The mapping of (7) onto (8) is rather more indirect and shows the importance of metaphor in word meaning with particular clarity. There are in fact a number of metaphorical (and other) processes in play here. The most basic process, once again, is reification, allowing us to conceive of a certain configuration of Jo's facial features as 'a look'. It is important to note that, literally speaking, 'a look' is clearly not a physical object located on the face, though the construction of such a metaphorical object is quite a familiar process in English, as illustrated by such expressions as *A sad look appeared on her face, Take that impertinent look off your face* and so on. As a second-stage operation this constructed 'look-object' then becomes associated with a particular kind of meaning or message by the process of metonymy. This association derives from the fact that internal emotional states are associated with certain facial 'expressions' and that this association is exploited in communication, so that relatively small changes in facial configuration (e.g. the raising of an eyebrow) can be interpreted as carrying meaning. Metonymy, then, 'converts' a certain arrangement of the facial features into a message or meaning. Reification then applies again to convert this message into an object through a metaphor that we will consider in the fourth section of this chapter – the 'container metaphor'. This treats the 'meaning' associated with a particular facial expression as an object that can be transferred from 'A' to 'P'.

This argument both confirms and elaborates on points made in earlier chapters. It confirms the notion that language is a classificatory instrument by claiming that the use of the word *give* in all these examples allows them all to be constructed as members of the same category at some level, whereas the polysemy-based approach in effect treats them as unrelated. It also confirms the point that metaphor can play a crucial role in constituting the strands that bind the members of a category together. For the purposes of the present argument, the main point is that it demonstrates the crucial role of metaphorical processes in the most fundamental aspects of language use. It seems to provide a much more satisfactory account of the distributional patterns and meanings of very basic items of vocabulary than alternative models.

Why is metaphor and the concept of 'likeness' so basic to language? The reason almost certainly has to do with considerations of economy and openness. The fact that a wide range of situations can be constructed in terms of the process of 'giving' makes for significant economies in the lexical resources of the language. There are also conceptual benefits. As Lok noted, the perception of likeness makes our world 'thinkable'. It enables us to adapt both conceptually and linguistically to new situations without too much difficulty. One of the reasons why English (and no doubt other languages) have been able to adapt so easily to the computer revolution, for example, is that much of our basic vocabulary has moved quite smoothly into the new field. Words such as *run*, *crash*, *freeze*, *write*, *save* and many others are in everyday use in this domain, applying to specific computational operations (*DOS is running*, *The system has crashed*, *When it freezes*, *you have to reboot*, *It's saving the file to disk*). In most cases, the application of the word to the new domain involves both semantic extension and, paradoxically, specialisation (there is a subtle difference between 'writing to disk' and 'saving to disk'). In all of these cases the process of chaining through metaphor is crucial.

It is interesting to note parenthetically that Whorf suffered from a curious myopia with respect to the semantic flexibility of English words, whilst noting the importance of this phenomenon in the Amerindian languages that he studied.

> The way the constituents are put together in these sentences of Shawnee and Nootka suggests a chemical compound, whereas their combination in English is more like a mechanical mixture . . . The typical Shawnee or Nootka combinations appear to work with a vocabulary of terms chosen with a view not so much to the utility of their immediate references as to the ability of the terms to combine suggestively with each other in manifold ways that elicit novel and useful images. (Whorf 1971c: 236)

In illustration of his point, Whorf cites two examples from Apache (p. 241):

(9)   *To-no-ga* (*to* = 'water', *no* = 'downward motion', *ga* = 'whiteness')

(10) *Gohl-ga* (*gohl* = 'manifests', *ga* = 'whiteness')

Whorf glosses (9) as 'there is a waterfall' ('whiteness moves downward as water') and (10) as 'there is a clearing in the forest' ('whiteness manifests itself'). Although Whorf was understandably struck by the novelty of these combinations, it seems that the familiarity of his own language blinded him to the novelty of the combinations in which the basic words of English occur. It is possible that these might appear no less exotic (and perhaps no less poetic) to an American Indian than the Apache combinations seem to us.

Metaphor in discourse

Some time ago, as I drove into an underground car park, my seven-year-old daughter asked me why the car radio had suddenly stopped working. My spontaneous (and probably somewhat un-helpful) reaction was to say that it was because of 'radio shadow'. This small example illustrates a rather different (and perhaps more important) way in which metaphor operates in the interpretation of language. It differs from the examples discussed in the previous section in that it is difficult to tie the process here to a particular word. What is happening, rather, is that one domain of experience (that of radio transmission) is being structured in terms of a differ-ent domain of experience (the perception of light) through the use of language. The metaphorical process is operating at a more general level.

In recent years linguists have devoted considerable attention to this use of metaphor in discourse. Lakoff and Johnson, in particu-lar, have identified a wide variety of metaphorical practices of this kind. As part of the process of learning English, children learn not only to talk about certain domains of experience in terms of other (usually more basic) domains but to structure them and concep-tualise them in those terms. In identifying such discursive practices, Lakoff and Johnson have gone a considerable way towards ident-ifying the ideology of our culture. The range of metaphors dis-cussed by Lakoff and Johnson is extensive. We will have space to consider only a few here, with the aim of bringing out some of their more important characteristics.

The first point is that the structuring of experience operates through conventional ways of using a particular language, some of which (though not all) are specific to that language, that culture. Consider for example, the metaphor 'argument is war', as exempli-fied by the following conventional ways of talking about argument (Lakoff and Johnson 1980: 4):

(11) *Your claims are indefensible*
(12) *She attacked every weak point in my argument*
(13) *His criticisms were right on target*
(14) *If you use that strategy, he'll wipe you out*
(15) *She shot down all my arguments*
(16) *Let me try to defend my position*

Not only is this clearly not an exhaustive list of examples of this metaphor, it also is equally clear that it would be impossible to compile a complete list. As a result of being exposed to these ways of talking, we have come to construct the whole process of argument in terms of battle, so that the vast, potentially infinite, array of concepts that are available for talking about war can be marshalled for discoursing about argument. As new means of warfare become available, these can be applied quite naturally to the domain of argument (*I'm afraid Jo's proposal went down in flames, Alan's missiles just didn't home in, I thought Kim was going to try a pre-emptive strike*). The metaphor, in other words, is highly productive. Its viability derives from the fact that there are many perceived similarities between argument and battle. In a meeting, for example, there are often different 'sides', each with mutually incompatible goals and the meeting provides the place in which the issue between the two sides has to be 'fought out' and decided. The model is highly 'motivated'.

The metaphor 'argument is war' is a specific manifestation of a more general process – the construction of relatively abstract domains in terms of more concrete domains. It is this principle that accounts for the fact that argument is structured in terms of battle rather than the reverse. The metaphors noted above, in which events and actions are constructed as physical objects, are part of a more general set in which abstract concepts are subject to reification:

  – 'the mind is a machine' (*My mind was racing, I'm really rusty today, I'll mull that over, My mind just isn't operating*)
  – 'the personality is a brittle object' (*He's going to pieces, She broke down, The experience just shattered her, He's a broken man, Get yourself back together again, She's really got it all together*)
  – 'the visual field in a container' (*It's out of sight, It's coming into view now, The sun's in my eyes*)
  – 'love is a substance' (*I have very little love left for him, She has such a lot of love to give, How much love do you have for her?*)

The concrete domain of physical space, in particular, is one that plays a significant role in a wide range of metaphors. These are called 'orientational metaphors' by Lakoff and Johnson (1980: 14–21).

- 'to understand someone is to be near them in physical space' (*I don't follow you there, We are right with you, She's way ahead of you, You've lost me*)
- 'life is a journey through physical space' (*I've come through that experience, A problem is looming ahead, We're running into difficulties here, I think he's on course, Thank God she's through her teens*)
- 'freedom of action is unrestricted movement in physical space' (*Stop crowding me, We've no room to manoeuvre here, You're cramping my style*)

Within the domain of physical space the contrast between 'up' and 'down' is a particularly fruitful source of metaphors.

- 'happy is up, sad is down' (*Cheer up, Why are you so down in the dumps?, I'm on top of the world, Everything's getting me down*)
- 'power is up' (*I have control over them, She is on top of the situation, She's at the height of her powers, We succumbed to a superior power, He's my inferior, He's under my control*)
- 'alive is up, dead is down' (*We'll have to have the cat put down, Lazarus rose from the dead, He's sinking fast*)
- 'healthy is up, sickness is down' (*I'm in top shape, They went down with the flu, I was really laid low by the virus*)
- 'more is up' (*our stocks are up, My savings have gone down, Profits have declined*)
- 'good is up, bad is down' (*Things are looking up, My opinion of Mary has gone down, His performance is definitely up on the previous one, Your standards have slipped, The quality of his work has gone down*)

Lakoff and Johnson note that such metaphors are strongly motivated. The concept of 'down' is associated with situations of inactivity such as sleep or death. Activity, on the other hand, is associated with upright posture. This fundamental distinction is the physical basis for these metaphors. At a more general level, the grounding of abstract domains in terms of the basic domains of physical action and physical space is perhaps a reflex of the fact that our general cognitive system develops from our initial interactions with the physical world as infants (the basis of our conceptual system being what Piaget calls 'sensori-motor knowledge').

It is crucial to note that conventional linguistic practices provide not just one way of structuring a particular domain but many. The convention of talking and thinking about argument in terms of war, though it is strongly entrenched in our conventional linguistic practices, is not by any means the only metaphor available to us. We can, for example, talk about arguments as if they were buildings (*I don't think this undermines my position, That point supports my claim, This may buttress your argument*), or as if they were games (*Who should go in to bat with that argument?, That remark didn't score many points, Ken was really on form in the meeting, We're starting from well behind the eight-ball here*). In some cases, the different ways of structuring a domain cohere with each other strongly. Aspects of war, for example, can also be conceptualised in terms of buildings, so that one can 'build up' one's forces in a particular area and one may fear that weaker areas may 'collapse' under pressure. These parallels may derive in part from the fact that many battles were focused on particular buildings (such as castles). In a siege, there is a very real sense in which a physical structure is a crucial part of the defender's army.

In other cases, however, metaphor provides real alternatives for the structuring of particular domains. In emphasising the structural coherence of many metaphors, Lakoff and Johnson tend to overlook this point. For example, as part of their argument that many metaphors are culture-specific, they invite us to imagine a society in which argument is structured not in terms of war but in terms of dance (Lakoff and Johnson 1980: 5).

> Try to imagine a culture where arguments are not viewed in terms of war, where no one wins or loses, where there is no sense of attacking or defending, gaining or losing ground, Imagine a culture where an argument is viewed as a dance, the participants are seen as performers, and the goal is to perform in a balanced and aesthetically pleasing way. In such a culture, people would view arguments differently, experience them differently, carry them out differently, and talk about them differently.

This argument suggests that metaphors derived from dance are not applicable to argument in our culture. In fact the situation is not so straightforward. It is perfectly true that the construction of argument in terms of dance is not as conventional as is the structuring of argument in terms of battle. But there are a number of general metaphors derived from dance that can be applied without great difficulty to the process of argument: *Richard waltzed through Alan's objections quite effortlessly, Helen showed some fancy footwork in dealing with the first item on the agenda, I wish Ken would stop all these pirouettes and come to the point.* Practically all our activities can in fact provide metaphors of quite general application: *I find Kim quite difficult to read, I wish he wouldn't embroider all his stories, She just sailed through the exam.* It is extremely difficult to envisage any absolute constraints on this process of constructing one domain in terms of another, providing that there is some kind of basis or motivation. Metaphor is quite clearly a major source of creativity in the everyday use of language.

It will be useful at this point to reconsider briefly the earlier discussion of linguistic relativity (Chapter 2) in the light of the notion of metaphor being developed here. Whorf's argument, too, was concerned essentially with the connections between various aspects of experience. He proposed that the structure of our native language causes us to see certain phenomena as being related to each other, whereas speakers of other languages see them as unrelated. The reason why a Shawnee Indian might consider the situation designated by the English sentence *I pushed his head back* as similar to the one referred to by the sentence *I dropped my paddle in the water* is that there is a word in Shawnee, *kwaškwi*, denoting a conceptual element 'force-applied-resistance encountered', around which each situation can be constructed. That is, the nature of the Shawnee language leads its speakers to construct their perceptions of each of these situations with reference to the concept 'force-applied-resistance encountered'. English speakers, on the other hand, are led to interpret one situation with reference to the concept of 'intentional force applied to object' (*push*) and the other one in terms of the concept of 'accidental exposure of object to gravitational force' (*drop*) and thus to see them quite differently. The connection between the issues raised by Whorf and those raised by the discussion of metaphor is clear. In each case the central question is: how does language influence the ways in which we order and categorise our experiences of the world.

There are important differences, however, between the discussion of linguistic relativity and that of metaphor. Whorf's arguments are concerned primarily with linguistic **structure**. Since structure is a fairly stable phenomenon, evolving slowly over long periods of time, his arguments suggest that world-view is relatively static. For Whorf, moreover, world-view is homogeneous, shared by all the speakers of a particular language. The discussion of metaphor, on the other hand, is based not on **structure** but on **usage**. There is nothing in the structure of English that leads us to speak of argument as war and there are many other languages in which this happens. We do so, rather, because of the fact that we perceive features that are common to the two kinds of activity. In this case, then, it is not that language structures perception. Rather, patterns of language usage follow from the prior foundation of cognitive structures. On the other hand, it is worth noting again that, if we consider the situation from the point of the child learning a language, the conventional ways of speaking that are current in the community must exert a strong influence on how she or he comes to conceptualise many important areas of experience.

Why does language work in this way? The reason must have to do with the infinitely varied nature of our experience of the world. In order for a finite system to be able to cope with this complexity, we need to establish categories of experience through processes of association and transformation. Some of these are universal to all human cultures, some are culture-specific.

A particularly interesting example of culture-specific modes of perception is cited by Lakoff (1987: 313) from the work of Claudia Brugman (Brugman 1983, 1984). In Chalcatongo Mixtec, an Otomanguean language of Western Mexico, there is a general projection of body-part terms onto the domain of spatial orientation.[1] Consider (17), for example, which means 'the stone is under the table'.

(17) yuù wǎ híyaà cìì-mesá

Literally this sentence translates as 'the stone is located at the table's belly'. Similarly, if you want to say 'I was on the roof of the house' in Mixtec, you say that you were located on the 'back' of the roof. 'My son is lying on the mat' is expressed as 'my son is lying on the mat's face' (Lakoff 1987: 314). In each case one object is located with respect to the other object by conceptualising the latter as a kind of animal, so that a body-part can be used in the specification of place. It is important to note that these Mixtec examples are not isolated idioms. Rather, there is a general conceptual system for understanding spatial location that operates in every utterance concerned with this area and that is quite different from the English way of dealing with it. Situations of this kind highlight the general problems involved in translation from one language to another. At one level, it is of course possible to give English equivalents for Mixtec sentences involving these terms. We can translate yuù wǎ híyaà cìi-mesá, for example, as *The stone is under the table*. However, important aspects of the way in which speakers of Mixtec conceptualise this situation have clearly been lost in this process.

Let me conclude this section by considering a short, somewhat banal newspaper report, illustrating in concrete terms just how pervasive the process of metaphor is.

(18) *Teen heart-throb Jason Donovan, who **plays** Kylie's on-screen husband in the **hugely** popular soapie 'Neighbours', also won a Silver Logie for most popular male performer, and 'Neighbours' – a constant ratings **bonanza** for the 0–10 **network in** its 7 p.m. **timeslot** – **snatched** most popular Australian drama series.*
*Kylie, dressed in a body-**hugging** black and tan dress, was **swamped** by fans when she arrived at the **awards** with Donovan.*
*Last night's **glittering** ceremony **caps** a **stunning** year for Minogue, who has become an Australian teen **phenomenon** and whose **hit single** 'I should be so lucky' is still **number** 1 on the British **pop charts**.*
*Logie **veteran** Bert Newton, a four-time Gold Logie winner, was specially honored with **elevation** to the Logie **Hall** of Fame.*
*'I'm thrilled, absolutely delighted', he said of the honor. 'I've **given** two-thirds of my **life** to **television'**.*[2]

It can be argued that all the words in bold face in the above text involve some degree of abstraction away from the core meaning of the item and that their meaning is in some sense metaphorical. We will discuss selected examples briefly.

The application of *play* to the process of acting is clearly related to the core notion of 'play' as non-serious activity and seems to be partly motivated by the fact that much of children's play is based on pretence. The central meaning of *huge* relates to the concept of physical size but extends to express the idea of intensity, when it enters into construction with certain concepts like popularity or success. The notion of a television company as a 'network' may be motivated by two factors – the existence of separate regional centres linked to a central organisation but possibly also by the idea that the pathways of the broadcasting operation itself are like the filaments of a net.

The concept of 'timeslot' derives from a very general metaphor 'time is space'. This metaphor manifests itself most obviously in the fact that prepositions in English can be used in conjunction either with locative or temporal expressions. We can see someone '**at** the pub' or '**at** two o'clock'; they may leave us '**on** the station platform' or '**on** Tuesday'; I can arrange to meet you '**in** the High Street' or '**in** three weeks' time' and so on. Periods of time are spaces within which we exist and move, and this allows us to conceive of a short period of time occurring at a particular moment of the day as a 'slot' that can be filled by a television programme.

The term *hit* – and more generally the notion of physical impact – participates in two rather different metaphors. This seems to derive from the fact that the process can be conceptualised either from the point of view of the agent or from that of the patient. In the former case, the primary metaphorical meaning relates to success (*a hit single*). When seen from the point of view of the patient, physical impact is used to express emotional effect (*a stunning year*). Emotional effect can also be constructed in terms of the concrete medium of visual effect (*a glittering ceremony*). Many other examples of each of these metaphors readily spring to mind: *You've hit the jackpot, We missed the opportunity, you need to raise your sights* ('success is hitting a target'), *a striking concept, a touching film, your offer really bowled me over* ('emotional effect is physical contact'), *a brilliant idea, a shining example, a dazzling performance* ('emotional effect is visual effect').

The possessive suffix -*s* illustrates the point that metaphorical processes can also apply to grammatical forms. The range of concepts and relations denoted by -*s* is quite extensive. In *Last night's glittering ceremony* the form seems to designate the concept of 'temporal situation' (another example of the time-as-space metaphor). In other cases it may denote an agentive relation between a participant and an event (*Jo's arrival*), a patientive relation (*Harry's defeat*) or a somewhat indeterminate relationship (*Kim's future*). What is not clear here is whether the various relations identified by the suffix (and by other forms prototypically denoting possession) are an idiosyncratic set or whether they are perceived as being related in some way to the core concept of possession. In what sense, for example, can the night be said to 'possess' the ceremony? The difficulty is that the core concept of 'possession' is not in fact a particularly clear-cut category. I own my nose, for example, in a rather different sense from the way in which I own my car, and both of these are different again from the sense in which I own my brother or my daughter. Perhaps the most obvious feature that is closely connected to these and to many other senses of possession is the notion of physical proximity – objects that I own tend to be located near me or in places associated with me (such as my home). And since we conceive of time and space as closely related, physical proximity is closely akin to temporal proximity. It can be surmised, therefore, that it is the temporal association between 'last night' and the 'ceremony' that allows us to conceive of the relation between them as one of possession. But why should we conceive of the night as possessing the ceremony rather than the reverse? This clearly follows from the fact that the temporal position of 'last night' is fixed in relation to every other moment of time, quite independently of the ceremony. The latter, on the other hand is arranged in advance and is 'assigned' to the particular temporal period designated by the phrase *last night*. In other words, the ceremony is situated with respect to the temporal period in question rather than vice-versa and it is this inequality in the relationship that causes us to see the time as possessor, the event as possessed. The relationship is, of course, a quite general one, illustrated in such expressions as *yesterday's accident, today's match, tomorrow's meeting*. Again the interesting point about this example is that it is part of a complex ideological system involving perceived relationships of specific kinds between space and time on the one hand and space and the somewhat abstract concept of possession on the other.

The container metaphor

We turn now to a metaphor that is of special interest, since it in-

volves a particular perspective on language itself. There is a view
of language and communication that is so widespread in our culture that it undoubtedly constitutes an important part of our
general ideology. According to this view the process of communication is conceptualised in terms of transport. Meanings exist as
object-like entities in the minds of individuals. They are available
for 'insertion' into language in the form of speech or writing and
the role of the hearer or listener is to extract these meanings from
the text. In other words, language acts as a **vehicle** for transfering
meanings from the mind of the speaker to the addressee. The
meanings that are so transfered have essentially the same form in
the minds of both transmitter and receiver when communication
has taken place. This view of language and communication is
generally known as the 'container view' (Reddy 1979, Lakoff and
Johnson 1980: 11–13, Moore and Carling 1982: 149–75, Lakoff
1987: 67–74). It is deeply embedded in our culture both in the way
that we think and talk about language and communication, manifesting itself in the expressions below.

(19) *It's hard to get that idea across to her*
(20) *It's difficult to put this idea into words*
(21) *Insert those ideas elsewhere in the paragraph*
(22) *I don't think I'm getting through to her*
(23) *I'm not getting any ideas out of this text*
(24) *Why don't you put that idea on paper?*
(25) *I didn't absorb anything from the lecture*
(26) *I just can't take in what he's saying*

One of the problems with the container view is illustrated by the
example cited earlier, involving the concept 'radio shadow'. Such
an expression will make sense to a hearer only if that person has a
particular way of understanding the world, incorporating knowledge of the fact that there is a similarity between the diffusion of
light and the transmission of radio signals. The term *radio shadow*
interacts with this knowledge to produce a meaning. It does so by
reacting with the hearer's knowledge that a 'shadow' in the literal
sense is caused when a solid object prevents light rays emitted by a
light source (such as the sun) from directly reaching a specific area.
This knowledge is then used as the basis for reference to the process of radio transmission. The analogy derives its validity from

the fact that solid objects can prevent radio waves from reaching certain areas in the same way that they affect light waves. As far as our view of language is concerned, the crucial point is that this information, so crucial to the interpretation of the utterance, is not in the utterance itself. It is part of the knowledge base that most hearers bring to the interpretation of the utterance. However, in the case of a very young child, who might have quite a different theory of radio (who might believe, for example, that the people heard on the radio are in fact very small people living in the set), the explanation would make no sense at all.

The general point is that utterances are not vehicles that transfer meanings from speaker to addressee. Rather, they interact with a particular set of conceptual structures to **produce** meaning. On this view, which we will call the 'epiphenomenalist theory' (following Moore and Carling 1982: 10), the role of language is more like that of a catalyst in a chemical reaction than like that of a vehicle in a transport operation. A chemical reaction will not take place unless other substances besides the catalyst are present. In communication, the addressee's knowledge base is the analogue of these other substances.

One consequence of moving away from the container view is that it throws into question the assumption that communication produces object-like meanings in the mind of the addressee that are essentially identical to corresponding objects in the mind of the speaker. Let us consider a further example to illustrate this point. A car stops at a service station and the driver tells the mechanic (we will assume that this is a male mechanic) that the engine is not running well. The mechanic spends a few minutes investigating the situation. Finally he says *It's a distributor problem.* In the epiphenomenalist theory of communication, to ask what this text means is not to ask what meaning the text 'contains' but to ask what kind of mental structures it causes the interpreter to produce. The answer to this question will crucially depend on the character of the knowledge base of the interpreter.

Consider the reactions of three different interpreters, X, Y and Z. Interpreter X has an extensive knowledge of car mechanics and the utterance will therefore trigger a rich set of processing strategies leading to a complex array of output structures. X will be able to visualise the internal structure of the distributor assembly, to formulate certain hypotheses concerning the condition of

the points or the condenser, to relate these hypotheses to the observed symptoms and possibly to visualise the processes required
to correct the problem. Interpreter Y on the other hand has some
vague knowledge of the functioning of a car engine, and of the role
played by the distributor, but no detailed first-hand experience of
repair or maintenance. Y's interpretive processes will be much
more schematic than those of X, and the output structures less
well developed. There may be some conceptualisation of the external appearance of the distributor, its position on the engine and
the nature of its connections with other components, but without
any specification concerning its internal composition or the processes required to repair it. For interpreter Z, who has no knowledge of car mechanics, the text will mean very little.

There are several points to be made about this example. The
first is that the range of mental structures capable of being produced by this utterance is extraordinarily variable, potentially infinitely so. This variability is a function of the infinite range and
infinite variability of the knowledge bases capable (in principle) of
being applied to the interpretation of the text. In this situation it
would make little sense to attempt to divide interpreters into those
who had 'understood' the utterance (i.e. identified 'the meaning of
the text') and those who had not. If we interpret the question
'what does this text mean?' to mean 'what kinds of conceptual
structures does this text produce', we have to accept that there are
no clearly defined constraints on the nature of such meanings. It
would be quite misleading to speak (and think) in terms of there
being a single, unitary 'object' that we can refer to as 'the meaning
of the text'.

One corollary of this argument is that it divorces the notion of
meaning from that of speaker intention. There are those who
argue from within the container metaphor that 'texts mean what
their authors intend them to mean' (Knapp and Michaels 1987).[3]
The problem with this argument is that the notion of speaker intention is not well defined. In the case of the car mechanic, since
the speaker has just carried out a close inspection of the internal
apparatus of the distributor, he presumably has a very clear picture of the condition of the points and of the condenser, the colour
and condition of the connections with the other components and
so on. But how much of this information, if any, does he intend to
convey when he says *It's a distributor problem*? It would be ab-

surd to seek an answer to this question from the speaker himself, by asking him, for example, how detailed a picture of the distributor he expected the interpreter to construct, whether he intended to produce an image of the unit as seen in its assembled condition or in terms of its component parts and so on. Nor do the words of the utterance itself provide any more helpful clues in this respect. The general point, as we noted in Chapter 1, is that any utterance grossly underspecifies the situation on which it reports. Such underspecification is essential, as Slobin points out in the extract cited on page 8, since the task of encoding all the features of a given situation is simply not feasible, nor is it one in which either the speaker or the addressee has any interest. Underspecification is effective because of the fact that the addressee's knowledge base performs a major part of the task of meaning construction. An inevitable corollary of this process, however, is that meaning escapes the control of speaker intention.

This argument should not obscure the relevance of the conceptual orientation of the speaker to the construction of text. The choices available to speakers will be determined by their own internal conceptual structures and these in turn will derive from speakers' experience of language and general processes of socialisation. Particular selections within that overall system of choices will result from speaker judgements concerning the interaction between linguistic factors and contextual factors, including the knowledge base of the addressee. In abandoning the container metaphor, however, we do have to reject the idea that speakers simply select those sentences that carry meanings corresponding to those in their minds. Rather, texts are the product of a complex interaction between social, psychological and linguistic factors impinging on the producer of a text at a particular time in a particular situation. That is, the processes operating in the production of text are profoundly ideological.

Metaphor in 'nukespeak'

As a specific example of the ideological potential of metaphor let us consider briefly a phenomenon that has received a certain amount of attention from linguists – the language of nuclear weapons or 'nukespeak' (Chilton 1985). From the first appearance of these weapons, the discourses of nukespeak have drawn upon a wide variety of metaphors, operating at many different levels and mediating many different perspectives.[4]

One interesting feature of nukespeak has to do with the kind of names applied to such weapons. The names applied to the first atomic bombs were 'Little Boy' and 'Fat Man' – apparently references to Truman and Churchill. The jocular nature of these names has a military flavour and is probably a reflex of military discourses concerning politicians as well as of the fact that the existence of the bombs was known to only a restricted group of people. As these weapons became more familiar, they required some kind of 'public face', so that a fundamental reinterpretation took place. With the coming of intercontinental ballistic missiles, nomenclature from Greek classical mythology was adopted: 'Jupiter', 'Titan', 'Zeus', 'Atlas'. More recently the area of mediaeval chivalry has been invoked by names such as 'Lance' and 'Mace' and the metaphorical construction of these weapons as hand-held instruments has operated through names such as 'Harpoon' and 'Tomahawk'. As to the question of why these weapons have names in the first place (since they all have their own code numbers), Chilton suggests that the naming process is a part of an attempt to promote their acceptance, to incorporate them into our everyday understanding of the world, to legitimate them in terms of our past and our cultural heritage.

The early appeal to Greek mythology in European and American practices was part of a more general process involving the application of religious discourses, as if the 'awesome' power tapped by the new weapons was of divine origin. These discourses were in fact present from a very early stage. Here is an extract from a report on the 'Trinity' test (the first tests of the bomb at Los Alamos):

> *The explosion lighted every peak, crevasse and ridge of the nearby mountain range with a clarity and beauty that cannot be described. It was the beauty the great poets dream about. Then came the strong, the sustained awesome roar that warned of Doomsday and made us feel that we puny things were blasphemous to dare to tamper with the forces heretofore reserved to the Almighty.*[5]

In another example a radio commentator quotes from one of Truman's speeches using the voice quality, intonation patterns and rhythms of religious incantation.

If they do not now accept our terms, they may expect a rain of ruin
from the air the like of which has never been seen on this earth.

The metaphorical construction of the bomb as an instrument of
divine power operates here through all the components of the linguistic system – phonological, grammatical, lexical and semantic.
The theme was taken up by religious revivalists who interpreted
the bomb as a signal of the second coming and the end of the
Universe.

When British atomic tests were carried out in Australia in the
1950s, rather different discourses came into play.[6] There were different naming conventions, for example. In an attempt to 'indi-
genise' the programme, weapons were named after Australian
birds and animals (e.g. 'Wombat'). The general theme of the supernatural also took on quite a different character in this context,
being tied to notions concerning the vast age and size of the continent. The theme of archaicness was tied to particular perspectives
on one of the 'dark secrets' of the continent, uranium, which was
spoken about as if it were a revered and almost religious substance. Discourses concerning Aborigines were also part of this
ideology. The Australian testing programme has been particularly
traumatic for Aboriginal people living in the test areas in terms of
its impact on their traditional way of life, on their tribal lands and
on their health. Yet references to Aboriginal people in nuclear discourses at the time of the testing programme completely ignored
all these aspects. What happened, rather, was that ways of speaking about Aborigines attempted to tie them into the cluster of
meanings concerned with the supernatural mysteries of the continent, its age, its remote wildernesses, its immense size. One newspaper correspondent, for example, claimed to notice in the
mushroom cloud the profile of an Australian Aborigine formed by
the soaring flames. Another report assigned to Aborigines a mythical status, comparing them to those high priests from the northern
hemisphere, the Druids. The function of these general discourses
was clearly to make the whole testing programme acceptable to
the Australian public, to integrate the programme into an official
ideology which saw in it an opportunity for changing the somewhat marginal status of Australia in the 1950s, a means for the nation to gain a prominent position on the international stage. In
general, these observations shed interesting light on the ways in

which metaphorical processes can be harnessed to the task of reconciling a new phenomenon to different cultural frameworks, different mythologies.

More recently, in the official discourses of pamphlets emanating from the British Ministry of Defence and in speeches in the House of Commons, a rather different range of metaphors has been employed. A study by Christopher Beedham (1983) has shown that one of the most common practices is for nuclear weapons to be constructed in terms of economic, industrial and technological processes, as if these weapons were part of the nation's machinery for the production of wealth. This enables writers to apply such concepts as 'heightened effectiveness' to weapons and to exploit the theme of technological progress and modernisation.

> *The effectiveness of the Polaris force . . . is about to be heightened by the improvement known as Chevaline* (p. 20)

The metaphor 'nuclear weapons are part of the nation's industrial output' leads to the construction of the general concept of 'deterrence' as an element of national industrial productivity through the concept of 'value'. The same process can even be applied to the explosive power of a particular bomb. Thus, the deterrent effect of a weapon becomes its 'deterrent value' and potential nuclear explosions are 'high value air bursts over Southern England'. A somewhat different aspect of this general discourse, oriented more to the financial aspects of economic discourse than to its industrial aspects, leads to an alternative metaphor – the notion of the power of a weapon as its 'yield', though this effect is complicated by the fact that the metaphor derives ultimately from the agricultural domain. These discourses come together succinctly in a phrase such as *low-yield, enhanced radiation warhead*. Alternative discourses are structured around the metaphor 'nuclear weapons are ideas', so that terms such as *concept, capability, system* can be applied – *the Cruise Missile concept, our nuclear capability, the final launch of our ultimate capability, land-based system, submarine system, land-based support system*.

Metaphor gives rise to specialised ways of talking about this area. For example, the term *deliver* undergoes semantic extension, appearing here in a specialised usage: 'Nuclear weapons are not so basic as to be dropped on a city, they are delivered, like a letter'

(Beedham 1983: 26). Following on from this, missiles come to be referred to as 'delivery vehicles' ('as if they were perhaps some kind of milk float', Beedham remarks sardonically). Similarly, terms such as *release* and *dispatch* are applied to the 'launching' of a weapon, and even these produce some metaphorical effect. *Release* conjures up the image of a dog being unleashed in defence of its harassed owner, whereas *dispatch* suggests that the missile is some kind of message.

The question of motivation raises two rather distinct issues. In the first place, in order for these metaphors to be plausible, they have to be 'grounded' in some sense. The vast economic and industrial activity which goes into the production of arms (as well as the economic benefits that some see as resulting from this activity) help to motivate the metaphor 'nuclear arms are an element of economic production'. The rather more surprising metaphor of nuclear weapons as 'concepts' is tied to the discourse of modernisation with its theme of technological advance based on human intellectual endeavour.

The second aspect of the motivation question has to do with the question of how the metaphor arises, what functions it serves and how it serves those functions. We do not need to seek far to find the answers to the last two questions. It seems obvious that the invocation of industrial and economic discourses stems from a desire to mobilise favourable attitudes to the means of production of economic prosperity. It is much more difficult to oppose the injection of massive effort and finance into concepts such as 'modernisation', 'improvement', 'advance', 'enhancement', 'heightened efficiency', 'high value' than it is to oppose the same activities when they are simply directed to producing more powerful weapons of destruction. Similarly the metaphor 'weapons are ideas' ties the possession and possible use of weapons to the area of rationality.

The question of how these metaphors arise is somewhat more problematic. Beedham argues strongly that governments adopt these ways of speaking as a deliberate exercise in ideological manipulation.

Nukespeak is the language of pro-nuclear arms rhetoric which seeks to indoctrinate us with the belief that nuclear weapons are harmless and sensible. By imposing upon us a specific vocabulary for com-

municationn it simultaneously compels us to take on a particular political standpoint, particular opinions, particular thoughts . . . The
general public must guard against this deceit, must be wary of nukespeak, and must condemn its use by government officials. (Beedham 1983: 29)

Alternatively, one might argue that metaphor is so fundamental to
language and so closely tied to particular models of the world that
speakers are as much the victims of the metaphorical processes
constructed by their own models as are their readers – perhaps
even more so. Instead of proposing that government officials consciously seek ways of speaking about nuclear weapons that will
tend to create favourable attitudes, it seems just as plausible to
suggest that their own ways of thinking lead them naturally to the
kind of metaphors indicated above. Indeed, cognitive models may
be so powerful that their users tend to lose sight of the fact that
the processes involved are in fact metaphorical. On the other hand,
there is no doubt that governments do occupy a particularly
powerful position in this whole area. The close contact between
government institutions and the media, and the status of the former as 'experts', ensures that ways of thinking and speaking that
originate in the institutions of government will spread quickly into
wider public discourses.

Conclusion

Far from being a marginal phenomenon associated only with certain specialised uses of language, metaphor is clearly crucial to the
way in which we talk about and construct our world. Its fundamental role in language is illustrated particularly clearly by the
fact that the meanings of the most basic words are closely imbricated in metaphorical processes. If these words did not have the
kind of semantic flexibility that we have noted here, a flexibility
that operates on the basis of perceptions of similarity across the
data of our phenomenal experience, language would be impossibly
unwieldy. At a somewhat higher level, metaphor draws on our
knowledge of the physical world of concrete objects and spatial
relationships in order to structure a great variety of experiential
domains.

Metaphor is inextricably bound up with the process of classification from which our discussion began. The relationship between thought and language is particularly intricate here. In acquiring a language children are socialised by pervasive metaphors into modes of perception that are in many cases language-specific and culture-specific. It is important to note, however, that the process in question operates not through linguistic structure but through usage. In this sense, the argument here distances itself from the emphasis on the relationship between linguistic structure and perspective in the work of Saussure and Whorf. It is also important to emphasise that metaphors provide not one but a whole range of ways of structuring particular domains, so that the perspectives they offer are heterogeneous rather than homogeneous. They are also characterised by openness. As our world changes, so new metaphors come into play. This has been particularly evident in the field of computing, where metaphorical processes operate at a variety of levels. Individual words have moved into the domain through the process of semantic extension. At a more general level, the construction of machines as people has given rise to such locutions as *It wants you to press a key*, *It doesn't seem to like that*, *It's trying to telling you something* and many others. Computers can even be affected by 'bugs' and 'viruses'. Thus, metaphor has a crucial role to play in allowing language (which in some ways is a finite phenomenon) to adapt to an ever-changing world.

The nature of communication itself is clearly crucial to our general concerns in this book. Our argument started from the claim that communication is essentially problematic and that this derives in large part from the fact that language is an instrument of categorisation and selection. Linguistic categories are not a 'given' and particular texts constitute the site of negotiation, sometimes conflict, over classificatory processes. A major problem with the 'container metaphor' is that it glosses over these difficulties. It assumes that holistic meanings are placed into texts by speakers and extracted by hearers. It does not recognise the indirectness of the relationship between text and meaning, nor does it recognise the work done by hearers in the construction of meaning. It tends to assume that 'the meaning of a text' is homogeneous and essentially fixed by the authority of speaker intention. We are concerned here, however, to develop themes illustrating the flexibility and openness of textual meaning.

The process of metaphor clearly has important implications for our consideration of the relationship between language and ideology, as the 'nukespeak' example shows. Lakoff and Johnson's observation that metaphor is not a matter of words alone but of thought and action suggests that these discourses are not merely a means by which government officials attempt to impose a particular ideology on a gullible public. There is the more disturbing implication that the metaphors of nukespeak do indeed represent the ways in which officials conceptualise the world of nuclear weapons. In devoting careful analysis to this language, linguists may therefore have made some contribution not only to the study of propaganda but to more fundamental issues concerning the patterns of thought that underlie such discourses.

Notes

1. Goldman (1987: 455) cites what is almost the converse phenomenon. In Huli parent–child talk (Papua New Guinea), words for natural objects are used metaphorically to refer to parts of the (human) body.
2. *The Courier Mail*, Brisbane, 12 March 1988, p. 1.
3. These issues have been extensively discussed in the semiotics literature (see for example Derrida 1982: 307–30). For a detailed counterargument to Knapp and Michaels 1987, see Lee 1990.
4. The discussion of nukespeak is based in part on a radio interview with Paul Chilton in a series entitled 'Background Briefing', Australian Broadcasting Commission, Sydney 1985.
5. This text and others cited here are taken from the broadcast referred to in the previous note.
6. The discussion of Australian discourses is based on comments by Noel Sanders of the University of Technology, Sydney, in the broadcast referred to above. See also Sanders (nd).

5 Language, perspective, ideology

Language and perspective

So far we have considered the question of the relationship between language and world-view at a somewhat general level, concerning ourselves either with a world-view that differs markedly from our own (*The Inheritors*, *The Sound and the Fury*) or with ways of dealing with areas of experience that are shared by most of the speakers of a particular language (metaphor). In this and subsequent chapters we consider the linguistic reflexes of differences of perspective across speakers of the same language. In order to provide a specific focus for the discussion in this chapter, we will examine a number of newspaper reports concerning certain events in the African township of Soweto and in what was at the time the Rhodesian capital, Salisbury – now Harare – capital of Zimbabwe. The methods of analysis adopted here have in fact been applied to a wide range of situations, including modes of communication in academic and industrial contexts (Fowler and Kress 1979a, Kress and Fowler 1979, Hodge *et al.* 1979, Sykes 1985).

We begin with the following extract from a newspaper report on events in Soweto.

The black township of Soweto, which has been simmering with un-
rest since the riots on June 16 and the shooting of 174 Africans,
erupted again today.
    At least three Africans were shot dead, according to witnesses, al-
though police deny this. The black hospital of Baragwanath nearby
was reported to be 'overcrowded' with injured Africans.
    The Minister of Justice, Mr Jimmy Kruger, announced in Pretoria
this evening that he is reimposing the ban on public gatherings
which lapsed last Saturday. The ban will continue until the end of
the month. The nightmare of many whites in Johannesburg of a
black march on their city almost came true today when between

20,000 and 25,000 angry Africans began moving in procession out
of Soweto towards John Vorster Square, police headquarters in
Johannesburg, where they planned to protest against the detention
of black pupils.

Police with automatic rifles and in camouflage uniform headed
the marchers off after they had swept through a roadblock. They al-
legedly fired long bursts at the leading marchers and also rained a
barrage of tear-gas canisters on them. A reporter said he took a
dead African to hospital, and witnesses said at least two other Afri-
cans were lying dead in the veld.[1]

Part of the reason for choosing this text has to do with the fact
that it is the kind of report that one reads every day in the newspaper. It is a typical example of its genre. If one had to characterise the writer's viewpoint from this text alone, one would
probably surmise that he writes from a rather liberal position. A
close examination reveals, nevertheless, that the text mediates a
white rather than a black perspective. This report could not have
appeared in this form in, let us say, the Tanzanian *Daily News*.
This is not a criticism either of the writer or of the newspaper in
which it appeared. The writer, after all, is white and he is writing
for a white audience, an audience that can be assumed to bring a
particular set of expectations to their reading of this text.

The first marker of the white perspective occurs at the second
word of the text. The reference to *the black township of Soweto*
rather than simply to *the township of Soweto* is directed to an ex-
pectation on the part of the reader that people are white, unless
otherwise specified. One would expect a report in the Tanzanian
Daily News not to find it necessary to describe the inhabitants of
Soweto as black. Similar rules operate with respect to the specification of such attributes as nationality and gender. Whereas it would
be quite normal to read a report in an Australian newspaper to the
effect that *Two Americans had been arrested in Sydney on drug*
charges, it would be quite strange to read that *Two Australians*
had been arrested in Sydney on drug charges. We will see in the
following chapter that many newspaper reports also operate with
a general rule to the effect that people are male, unless otherwise
specified.

It is important in a discussion of this kind not to oversimplify
the factors that are at work in the selection or omission of particu-

lar linguistic features. Another factor involved in the decision to assign the modifier *black* here to the noun *township* is the relevance of ethnicity to the general situation that is the subject of this report. This observation takes us a step further than the stage reached at the end of Chapter 3. Throughout the discussion of the examples in early chapters, there was an assumption that each of the linguistic features discussed performed a single function – that of mediating the world-view or cognitive orientation of the central character. In fact, the normal situation is for several different factors to converge in the selection of textual features. That is, grammatical systems are characterised by multifunctionality. This is an important point, which will be taken up again later at a more general level in the discussion of the concept of discourse.

Another feature of the first paragraph that could be said to derive from a white perspective is the metaphorical process that treats the people of Soweto as some kind of natural force, specifically here as a volcano which had been 'simmering' with unrest and then 'erupted'. This is echoed in the later report that the marchers had 'swept through' a roadblock, like a river. Note, too, that the emotions of individuals and the actions that they give rise to are transferred onto the place where they live. It is 'the township' that has been simmering and that now erupts, rather than the Sowetans experiencing feelings of anger and deciding to march.

The effect of these processes of metaphor and metonymy is arguably to distance the reader from the subjects of the report. In speaking of the Sowetans as a natural force and as a place, the emotions of the people involved and the decisions which they make to engage in particular actions are eliminated from the process of interpretation. The situation is seen as resulting from some kind of inevitable set of natural laws rather than from human feelings and decisions. This tendency to downplay the agentive element in events initiated by relatively powerless groups is a general one.[2]

Again, however, it is important to make the point that the linguistic aspects in question here derive in part from factors other than those pertaining to perspective. The process whereby the Africans are seen as a volcano is a banality of journalistic style. In other words, its presence here can be accounted for to some extent by the fact that it is a characteristic of the genre. The same is true of the fact that the Africans are treated as a place. It would be quite unsurprising to find a newspaper article beginning with words such as *Liverpool is an unhappy city today*. The fact that we can see it as part of a white perspective on the events in question does not have to do with inherent qualities associated with the feature but with the way that it interacts with other features in this particular text.

One of the most striking linguistic aspects associated with perspective occurs in the third paragraph in the sentence beginning *The nightmare of many whites in Johannesburg of a black march on their city almost came true today when between 20,000 and 25,000 angry Africans began moving in procession*. Here the main event which the reporter sets out to describe is introduced in the subordinate clause of a sentence in which the main clause refers explicitly to the white perspective. Halliday's concept of 'theme' (Kress 1976: 174–88) is useful in describing this situation. 'Theme' is closely associated with sentence-initial position, so that we can say here that the thematic position is occupied by the phrase *the nightmare of many whites*. In a sense, the theme establishes the point of reference from which the sentence proceeds and to which the remaining material is related.

The relationship between theme and perspective is further highlighted by the final paragraph. The significant point here is the selection of 'the police' as theme in (1) and (2).

(1)   *Police with automatic rifles and in camouflage uniform headed the marchers off*

(2)   *They allegedly fired long bursts at the leading marchers and also rained a barrage of tear-gas canisters on them*

Note that this pattern of thematic choice is by no means inevitable. One alternative to (1) would be some structure such as *The marchers were headed off by police with automatic rifles and in camouflage uniforms* and (2) could be recast as *The leading marchers allegedly encountered long bursts (of rifle fire) and were also bombarded with tear-gas canisters*. One of the main functions of structures such as the passive and of 'patientive' verbs (such as *encounter*) is to provide a range of thematic choices for the expression of a particular proposition – to provide alternatives to the choice of agent (where there is one) as theme. What is striking is that different thematic choices express quite different perspectives.

The structure *Police rained tear-gas canisters on the marchers* mediates a perspective in which the canisters move away from the reader; by contrast, *The marchers encountered a barrage of tear-gas canisters* facilitates a reading in which they move towards us.

There are a number of other textual features here which may be associated with the features discussed above but whose status in this respect is somewhat marginal. It is noticeable in the first two sentences that incidents involving the shooting of Africans are expressed in such a way that the people responsible for the shooting are not specified. In the first case, this effect is produced by the use of the nominalised structure *the shooting of 174 Africans*; in the second case a truncated passive structure is used: *At least three Africans were shot dead*. It is arguable that one effect of the nominalised structure here is to reify the event in question, and thereby to abstract away from the event, to diminish its violent nature (Fowler and Kress 1979b: 207). In this way one could argue for a connection between this structure and those processes of metaphor and metonymy mentioned above which appear to produce the same effect. The elision of the agent in both structures can be similarly interpreted as transforming the nature of the event from one in which a person or a group inflicts violence on others into one which happens to people but without any obviously responsible agent. However, another more straightforward account is that the main rationale for the use of both structures relates to the fact that 'agent deletion' has to do with the norms of interpretation that the reader can be expected to apply here. In particular, there is no difficulty in identifying the agent in this case, so that it would be redundant to specify it. Once more, it seems not unlikely that a variety of factors of this kind converge on the selection of the forms in question.

I have argued that the linguistic features identified above derive at least in part from a white perspective – that they result from choices different from those which a black journalist might have used in reporting these events for a black audience. There are other features which possibly derive from a white perspective in a different and perhaps more insidious sense. One of the more obvious examples of this point is the writer's reference to the *detention of black pupils*. The point is that the writer does not really have a choice here in so far as the use of the term *detention* is concerned and a black journalist might well find herself/ himself forced to use the same term. This does not mean, however, that it is without ideological content. The reason why the use of the term *detention* is for all practical purposes obligatory here has to do with the fact that it is an 'official' term (and therefore, in this context, a 'white' term). It is the term that **has** to be used if one wishes to refer to the situation of imprisonment without trial in South Africa, just as *internment* has been at certain times the appropriate term for the same situation in Northern Ireland.

The need for a term of this kind arises in the first instance in official transactions, following from the enactment of laws creating the phenomenon. The relevant enabling legislation defines a special set of circumstances, distinct from those concerning 'ordinary crimes', in which people may be imprisoned without trial. In the discussions between the officials concerned with advocating and drafting this legislation, the need arises for a term to refer to it – the concept needs to be lexicalised. It is interesting to note that when needs of this kind arise, it is not normal to invent a totally new word for the new concept. What happens, rather, is that an existing word is applied to the new situation by the process of metonymic extension discussed in the previous chapter. It is at this point that the process of ideological manipulation becomes possible, since the selection of the new term is based on the perception of similarity between the new situation and the one that is to supply the term in question.

Consider the semantics of the term *detain*, from which *detention* is morphologically derived.[3] X can be said to detain Y if:

(a)   Y is in place A.

(b)   Y wishes and intends to move from place A to place B.

(c)   By virtue of some power or control that X has over Y, X prevents Y from moving from A to B.

(d)   The period in which this control is to be exercised is relatively short.

(e)   Therefore in the near future Y will carry out his intention to move to B.

(f)   X's power over Y is not absolute – Y could move from A to B immediately if Y really wished to do so, but does not out of some sense of deference to X.

Clearly there are strong similarities between a situation where Y is placed in prison without trial by X and the situation 'X detains Y' as described above. There are also important differences, however. For one thing, 'detention' is not specific as to place. X is not a person but an institutional structure. There is no guarantee that conditions (d) and (e) apply (Nelson Mandela's detention being a particularly salient case in point) and X's control over Y is enforceable via the medium of institutional power. We can therefore say that in extending the term *detention* to the situation of imprisonment without trial, many of the characteristics of the situation identified as *detention* in the basic, non-technical sense are suppressed. It is precisely in this way that the term can function as a euphemism. The term carries over to the situation of imprisonment without trial a range of meanings suggesting relative innocuousness that can lull the reader into the construction of semantic representations involving a considerable degree of abstraction away from the reality that they represent.

To summarise this point: I have argued that the term *detention* is created as a technical term in official discourses by the process of metonymic extension. This process is ideologically controlled in that it is based on perceptions that involve the suppression of unpalatable semantic features. Its emergence in official discourses is simply the first step in its extension to other discourses. It appears next in institutional discourses – for example those discourses that are produced in the interaction between officials and journalists. From these institutional discourses, it spreads ultimately into general discourses. In all these situations, it continues to operate (at least for a time) as a euphemism, and therefore as an instrument of social control.[4]

Ideological transformation of discourse

In the foregoing, I have argued that there are specific linguistic reflexes of the well-known fact that events are perceived and reported through a given ideological perspective. A particularly elegant example of this has been provided by Trew (1979) in his analysis of a number of newspaper reports dealing with similar events. An attractive feature of Trew's analysis is that he focuses on a series of reports appearing over several days in two British newspapers. By taking this diachronic perspective, he is able to demonstrate the process of ideological transformation at work.

The argument is illustrated by a number of extracts from *The Guardian* and *The Times* over a period of three days. (There are certain differences of interpretation and emphasis between the following discussion and Trew's analysis.)

DAY 1   *The Guardian*

Police shoot 11 dead in Salisbury riot
Riot police shot and killed 11 African demonstrators and wounded 15 others here today in the Highfield African township on the outskirts of Salisbury. The number of casualties was confirmed by the police. Disturbances had broken out soon after the executive committee of the African National Council (ANC) met in the township to discuss the ultimatum by the Prime Minister, Mr Ian Smith, to the ANC to attend a constitutional conference with the government in the near future.

DAY 1   *The Times*

Rioting blacks shot dead by police as ANC leaders meet
Eleven Africans were shot dead and 15 wounded when Rhodesian police opened fire on a rioting crowd of about 2,000 in the African Highfield township of Salisbury this afternoon.

The shooting was the climax of a day of some violence and tension during which rival black political factions taunted one another while the African National Council Executive committee met in the township to plan its next move in the settlement issue with the government.

Since we have noted the crucial importance of language as a classificatory tool, let us consider first the question of whether the events reported here are to be classified as a 'demonstration' or as a 'riot', together with the (perhaps surprisingly) separate question of whether the participants are to be classed as 'demonstrators' or 'rioters'. In the *Guardian* report there is some equivocation over these points. The event is designated as a 'riot' and the agents of the shooting as 'riot police' but those killed are referred to as 'demonstrators'. This equivocation clearly derives from inherent complexities characterising the events in question. One would guess that most of the people involved in this situation were engaged in activities more accurately described as 'demonstrating' than 'rioting' – marching, carrying banners, shouting political slogans. On the other hand there were undoubtedly some involved in more violent activities – breaking shop windows, setting fire to cars, throwing stones and petrol bombs at the police. The question as to whether the event as a whole is to be categorised as a 'demonstration' or a 'riot' is therefore problematic (as indeed is the concept 'the event as a whole'). Strictly speaking, it would be accurate to refer to the people who were shot as 'demonstrators', if none of them had been involved in violence (though even this is somewhat problematic if we think of them as participating in a total event involving violent acts), and to refer to them as 'rioters' if all of them were. It is difficult to believe that either of these scenarios was entirely accurate (though one would guess the former to be more so than the latter). It is interesting to note that there is no hint of these problems in the *Times* report – the dead are unequivocally referred to as 'rioting blacks'. This suggests that at this stage the perspective of *The Times* is somewhat less sympathetic to the Africans than that of *The Guardian*.

There is some support for this view in other features of the Day 1 reports. Consider, for example, the way in which the actions of the Africans – quite apart from the question of whether they are categorised as 'riot' or 'demonstration' – are treated semantically and grammatically. In the *Guardian* report the actions are treated as a **space** within which the shootings take place (*Police shoot 11 dead in Salisbury riot*). This possibility is made available (a) because the process of nominalisation allows the events to be designated by a Noun Phrase and (b) because one characteristic function of Noun Phrases is to designate places. A further relevant factor is that events of this kind typically involve large numbers of people occupying significant areas of physical space, so that it is quite natural to conceptualise the situation in locative terms. The view of the riot/demonstration as a space within which the police shot the rioters/demonstrators unequivocally assigns the agentive role to the police.

The Times, however, treats the events not as a **space** but as an **attribute** of the participants involved (*rioting blacks*, *rioting crowd*). This possibility derives from the grammatical fact that the so-called 'participial' forms of verbs – i.e. present participles such as *talking* (*a talking doll*), *singing* (*a singing bird*) and *rioting* (*a rioting crowd*) as well as past participles such as *broken* (*a broken window*) – are closely related to adjectives. Again there is an underlying semantic basis for this similarity between actions and attributes. If 'talking', for example, is an activity that a particular doll performs, then it is also an important property that she possesses. And when someone smashes a window, the process of 'breaking' is not only something that has happened to the glass in the past but also a salient aspect of its present characteristics.

The decision to treat the process of 'rioting' as an attribute rather than as a space clearly facilitates the notion that it was this aspect of the situation that led to the shooting. That is, the *Times* report derives from a view of these events as flowing not from the actions of the police but from those of the actions/attributes of the Africans. In this sense the contrasting grammatico-semantic classifications in these texts interact with differences in the way the events are named, indicating quite different attitudes and sympathies.

There is further evidence for this interpretation. It is noticeable that *The Guardian* uses active structures in both the headline and in the text (*Police shoot 11 dead … riot police shot and killed 11 African demonstrators*) whereas *The Times* uses passives (*Rioting blacks shot dead by police, Eleven Africans were shot dead*). The effect of the passives is to further attenuate the agentivity of the police, particularly in the case of the truncated passive with agent deletion. One further difference between the two texts is the overt reference in the *Times* report to the existence of 'rival black political factions' contrasting with the absence of any reference in the *Guardian* report to 'factionalism' of this kind. The *Times* description of the shootings as the 'climax' of the violence and tension associated with this situation clearly prepares the way for the ultimate responsibility for the riots (and therefore the killings) to be assigned to African disunity.

To summarise the discussion so far. The *Guardian* report shows equivocation over categorisation of the situation as 'demonstration' or 'riot', clearly identifies the police as agentively involved in the shooting and treats the general situation as a place in which the shootings occurred. The only agentive link clearly established is between 'police' and 'shot and killed demonstrators'. The *Times* report presents the situation unequivocally as a 'riot', sets up a causative link between the rioting and the shootings by treating the riot as an attribute of the participants and attenuates the role of the police by the use of passives and intransitive structures. *The*

Times also signals its intention to extend the causative chain from (A) to (B):

(A) 'riots' ⟶ 'killings'
(B) 'factionalism' ⟶ 'riots' ⟶ 'killings'

Let us consider how these perspectives work themselves out in the grammatical treatment of the situation in the reports that appeared on subsequent days.

DAY 2 *The Guardian*

Façade of Africa's unity collapses in the Rhodesia riots
The divisions within the African nationalist movement deepened today as police announced that the number of dead in yesterday's riots in townships on the outskirts of Salisbury had risen to 13.

DAY 2 *The Times*

Split threatens ANC after Salisbury's riots
After Sunday's riots in which 13 Africans were killed and 28 injured, a serious rift in the ranks of the African National Council became apparent today.

One of the most striking points about these two texts is that the difference in perspective that characterised the Day 1 reports now seems to have disappeared. This is due to the fact that *The Guardian* has moved to the position adopted by *The Times* on the first day in which the primary factor precipitating the killings is seen as the riot rather than the police action. (*The Guardian*'s equivocation over the riot/demonstration issue has also disappeared.) This is mediated through a rather subtle change in *The Guardian*'s presentation. As in the first text the riot is still seen as a **place** where the killings occurred but there has been a shift from (3) to (4).

(3) *Police shoot 11 dead in Salisbury riot*
(4) *The number of dead in yesterday's riots*

It is useful to consider these examples in the light of a parallel pair, (5) and (6).

(5) *Police kill 11 in earthquake*
(6) *Eleven killed in earthquake*

In (5) the police are firmly assigned to the agentive role, with the earthquake simply occupying the role of circumstance in which the killings took place. Although there is no change in the grammatical function of the earthquake in (6), there is a marked shift in its semantic role. The selection of the truncated (agentless) passive structure in (6) allows the earthquake to be interpreted as filling the agentive role. Similarly the shift from (3) to (4) facilitates the transfer of the notion of agentivity (and therefore of responsibility) from the subject of (3) (*the police*) to the circumstance of (4) (*the riots*). Thus, by Day 2, *The Guardian*'s view of agentivity relations has clearly moved closer to that of *The Times* on Day 1.

There are also indications that *The Guardian* is also moving to extend the chain of causation from (A) to (B):

(A) 'riots' ⟶ 'killings'
(B) 'factionalism' ⟶ 'riots' ⟶ 'killings'

This is far from obvious at first blush, since the headline (*Façade of Africa's unity collapses in Rhodesia riots*) appears to establish the opposite causative relationship between the riots and the disunity. The headline is parallel to (4) above, and clearly establishes the riot as the agent of the process of collapse. It is important to note, however, that what is reported to have collapsed is not African unity but the **appearance** of unity. Implicit in this view is the existence of disunity prior to the riots. This leads naturally to the notion that the riots were the result of this prior disunity.

Disunity ⟶ Riots ⟶ { Killings
                                         Collapse of appearance of unity

This message is reinforced in the use of definiteness in the *Guardian* report. The fact that the first Noun Phrase (*the divisions within the African nationalist movement*) is definite means that the existence of such divisions is treated as 'given' information. In other words, part of the position constructed for the reader by this feature is a belief in the existence of these divisions prior to the riots.[5] It is also worth noting that the subject Noun Phrase of the *Guardian* headline (*façade of African unity*) is also definite, in spite of appearances. That is, the Noun Phrase is a reduced form of *the fa-*

çade of African unity, the abbreviation resulting purely from the fact that it is part of a headline. (As an independent sentence the headline is not grammatical without the definite article.) This Noun Phrase too, therefore, constructs a reader position characterised by the belief that disunity existed prior to the riots, supplemented by the belief that the disunity was not apparent – there was a façade of unity. Clearly by this stage *The Guardian* has moved very close indeed to a position in which the fundamental cause of the situation is African disunity.

Interestingly, the *Times* report does not appear to have moved quite so far. The contrast in the use of definiteness is particularly striking. *The Times* uses an indefinite Noun Phrase to refer to African disunity (*A serious rift . . . became apparent today*), not therefore making any assumptions about the prior existence of the rift. Certainly the proposition that 'a rift became apparent' is not incompatible with the idea of its prior existence (it may simply have been hidden) but it does not presuppose it. Similarly the subject Noun Phrase of the headline (*Split threatens ANC after Salisbury riot*) is clearly indefinite in this case, the existence of a split being presented as new information. The strong implication of the headline, in fact, is that African disunity is simply a future danger rather than a past or present reality. The contrast between the position of the two newspapers on this question of the prior existence of disunity is also highlighted by contrasting predicates. In the *Guardian* report, the divisions 'deepened' (presupposing prior existence); in the *Times* article a rift 'became apparent' (it may or may not have been present previously). If anything, *The Times* seems to have stepped back somewhat from the position hinted at in its Day 1 report. At this stage disunity appears to be seen as a result of the riots rather than a cause.

However, the editorial of the same edition of *The Times* moves explicitly to the position that has been merely hinted at so far – the view that these events are to be traced back ultimately to African disunity.

DAY 2   *The Times* (leader)

The riots in Salisbury
The rioting and sad loss of life in Salisbury are a warning that tension in that country is rising as decisive moves about its future seem

to be in the offing. The leaders of the African National Council have ritually blamed the police, but deplore the factionalism that is really responsible. The brawling between supporters of Zanu led (from abroad) by the Rev. Ndabaningi Sithole, and the henchmen of Zapu, led by Mr Nkomo, both nominally under the control of Bishop Muzorewa, recalls the vendettas between the two nationalist parties in the early days of the Smith government and before. It will certainly give fresh life to the whites' belief that African politics is based on violence and intimidation.

A number of further conceptual and linguistic transformations have taken place here. The relationship between the rioting and African deaths has once more been reinterpreted. Instead of seeing the former as a **place** in which the latter occurred, or as an **attribute** of the people involved, the two are now simply conjoined as linked events (*The rioting and sad loss of life*). This facilitates a perspective in which the relationship between them is not perceived in terms of causality; rather they can each be seen as parallel events, deriving from a common source: the factionalism that is 'really responsible'. It is interesting, too, to see that the process referred to in the Day 1 texts as *shot and killed, shot dead*, is now referred to as *loss of life*. The transformation from an agentive, dynamic process into a non-agentive, stative situation is another reflex of the general process of distancing and abstraction that characterises the development from the Day 1 to the Day 2 reports. Yet another indication of this is the treatment of the riots and deaths not as events in their own right but as semiotically charged. They are now seen as 'warnings that tension in that country is rising'. In other words, a process of abstraction has applied to them conferring on them the status of communicative acts, specifically 'warnings'.

The newspapers are, of course, engaged in a quite legitimate enterprise here. It is undoubtedly part of their role to interpret events and it is entirely appropriate that different kinds and levels of interpretation should be explored at different stages of the reporting exercise. To observe that there is a process of abstraction involved in the reporting sequence here is not to pass a value judgement on it. Our concern is simply with the linguistic reflexes of that process. For our purposes, the relevant point is that changing perspectives can be traced here through the operation of a wide variety of linguistic features, lexical, grammatical and metaphorical. The situation differs from that examined in previous chapters in that we are dealing not with a static world-view but with a situation in which tensions between different perspectives and positions work themselves out dynamically.

On the other hand, it is certainly arguable that the tracing of the root cause of the Soweto deaths to African 'factionalism' (with all the derogatory overtones of that term) is essentially a white interpretation. Trew's argument is that the notion of factionalism as a major underlying cause of Africa's problems is a crucial aspect of a Western ideology of Africa, deriving from colonialism. Patterns of colonialist domination created entities which were seen as essentially homogeneous from a white perspective, precisely because they were established as colonial units. From an African perspective, however, the 'units' in question were heterogeneous. In a white perspective, 'factionalism' is an aberration, since it involves deviation from some underlying ideal unity that ought to characterise situations of this kind. Trew (1979: 105) makes the connection between this point and the associated issues of peace versus violence in the following terms:

> The view of 'African politics' in this ideology is, roughly, that it is the site of factional division determined by tribalism, and based on violence and intimidation, with the whites concerned merely to promote progress, law and order.[6]

From a black perspective, however, political heterogeneity is a quite normal state of affairs, deriving from the complex post-colonial situations that Africans have inherited. It is therefore appropriate to conclude this chapter with a statement of a black viewpoint on these events:

Daily News, TANZANIA (editorial)

Rhodesia's white supremacist police had a field day on Sunday when they opened fire and killed thirteen unarmed Africans, in two different locations of Salisbury and wounded many others. Their pretext was that the men had been rioting . . . Nobody will buy the statements from the Salisbury propaganda machine, that in fact all the [non-fatal] ways [of crowd control] were used. Rather, knowing the blood-thirsty nature of the illegal regime, it is much more conceivable that if any of the non-murderous methods were employed, they were merely a quick formality abandoned without valid reason, in order to rush to the 'real thing'.

For the ANC and Africa it would be wrong to imagine that this is only an isolated act, or that the regime will stop here. A correct ana-lysis of this latest outrage fits it in a pattern of acts of provocation against the people of Zimbabwe with the view to intimidating them so that they can slow down their tempo in demanding their rights.

It is a follow-up to the other relatively less violent acts of provo-cation which preceded it – the arrest and detention of the ANC leaders and the continued imprisonment of political prisoners. Zim-babwe nationalists must reckon with the fact that in their desper-ation, the illegal rulers of their country have now embarked on wanton use of the bullet on unarmed men to instil fear and des-pondency.

It is a phase which calls for greater cohesion in the liberation ranks, cohesion which will make it impossible for the enemy to divide the people for his benefit.

We appeal to our brothers of Zimbabwe to be extra vigilant so that they can correctly anticipate and interpret the enemy's machi-nations aimed at provoking them into a situation and taking ad-vantage of it to murder the people.[7]

Conclusion

We have examined here some of the linguistic reflexes of speaker perspective. Since texts are the product of the operation of choices at all levels of the linguistic system, we can shed some light on the nature of perspective by examining textual structure in the light of such choices. This process brings into play a wide range of linguis-tic features and processes. At the semantic level, the classificatory question proves to be both crucial and problematic. The events re-ported here provide a particularly clear illustration of the difficul-ties arising from the imposition of linguistic categories (for example, the opposition between 'demonstration' and 'riot' or be-tween 'killings' and 'loss of life') on the complex phenomena of human experience and the way in which ideological factors come into play in this process. Classificatory factors also enter into play in a different way through metaphor. The linguistic resources available for the encoding of human emotions and actions in terms of natural phenomena (such as volcanoes and rivers) are so much a part of the banalities of the genre that they pass almost unnoticed, yet they are not without significance. The kind of semantic extension that applies to terms like *detention* indicates yet another avenue by which ideologically laden connections can be established across different domains of experience.

At the grammatical level, processes such as thematic selection, nominalisation and passivisation mediate perspective in a variety of ways. What is particularly interesting about this group of processes is that, in spite of their formal differences, their functional roles exhibit remarkable similarity. Two main dimensions are involved. The first has to do with agentivity. Nominalisation and passivisation both allow for the downgrading or suppression of agents (*The shooting of the Africans, three Africans were shot dead*). Thematic choice allows for alternative encodings of agentivity, in some cases also involving downgrading and suppression (*Police fired at the marchers* versus *The marchers encountered a hail of fire*). The second dimension has to do with the organisation of propositional content in terms of the opposition between 'given' and 'new' information – a distinction that connects directly with the ideology-related phenomenon of presupposition. In the case of thematic choice and passivisation, this process operates through linear ordering. In nominalisation it operates through the incorporation of the definite article into the structure derived by the rule (*Someone shot unarmed Africans* —→ *the shooting of unarmed Africans*).

The production of text clearly has a good deal to do with the exercise of power. Given the way in which perspective is mediated through textual structures and textual processes, it would appear that those who control the production of text control the operation of ideology. It is important to recognise, however, the extensive social and generic constraints that impinge on textual production – constraints which impose severe limitations on the power of the producer of text. The most striking feature of the materials discussed here is their familiarity – the fact that the same expressions and phrases recur in text after text concerned with events of this kind. This suggests that the producers of these texts do not in fact exercise the degree of control over their products that has traditionally been attributed to them. Many texts are subject to extremely tight constraints deriving from the social context in which they are generated. This observation indicates the existence of a whole range of socially regulated ways of speaking (and writing).

In the next chapter we will attempt to give further substance to this claim by examining a number of such discourses deriving from the social category of gender.

Notes

1. Stanley Uys, *The Guardian*, August 1976.
2. For a particularly clear example, see Sykes 1985. The literature on language and gender also abounds with examples illustrating this point – see Spender 1980.
3. The use of *detention* in the South African context can of course be interpreted as an extension from *detention* as used in the school context. On this view, the initial extension from 'detain' to 'detention' in school exploits the kind of euphemistic possibilities discussed in the text. The further extension to 'detention' as imprisonment then exploits both these possibilities and those deriving from the relatively innocuous connotations of 'detention' as a school punishment. It is noticeable that the text from the Tanzanian *Daily News*, cited at the end of this chapter uses the term *imprisonment* rather than *detention*.
4. In this sense *detention* can be seen as an example of Beedham's (1983: 16) concept of 'ideonym', which he defines as a word 'having a strong element of ideological manipulation or guidance'. Beedham's examples of ideonyms are taken from the area of 'nukespeak' (see p. 83).
5. As we noted in Chapter 1 (page 12), assumptions of this kind, irrespective of whether or not they are valid, are extremely powerful and effective rhetorical devices.
6. There are echoes here of the discussion of the term *settlement* in the context of the European incursion into Australia, discussed in Chapter 1 (page 15).
7. *Daily News*, Tanzania, 3 June 1975.

6 *Language and gender*

Sexist discourse

In the previous two chapters we embarked on an investigation of the association between discursive practices and perspective. Chapter 4 was concerned mainly with the fact that certain metaphors are so central to the way in which speakers of English talk and write about important areas of experience that it is impossible to acquire the language without also acquiring these ways of perceiving and conceptualising the phenomena in question. In the previous chapter we moved to a more 'delicate' level by beginning to explore some of the ways in which differences of perspective across users of the same language operate through the selective use of linguistic resources and through particular discursive practices in the construction of texts. The question of perspective is clearly bound up with that of social identity. The components of our social identity – social class, ethnicity, gender, age and so on – have a crucial bearing on our experience of and relationship to social processes.[1] This chapter is concerned with the place of gender in these processes. There are two aspects to the question. The first section addresses the notion of 'sexist discourse'. The second deals with the more problematic question of possible gender differences in the area of language usage.

The concept of sexist discourse was identified, described and to some extent explained in intensive work on the topic, mostly carried out in the 1970s. Since the focus of research has shifted in recent years to the second topic identified above, it is to some extent an open question whether the notion of sexist discourse is still relevant to current discursive practices. The concept will be exemplified here largely from textual material from the 1970s. Certainly, heightened awareness has given rise to noticeable changes, fostered not least by the production of publishers' guidelines identifying the kind of practices that constitute sexist discourse and indicating alternatives (Cheshire 1984: 36). On the other hand, it is extremely doubtful whether the practices in question have fallen into total disuse. The question raises issues concerning the genesis, perpetuation and demise of discursive practices that are relevant to the general concerns of this book.

The concept of sexist discourse derives primarily from Lakoff 1975, (although the term was not used in that work). Lakoff's argument starts from the premise that there is a pervasive ideology which tends to downgrade, marginalise and exclude women. This very general perspective operates through a wide variety of linguistic practices. Since these practices are functionally related, we can draw a comparison with the discussion in Chapter 3 of *The Inheritors*, where we were concerned with a number of disparate linguistic features that were also functionally related, mediating a particular ideological orientation. It is their functional homogeneity that allows us to identify the practices in question as a discourse. The similarity between sexist discourse and the kind of discourse features identified in Chapter 3 is only partial, however. The linguistic features discussed earlier derive from a certain cognitive orientation which it is reasonable to see (from our perspective at least) in terms of cognitive deficit. However, the process involving the marginalisation and exclusion of women derives primarily from the social disadvantage from which women have suffered in most human societies in the course of human history. In other words the ideology with which we are concerned in this chapter has a social rather than a cognitive basis.

This point has important consequences for our understanding of the relationship between language and ideology in each situation. In Lok's case, his world-view plays a deterministic role with respect to his language, so that the linguistic features discussed in Chapter 3 are essentially a reflex of the underlying conceptual orientation. Whenever he is exposed to structures that mediate a different world-view (as happens from time to time in the book, given the more advanced conceptual orientation of some of the other members of his group), he simply fails to understand them. In the case of sexist discourse, however, the relationship between language and ideology is more complex. In this case the linguistic practices in question play a crucial role in the creation and perpetuation of perspective. They are part of the processes of socialisation that apply to us all – processes that essentially shape and mould our orientation to social reality. In this case perception does not play a determinative role with respect to language. Rather, linguistic processes and ideology constitute different aspects of the same phenomenon.

Most of the descriptive work in the 1970s focused on the domain of newspaper reporting, not because this was the only genre in which sexist discourse operated, but because the field provided a particularly rich source of exemplificatory material. Jean Ward (1984: 41–3) identified a number of (interrelated) principles of journalistic practice which constitute a particularly clear exemplification of sexist ideology. They include the following:

1. All people are male unless proven female.
2. A woman's relationship to a man (or men) is her defining identity.
3. A woman's appearance always requires comment, whether she defies or exemplifies a popular stereotype.
4. A woman can safely be identified as 'his wife'; it is unnecessary to identify her by name.
5. After marriage, a man remains a man and a woman becomes a wife.
6. Homemaking and parenting are not work.

These principles of language use and interpretation are exemplified in the textual fragments below.

(1) *Parliament, by an overwhelming majority, shelved the bill for six months. For the time being, therefore, Kenyans may continue to slap as many wives as they can afford. (Time 6.8.79)*

(2) *The 'documentary' delightfully explores the rivalries between different orchestral sections, as well as some of the personal ones, like the feud between a woman cellist who takes nips from a whiskey bottle ~~and a violinist~~ she accuses of molesting little girls. (Minneapolis Tribune 14.11.79)*

(3) *In fact, although no-one ever talks about it very much, booze has played as big a part in the lives of modern American writers as talent, money, women and the longing to be top dog. (Commentary March 1976)*

(4) *A woman Sandinista guards wounded guerillas fleeing a clash with Somoza forces. (Time 2.7.79)*

(5) *London – Legal history was made when a man was granted a*

> *high court order restraining a woman neighbor from enticing away his dog, a Pharaoh hound called Kinky* (Los Angeles Times, 30.8.79)

(6) *An Illinois man and wife were charged here Tuesday with illegal possession and intent to sell about 12 pounds of hashish worth about $30,000.* (AP 11.10.79)

(7) *Mundal Norway – On a summer's day in 1856, a farmer named Fredrik Mundal, his wife and their 6-year-old son, Ole, set out on a long and perilous journey from this remote village of 400 people, nestled beneath the mighty Jostedalsbre glacier along the spectacular Fjaerlands Fjord.* (New York Times 16.4.79)

(8) *The death penalty will be sought against a 24-year-old South Side man who pleaded guilty Tuesday to kidnapping, raping and murdering a doctor's wife last year, prosecutors said.* (Chicago Tribune 10.10.79)

(9) *Hernando Williams stunned a Criminal Court room Tuesday by pleading guilty to the 1978 abduction and murder of Linda Goldstone, the wife of a North Side doctor.* (Chicago Sun Times 10.10.79)

(10) *To her neighbors in the Baltimore suburb of Towson, MD, Jean M. Kirk is simply a pleasant, church-going, working housewife and mother of four. But then there's the T. Rowe Price Associates Inc. business card that carries the title of assistant vice-president.* (Wall Street Journal 13.11.79)

The literature devoted to this topic in the 1970s and early 1980s produced a wealth of evidence illustrating the pervasiveness of practices of this kind (for a general overview see Cheshire 1984). Certain examples are reminiscent of some of the processes illustrated in the previous chapter. For example, Stirling (1987) cites a number of texts showing how the development of a particular report can produce the kind of ideological shift noted in the second section of that chapter ('Ideological transformation of discourse'). In this case the shift manifests itself in the gradual backgrounding or elimination of women. Consider, for example, the following texts from different articles in the same edition of The Australian concerning a racehorse called *Hyperno*.

(11) *The multi-millionaire builder Mr George Herscu races Hyperno in partnership with his wife of 21 years, Sheila, the managing director of G. J. Coles, Mr Tom North and his wife, and Dr Ray Lake*

(12) *Four and a half months ago the owners of Hyperno, Mr and Mrs Tom North, Mr and Mrs George Herscu and Dr Lake decided to send Hyperno to Cummings*[2]

These reports clearly identify Sheila Herscu and Mrs Tom North (no first name given) as part-owners of *Hyperno*. However, the text of the picture caption associated with the report eliminates the two women from the list of owners, even though one of them actually appears in the picture.

(13) Picture caption:
A happy quartet after Hyperno's Melbourne Cup win ... from left, jockey Harry White, part-owner Mr George Herscu, trainer Bart Cummings and Mrs Herscu

A report in the same day's edition of the Brisbane *Courier Mail* also excludes Sheila Herscu from the list of owners.

(14) *He [Hyperno] is owned by Mr Tom North, managing director of G. J. Coles, builder Mr Geoff Herscu and Melbourne doctor Ray Lake*

Similarly the following story clearly identifies a Mrs Malt as the writer of a letter to the Queen, requesting her to intervene in the sale of a racecourse.

(15) *A horse-trainer's wife has asked the Queen to intervene in the proposed sale of the old Deagon racecourse. Grandmother Mrs Reg Malt wants the Queen to acknowledge a proclamation made by the Queen's grandmother, Queen Victoria. Mrs Malt has received a reply from the Queen's private secretary referring the matter to the Governor-General (Sir Zelman Cowan)*[3]

Yet the accompanying picture shows only Mr Malt, identifying him as one of the initiators of the appeal.

(16) Picture caption:
Horse trainer Mr Malt of Deagon, with the letter received by his wife from the Queen's Secretary

In identifying Mr Malt as co-author of a letter which his wife seems to have composed herself, this text also highlights the way in which the apparently simple notion of agency can be problematised through the operation of ideology – a point which arose in Chapter 1 in the context of the discussion of the extract from *A Passage to India* (p. 21). A further example of the way in which the notion of agency is constructed through ideology, involving complex interactions between gender and power, is illustrated in the following extract from the Brisbane *Telegraph*.

(17) *Smiles all round as Lord Snowdon has his daughter, Lady Francis Armstrong-Jones, now three months old, christened at the quiet Sussex village of Staplefield. Holding the baby is Lord Snowdon's wife, the former Lucy Lindsay-Hogg*[4]

One would surmise that 'the former Lucy Lindsay-Hogg' was as heavily involved in making the arrangements for the occasion as she clearly was in the ceremony itself, yet the situation is constructed in terms of Lord Snowdon as the sole agent of 'his' daughter's christening.

One particular practice that has received considerable attention in the literature on language and gender is the use of male pronouns and other male-oriented terms (*man, chairman, newsman, salesman* and so on) to refer to people in general. The claim that these terms are male-oriented is not universally accepted. The fact that dictionaries tend to identify a word such as *man* as having two distinct senses – one in which it is used to refer to a male human being and a second in which it refers to the whole human race – could be cited as evidence supporting the view that the word has a truly generic sense. The notion that *man* 'has' or 'possesses' two distinct senses is clearly a specific manifestation of the container metaphor, discussed in Chapter 4. The claim is that in any given text it 'has' either one meaning or the other, that it excludes women in a text such as (16), for example, but includes them in (17).

(18) *A man came into the room wearing a dark suit*
(19) *A man has the right to privacy*

A slightly different argument is sometimes based on the concept of author intention. In the following text a professor of English argues that if a writer (or speaker) uses a masculine pronoun with the intention of including women, then this determines its meaning.

> If an author writes, 'Everybody must do his best', it is quite obvious from the context that *his* is not restricted to males ... In using *his* there is never any intention of overlooking any section of society.[5]

There is clearly a relationship between this appeal to the authority of author intention and the notion of polysemy. If a word has a number of discrete meanings, then the author's intended meaning (if we can reconstruct it) seems to be the obvious authority for resolving any possible ambiguities.

These arguments are not, however, consistent with the view of meaning that we have been developing in this book. In earlier chapters we have argued that meaning is not a product of author intention and that the various meanings of a word are not as unrelated as the notion of polysemy would suggest. Nor are the arguments consistent with a wealth of both theoretical and experimental evidence that is now available to us. Consider first the claim that the various meanings of a particular word are discrete entities. This is undoubtedly true in a number of cases. For example, the fact that *bank* can mean both the 'side of a river' and a 'financial institution' is a pure accident of history. Such examples are cases of 'homonymy'. In the context of the lexicon as a whole, however, homonymy is rare. In most cases where a word is analysed as having multiple meanings, there is a clear rationale for the situation. Consider, for example, the fact that the word *glass* can mean (a) a material out of which certain objects are made (*It's a glass bottle*), (b) certain containers made of that material (*I've just broken a glass*), (c) the contents of such a container (*I drank the whole glass straight down*), (d) a barometer (*The glass is falling*). Clearly this is not a case of homonymy – the fact that *glass* has this particular range of meanings is not an accidental matter. This example is typical of the general situation in the lexicon in that most words have a range of interconnected meanings. Moreover, we have identified the reasons for this situation in the previous chapter. It derives from all the metaphorical and metonymic processes that are involved in the constantly ongoing process of adjustment of language and linguistic practices to an ever-changing world. These, then, are some of the theoretical arguments for the claim that the meanings of *man* are not discrete.

One piece of concrete evidence for the view that *man* is not a case of homonymy is the fact that elements that are homonyms in one language normally correspond to quite distinct terms in other languages. Thus, English *bank* in the sense of 'side of a river' corresponds to *rive* in French, whereas *bank* in the sense of 'financial institution' corresponds to *banque*. On the other hand, the word *verre* in French has a very similar range of meanings to its English counterpart – it can be used to refer to the material out of which glass objects are made, to the containers made out of glass and to the contents of such containers. Similarly, the word *homme* in French can be used to refer either to males or to people in general.

Further evidence for the view that 'the two meanings' of *man* are not as discrete as the dictionary would suggest comes from a large number of experimental studies showing conclusively that generic masculine (GM) terms lead to the construction of male images. Silveira (1980: 170) summarises this work in the following terms.

> The GM words studied have been *man* and/or *men*, the suffixes *-man* and/or *-men*, *mankind*, *he* and *his*. The comparable non-GM statements have included the appropriate noun or suffix form of *people* and *person*, terms for human activity, *individual* and/or *human being*, *they* and *he or she*, *their* and *his or her*, the invented pronouns *e*, *E*, *tey* and a sentence with a noun but not a pronoun.
>
> Several of the studies asked people to illustrate the sentence, by bringing in pictures to class, selecting from pictures provided by the experimenter or drawing a picture. Other studies asked people to name or write a story about the person referred to in the sentence. Still other studies asked straightforwardly whether the sentence could refer to a woman. Two reaction time studies followed the sentence with a picture of a woman, man, or non-person and timed people as they answered that the picture did or did not fit the sentence.
>
> In all 14 studies the GM terms caused more male-biased responses than did the more neutral wording. Thus, pictures illustrating generic *man* contained more males than pictures illustrating *people*. Characters referred to as generic *-man*, *he* or *his* were given a male

identity more often than characters referred to as *person, their, they, he or she* or *his or her*. Sentences containing generic *he* were said to exclude women more often than were sentences containing alternative wording, but neither type of sentence was said to exclude men. Reaction times were significantly slower to female than to male pictures only after *man* and *he* sentences, not after sentences with *people* or alternative pronouns.

This evidence is relevant not only to the specific question of word meaning but to more general questions concerning the nature of communication. These studies illustrate the point that communication is not a question of the transmission of some speaker-initiated (and speaker-controlled) message but crucially involves the construction of meaning by the hearer. The question to which this experimental work is addressed concerns the nature of the mental structures produced by hearers in response to the occurrence of GM words. We see here the strong tendency for hearers to construct male images for GM terms, irrespective of the images that the speaker or writer may have had in mind when using them.

The speaker's mental structures and intentions (problematic as these concepts are) are not without interest, however. As noted in the previous chapter, the epiphenomenal model of communication identifies the relationship between the speaker's mental structures and those produced by the hearer as a topic of considerable interest. A number of examples cited in the literature shed light on this question in relation to the use of GM terms. Consider in particular the following:

(20) *Man can do several things that the animal cannot do … his vital interests are life, food and access to females* (Erich Fromm)[6]

(21) (Of 'man' in the generic sense) *His back aches, he ruptures easily, his women have difficulties in childbirth* (Loren Eisley)[7]

The ease with which the writer moves here from a generic use of *man* to a male-oriented use of *his* (referring back to *man*) suggests strongly that the mental structures that gave rise to this text comprised male images for the notion of 'people in general'. As far as the hearers' responses are concerned, some of the experiments cited by Silveira show that women are slightly less prone to construct male images in reaction to GM terms than are men. Clearly, then, there will be occasions where there is a discrepancy between the mental structures that give rise to the use of a GM term in the mind of the speaker and those produced by the hearer. This small example highlights once again some of the complexities involved in the production of meaning. In particular, it points to the importance of factors relating to social identity and social perspective in this process. It is clearly quite misleading to adopt a model of communication suggesting here that the speaker 'inserts' some non-gender specific meaning into the term *man* in sentences of this kind and that the only legitimate role of the hearer is to 'extract' such a meaning from the utterance. What actually happens is that processes governed by complex interactions between ideological and social factors come into play both in the production and in the interpretation of text.

Another issue arising here has to do with the question of whether gender bias derives from the structure of English. Carolie Coffey (1984: 512), for example, has argued this in the following terms:

> One day in class as I glanced at my lecture notes concerning Whorf's linguistic hypothesis, I suddenly realized that the grammatical forms I had used to write these notes were now obsolete! 'Whorf asserts that the grammatical structure and vocabulary content of language greatly influences the manner in which man perceives himself, the universe, and his relationship to it.' I asked my students to write the sentence verbatim. Then I asked them to write a second sentence: 'Whorf asserts that the grammatical structure and vocabulary content of language greatly influences the manner in which we perceive ourselves, the universe and our relationship to it.' Looks of surprise and dawning smiles spread across the faces of students in the class. They had directly **experienced** Whorf's hypothesis.

There is no doubt that Coffey is right to identify the first version of her notes as embodying a practice that excludes women. But she is surely incorrect in claiming that the issue has to do with language **structure** in the sense of 'the grammatical structure and content of language'. The fact that she is able to reformulate the proposition in a way that is not exclusive shows quite clearly that the basic problem here does not have to do with the **structure** of the English language but with the way in which it is **used** – i.e. with the operation of a particular discursive practice.

It could be argued that the distinction between usage and structure here is somewhat fuzzy – that the lack of a sex-neutral third-person singular pronoun and the absence of a singular non-gender-oriented term for 'people in general' in English are factors that have contributed to the creation and perpetuation of the practice identified here.[8] What this means is that structural factors may tend to encourage the persistence of certain ways of speaking but it would be wrong to regard them as having the power to totally inhibit new discourses, new forms of meaning. In a sense, the hypothesis that a male-oriented ideology is inscribed in the **structure** of English is another facet of the container metaphor, since it implies that male-oriented meanings are **properties** of words and that it is therefore impossible to use the language without simultaneously applying these biased meanings.

This point raises the question of language change. If it were the case that bias was incorporated into the very fabric of English, then we should have to take a somewhat pessimistic view of the prospects for change – at least in the short term – given the fact that the grammatical component of a linguistic system tends to be resistant to innovations. However, given favourable conditions, new discursive practices can emerge very rapidly, once the social need for them has become apparent. In recent years we have seen a growing awareness of the problem identified here and the development of alternative discourses.

Female discourse, male discourse

We turn now to the quite different hypothesis that there are contrasting female and male discourse styles. These notions are considerably more problematic than the concept of sexist discourse and they raise a host of conceptual and methodological problems. In terms of what kind of features or components are such concepts to be defined? To what extent can such concepts be divorced from contextual factors? How might such contrasting styles arise and how might they be interpreted and explained?

Again it is useful to start from Lakoff 1975. Lakoff claimed that there were a number of lexical, grammatical and phonological features that characterised women's language. Lexical differences were said to relate to the use of certain colour terms (e.g. *beige, ecru, aquamarine, lavender*) and to certain adjectives of approval (*adorable, sweet, charming, lovely, divine*). A postulated grammatical difference concerned the use of tags (forms such as *isn't it?*, *won't you?*, *aren't they?*), which women were thought to use more frequently than men. Phonological differentiation was illustrated in terms of rising intonation contours in utterances such as *oh, about six o'clock?* (in reply to a question such as *When will dinner be ready?*), where it was thought that men would tend to use a falling contour. She also suggested (Lakoff 1975: 18) that women's speech 'sounds much more "polite" than men's'.

This characterisation of the concept of the female register in terms of a specific set of lexicogrammatical features was almost certainly influenced by contemporary developments in sociolinguistic analysis. Labov and others had published findings of sociolinguistic surveys indicating that there was evidence of gender-related accent variation – in particular that in many phonological variables women tended to use 'standard' variants more frequently than men from the same social class (see Trudgill 1972 for a particularly clear statement). It is possible to interpret Lakoff's paper as an attempt to extend this approach to areas of lexis, grammar and prosody. (For a discussion of the theoretical implications of such a move see Lavandera 1978.)

One issue arising from the original paper is whether the concept of a 'female register' necessarily implies that of a male register. Lakoff's discussion tends at times to construct female style in opposition to some kind of 'neutral' style, accessible to both men and women, from which she is led to identify the need to choose between the two as one of the difficulties confronting women in many situations (Lakoff 1975: 12). However, this way of constructing the female register relies essentially on the idea that there are 'sex-exclusive markers' (linguistic features that are used by only one sex) rather than 'sex-preferential markers' (features used more frequently by one sex than by the other). For example, if it is the case that adjectives of approval such as *lovely, gorgeous, divine* are used exclusively by women but *great, terrific, neat*, and so on are used by both sexes, then it is not unreasonable to see the situation in terms of an opposition between female and neutral discourses. On the other hand, if the more typical situation is for there to be features (e.g. tags) that are used by both sexes but more frequently by women than by men, then it is misleading to interpret this situation in terms of an opposition between the female register (frequent use of tags) and a 'neutral' register (less frequent use of tags). Such an analysis is a reflex of an androcentric ideology, since it is tantamount to seeing the male style as the unmarked, the 'normal' style and the female usage as deviant.

The property that characterises Lakoff's somewhat disparate features as a 'discourse' has to do once again with the fact that they are interpreted as functionally homogeneous. The explanation proposed is that, like sexist discourse, the characteristics of the female register derive from the social disadvantage of women. All of these features are interpreted as belonging to the language of diffidence or powerlessness.

The area of fine colour discrimination is said to be one that is of relatively little import, having been assigned by men to women, since it is marginal to areas of real power. The sex-exclusive adjectives of approval are similarly seen to be applicable to ideas that are 'essentially frivolous, trivial, or unimportant to the world at large' (Lakoff 1975: 12). The other features are interpreted as general markers of diffidence. There are major problems with these claims, to which we will return later in the discussion. For the moment, however, it is of more direct relevance to our argument to observe how this way of defining the concept of the female register has been overtaken by a rather different approach.

Recent work has distanced itself from Lakoff's argument in a number of ways. It has rejected the idea that linguistic differentiation can be defined with respect to a particular set of monofunctional lexicogrammatical features, moving towards the view that the phenomenon has to do rather with different discursive practices, contrasting rules of interaction and interpretation. It has rejected the view that women's language is powerless, focusing instead on the strengths of women's talk. It has rejected the idea that differentiation can be accounted for in terms of macro-level social disadvantage, seeking explanations rather in micro-level patterns of interaction.

The view that gender differentiation in English is marked not by lexical, grammatical or phonological features but by distinct discursive practices stems in the first instance from a number of studies by West, Zimmermann, Fishman and Hirschman of cross-sex conversations (Zimmermann and West 1975, Thorne and Henley 1975: 249, Fishman 1983). The findings of these studies can be summarised as follows (Maltz and Borker 1982: 197–8).

1. Women display a greater tendency to ask questions.
2. Women do more of the routine 'shitwork' involved in maintaining social interaction.
3. Women show a greater tendency to make use of positive minimal responses (e.g. *mm hmm*).
4. Women are more likely to 'adopt a strategy of silent protest' after they have been interrupted.
5. Women tend to acknowledge the addressee with more frequent use of the pronouns *you* and *we*.
6. Men interrupt women more frequently than women interrupt men.
7. Men are more likely to dispute their partners' statements.
8. Men are more likely to ignore the comments of the other speaker, or to respond unenthusiastically to others' utterances.
9. Men use 'more mechanisms for controlling the topic of conversation' (in developing topics and introducing new topics).
10. Men make more direct declarations of fact or opinion than do women.

Like Lakoff, West and Zimmermann (1977) attribute these patterns to power differences. They note, for example, that similar patterns (particularly interruptions) can be found in talk in other asymmetrical situations, such as talk between parents and children. Similarly Fishman (1983: 100) explains these patterns in terms of the 'socially structured power relationship between males and females', a relationship that assigns to men control over 'what will be produced as reality by the interaction'.

However, Maltz and Borker (1982) propose quite a different explanation. They argue that the answer to this question is not to be found in macro-level questions of social disadvantage but in differential experience of micro-level patterns of interaction in general processes of socialisation. On this view the 'learning of gender-specific cultures' leads to the emergence of different ways of speaking in boys and girls at an early age (Meditch 1975, Haas 1979), a process that is reinforced by contrasting behaviour patterns in adolescence. Maltz and Borker argue that boys tend to belong to large, hierarchically organised peer groups in which the use of language is oriented to the assertion and maintenance of power. Girls, on the other hand, tend to form close friendships with just one or two other girls. For them the concept of 'best friend' is particularly important (see also Cheshire 1978: 66). Since these relationships are egalitarian, language performs quite a different role, functioning to support and facilitate the relationship and to smoothe over any pressures and conflicts that may threaten it. Hence the emergence of a general female orientation to co-operative strategies in the use of language and a male leaning towards a competitive discourse style.

Maltz and Borker cite the interpretation of questions and minimal responses as specific manifestations of these differences. They suggest that women tend to use questions to promote and foster conversational interaction and to use minimal responses (*mm hmm*) to signal that they are listening and to encourage the speaker to continue. Men, on the other hand, tend to use questions to elicit information and to use minimal responses to signal agreement with the speaker. If it is indeed the case that different interpretive strategies of this kind are at work, it is easy to see how cross-sex conversations could give rise to the same kinds of misunderstanding that occur in cross-ethnic conversations. As far as minimal responses are concerned, Maltz and Borker (1982: 202) make the following point:

> [These observations seem] to explain two of the most common complaints in male–female interaction: (1) men who think that women are always agreeing with them and then conclude that it's impossible to tell what a woman really thinks, and (2) women who get upset with men who never seem to be listening. What we think we have here are two separate rules for conversational maintenance which come into conflict and cause massive miscommunication.

The general re-interpretation of the origins of linguistic gender differentiation has gone hand in hand with a re-evaluation of the properties of the female register. Jennifer Coates, for example, has pointed out the high level of skills demonstrated by women in the collaborative production of conversational texts. The following extract from a conversation concerning the question of whether it is taboo to miss a mother's funeral provides a small illustration.[9]

(22) (a) B: *Oh we ... it's so odd you see because we had this*

    (b) A: *mm*
            B: *conversation at dinner tonight ... because Steve*

(c) B: *MacFadden's mother died at the weekend ... and she ...*

(d) B: *well she lived in Brisbane ... They were at Brisbane ...*

(e) B: *so he's going over there ... Australia ... So he's going*
    E: *What ... Australia?*

(f) B: *to the funeral ... it's obviously gonna cost him a*
    D: *Oh my god*

(g) B: *fortune ... and John said ...   he was just*
    E: *fortune* (whispers)   *'s about £400*

(h) B: *astonished ... I said ... well I wouldn't go Steve ...*

(i) B: *and the and the ... as you say it was just taboo ... I*

(j) B: *mean as far as Steve was concerned I mean that was*
    C: *mm   mm*

(k) B: *just   no ... and I ... and my response*
    D: *You just can't say that*
    ? :   *no*

(l) B: *I must "oh John" ... but sorry ... it's so odd that you*
    C: *I didn't go over for*

(m) B: *should ...*
    C: *my father*
    (Coates 1989: 100)

Coates notes the way in which, although B holds the floor, the other participants show their active involvement and support in a variety of ways – with well-placed minimal responses (lines (b), (j)), by repeating her words (*fortune*, line (g)), or by repeating what she is saying in different words (*you just can't say that*, (line (k)) and by asking for clarification (*What ... Australia?*, line (e)).

Coates has devoted particular attention to the use by women of the various exponents of 'epistemic modality' – elements concerned with 'the speaker's assumptions, or assessment of possibilities . . . the speaker's confidence or lack of confidence in the truth of the propositions expressed' (Coates 1987: 112). These comprise not only the modal auxiliaries (particularly *may*, *must*, *will*) but also modal adverbs *perhaps*, *maybe*, *possibly*, other modal forms (*possible*, *possibility*, etc.), tags, hedges such as *I think*, *I presume*, *I suppose*, *sort of*, *kind of*, *quite* and other related expressions. On the basis of careful textual analysis, Coates shows quite convincingly that to identify these elements simply as expressions of doubt and diffidence is to ignore the complexities that characterise their functional potential in context – their 'polypragmatic nature' (p. 114). In particular, the focus on doubt and diffidence (concepts that are oriented to the expression of propositional meaning) tends to obscure their important role in the production and maintenance of conversational interaction.

Consider, for example, the function of tags. A number of studies (Holmes 1984, Cameron *et al.* 1989, Coates 1989) concerned with the interpretation of tags in context has shown that their most common function is not to solicit information or to express diffidence but to facilitate the participation of others. This point is illustrated in the following texts from Coates 1989: 115–6).

(23) E: *But I mean so much research is male-dominated ... I mean*

   A: *mm*
   E: *it's just stàggering ìsn't it*

(24) D: *It was dreàdful, wàsn't it*
   E: *appalling Caroline absolutely*

   E: *appalling*

(25) A: *and they had they had a very accurate picture of him didn't*

   A: *they ... they roughly knew his age*
   D: *at one point they knew*

   A: *yeah*
   D: *about his gap teeth too didn't they*   *then they got*

   D: *rid of that*

A typical function of the tags in these cases is to provide the addressee with an opportunity to participate if she wishes (significantly they tend to be followed by a pause), an opportunity that is sometimes taken and sometimes not. Tags can also be used to underline the obviousness of the associated statement or to 'check the taken-for-grantedness of what is being said' (p. 117).[10] Coates suggests that in general speakers use tags to monitor the development of the conversation, to check on the 'co-operative progress of the discourse'. These insights into the complexity of the relationship between form and meaning constitute a significant advance on earlier interpretations of tags as simple markers of diffidence or powerlessness.

Coates makes similar points about the whole range of epistemic modal forms. Expressions such as *sort of*, for example, are often used not to express doubt about the associated statement but as a way of checking that the proposition is acceptable to listeners (Coates 1987: 120). For example, a speaker commenting on the appearance of an old friend says *She looks very sort of um ... kind of matronly really*, the modalisers allowing her the face-saving possibility of retreating from the description, if it turns out to be unacceptable. It may also signal a speaker's difficulty in finding the right words. In (26) a speaker signals that the expression *pen portrait* is not to be interpreted too literally:

> (26) *before the Ripper was caught they gave a sort of um ... pen portrait* (Coates 1987: 119)

Similarly forms such as *I mean, I think* often function as turn-holders, giving the speaker time to find the right words or to decide what point to make next without losing the floor. Even when the function of these forms is to signal hesitation, this is often part of a strategy for facilitating open discussion. In any event, as Gillian Brown (1977: 117) remarks, 'it is not appropriate behaviour in situations of informal conversation to pack your speech with information and deliver it in formal complete sentences'.

This discussion clearly provides a much more positive evaluation of the female register features than that which characterised early work in this field. At the same time, it raises difficult issues concerning the question of whether these features are involved in linguistic gender differentiation. Given the functional complexity of these forms, it will clearly not do simply to count the occurrences of these features in conversational interactions and to draw general conclusions about stylistic gender differentiation in this area. Coates (1989: 114) suggests that women probably do exploit these forms more than men but qualifies this view by noting that the comparative frequencies she found are based on a very restricted corpus. One factor that makes the question extremely difficult to investigate is the strong influence of context on the use of these forms. Coates (1989: 115) notes, for example, that men tend to talk about 'things' – home beer-making, hi-fi systems, etc., whereas women tend to talk about people and feelings. Since thing-oriented topics are less sensitive, less face-threatening than people-oriented topics, it seems likely that differences of this kind have a major influence on the use of epistemic modal forms. Even when there is some attempt to control for topic, there is no guarantee that different speakers will orient themselves to the topic in the same way. For example, a conversation on the merits of Boston as a place to live (a topic selected by Crosby and Nyquist (1977) for the study of linguistic gender differentiation) can be constructed in terms of quite different orientations ('thing-orientation' and 'people-orientation' are but two out of a large range of possibilities). Complexities of this kind pose major problems for attempts to draw valid comparisons between different texts.

In order to emphasise the fact that the issues raised here are open, we will conclude this chapter with a discussion of a conversation between four males. We will focus on three points. First, the text shows that the kind of co-operative strategies evinced by females in the construction of text are also accessible to males (though the example does not of course demonstrate that these strategies are used as frequently – or perhaps as skilfully – by males). Secondly, it also demonstrates that the kind of factors that give rise to the use of epistemic modal forms in conversations between women also operate in conversations between men. Thirdly, the text shows that co-operative and competitive (more specifically confrontational) strategies can co-exist and interact in the same text. Thus, the text points forward to the remaining chapters of this book, which focus on the phenomenon of discursive interaction. In this sense the issues raised by the language/gender debate provide a useful transition between the early chapters (oriented as they are to the notion of relatively homogeneous discourses) and the later chapters, dealing with discursive heterogeneity.

The text below is taken from a slightly more formal situation than the examples of women–women conversations exemplified above – a factor which probably accounts for the lower incidence of simultaneous speech across speakers. It is part of a sociolinguistic interview conducted in 1987 at an Australian High School in Brisbane. The conversation is between the writer (identified in the transcript as 'A') and three 15-year-old boys. The group was self-selected in the sense that one of the boys (chosen by a random sampling method described in Lee 1989b: 54) had selected the other two participants. The aim of this 'interview' (a somewhat misleading term, since the interaction was relatively unstructured) was to create an informal context favourable to the emergence of a casual speech style (Labov 1972a: 85–99). An indication that it was reasonably successful in this aim is the high frequency of non-standard phonological and grammatical variants (and the fact that at one point speaker C felt relaxed enough to interrupt the session in order to demonstrate his skills in break-dancing).

The interview was conducted in a school in the Brisbane suburb of Woodridge, a predominantly working-class area and one noted as an area of major social problems (Lee 1989b: 53). The three boys had already talked about a number of incidents in which they had run foul of the police, so that the topic of out-of-school activities which A introduces at the beginning of this transcript, is a sensitive one. The other difficult factor is that the conversation has so far been dominated by C and D. A wants to draw B into the conversation, but this participant is adopting a highly defensive stance (Labov 1969: 6). B's wariness is almost certainly due to the fact that he in particular has often absented himself from school and been in trouble with the police.

(27) (a) A: *Yeah, well what ... what else do you ... You've got quite*

(b) A: *a lot to do then when you're er ... you know out of*

(c) A: *school. What do you ... what do you do B ... with your*

(d) A: *spare time? Do you watch television a lot or you know*

(e) A: *just sort of go out of the house in the evenings or you*

(f) A: *know* ...　　*do you?*
　　B: 　　*play footy*
　　C: 　　　　　　　*nick off. The usual* ...

(g) A: 　　　　　　　　　*nickin' off, eh?* (laugh).
　　C: 　　　　　*yeah!*
　　D: *The usual thing for B* ...

(h) A: *Do you er stay out of school a fair bit or do you come in*

(i) A: *most of the time?*
　　B: 　　　　　*Come in most of the time.*
　　D: 　　　　　　　　　　*What about*

(j) B: 　　　　　　*eh?*
　　D: *the start of the year, B... eh?*　　... *getting busted*

(k) A: 　　　　*Did you* ... *tell me about that* ...
　　C: 　　*yeah!*
　　D: *by the police!*

(l) A: *What happened?*
　　C: 　　*Aw, Thursday we used to go up to the TAFE*

(m) C: *college* ... *we used* ...
　　D: 　　　*but before that* ...

The markers of epistemic modality in A's initial question – his hesitation in framing the question, the use of modalisers such as *you know*, *just* and *sort of* – stem from his awareness of the sensitivity of this topic, particularly when addressed to B. B replies curtly but C (probably trying to overcome B's defensiveness) injects a certain friendly aggressiveness into the situation by drawing attention to B's truancy (*nick off*). D immediately joins with C in picking up this topic (*the usual thing for B...!*). C then increases the pressure with a long ironic *yeah!* and even the interviewer joins in the general 'ganging up' (*nickin' off, eh?*). C responds by rejecting the charge (*Come in most of the time*) but D refuses to let him off the hook by taking over the major part in the general goading, reminding him of his troubles with the police at the start of the year (lines (i), (j)). C is content now with the supporting role (another ironic *yeah!*) and the interviewer pursues the theme, asking for details. This orchestration of the 'attack' on B, operating largely through prosodic features, is very much a cooperative endeavour, with first one, then another participant taking the lead in carefully coordinated exchanges, the whole illustrating an intricate interplay between cooperativeness and (good-natured) aggression.

A few minutes later the spirit of banter dissolves as all participants engage cooperatively in the production of a narrative. The story is initiated by C.

(28) (a) A: *You'd been muckin' about had you in* ...
      C: *... It's one Monday ... one Monday ... one*
      D: *... school...*

  (b) C: *Monday we were down workin' in craft, right?* ... *about*

  (c) C: *... what ... what period was it? Third period* ...
      D: *Third*

  (d) D: *period and the police were chasin' this (bloke) on the*

  (e) C: *this kid on the motorbike man!*
      D: *motorbike* (laugh)   *He came*

  (f) D: *an' he got up ... er ... down the back of the school* ...

  (g) D: *there's ... a road goin' down ... towards another róad*

  (h) A: *yeah* (slow low rise)
      D: *... and it er ... I mean ... he was goin' up* ...

  (i) A: *mm* (low)
      D: *there ... up towards the police station*   *but he*

  (j) A: *mm hmm* (mid-high rise)
      D: *musta seen 'nother police cár* ...

  (k) D: *so he turn ... he done er ... he pow..ered it round the*

  (l) A: *òh*
      C: *yeah!* (high-fall)
      D: *corner*   *an' almost ... he slid the bike out an'*

(m) D: *turn' round and came back and went ... up the street*

(n) A: *yeah* (low rise)
 D: *an' er ... he came up here went through*

(o) D: *the school. Police came up here ... they stopped ... they*

(p) D: *went ... bloke got out and got his baton and started*

(q) A: *strewth!*
 B: *there was*
 C: *yeah!* (low rise)
 D: *chasin' 'im ...*   *excellent!*

(r) B: *about four cops ... four cop cars ...*
 C: *er ... one panel van*

(s) D: *one paddy wagon an' then they found something*

(t) D: *or sumpen'!*

There are certainly some reflexes here of the hierarchical relationships within the group. D is a much bigger boy physically than the others and is clearly the leader. C, who tends to play the role of joker, introduces the narrative with great determination, insistently repeating *one Monday* until he is sure the story has been accepted by the group as topic, but the floor is then taken over by D following C's question (*what period was it?*, line (c)). From then on C is content to offer carefully timed supporting contributions at appropriate points – *this kid on the motorbike, man!* (line (e)), *yeah!* (lines (l), (q)). At the end of the narrative both B and C make contributions to fill out the picture (lines (q), (r)). There is also some fine differentiation in the interviewer's use of minimal responses. At line (i) D makes a very short pause after a short low-rise and D produces a very short minimal response (*mm*, low contour) to indicate support and continuing attention. A few moments later, however, D marks a dramatic development in the narrative (*He musta seen 'nother police cár*) with a more emphatic rise and a longer pause. A reacts with a much longer *mm hmm* (line (j)), produced with considerably more energy than the previous response and with a high rising contour, signalling acknowledgment of the dramatic turn in events.

Texts of this kind, which are surely far from atypical of male–male interaction suggest that the view of male discourse as predominantly competitive is as much of a stereotype as were the early interpretations of female discourse as diffident and powerless. This is certainly not to dismiss the large body of evidence indicating that there is a tendency for cross-sex conversations to be characterised by asymmetrical behaviours, indicating the operation of different conversational strategies. It may be that there is a tendency for males to adopt a different interactional style in these conversations than do women, for whatever reasons. As we have noted, however, the functional complexity of many of the relevant linguistic features in conjunction with the problematic role of uncontrolled contextual variables, suggests that extreme caution needs to be exercised in interpreting the results of work carried out so far. One important lesson that has been learned is that any analysis of the function of linguistic features needs to take account of the complex interaction between form and context in the production of meaning.

Conclusion

We conclude this chapter by attempting to sketch out an overview of the main factors that have impinged on linguists' attempts to describe and explain the various facets of the relationship between language and gender. Early work on the topic was strongly influenced by two prevailing strands of thought in linguistics. The first had to do with traditional concerns in the discipline with questions of structure rather than usage, based on a view of language as a homogeneous object. The second strand is the determinist view of the relationship between language and cognition deriving from Whorf. Starting from an informal perception of sex bias in language, linguists were led initially to seek the source of bias in linguistic structure and to argue from there that the process of language development was instrumental in the imposition of a 'man-made' linguistic code (Spender 1980). This applied both to the way in which language 'treated' people (differential treatment deriving from structural inadequacies in the linguistic system) and to differences between male and female discourses (many arguing that there were no appropriate linguistic structures mediating the female world-view). To the extent that there seemed to be a solution to these problems, this seemed to lie in the introduction of new unbiased structural elements – for example, *chairperson* to replace *chairman*, *Ms* to replace *Mrs* and *Miss*, a new neutral third-person pronoun – and in the development of new conceptual categories and terminology designed to encode women's experience. The problem, however, seemed to be a daunting one, partly because most aspects of linguistic structure are highly resistant to change (the 'closed' nature of the pronoun system being an obvious example), and partly because the creation and establishment of the current categorial system (envisaged as a relatively stable structure on this view) has been in operation over such a long period of time that the prospect of widespread and thoroughgoing change in the short term seemed remote.

More recent work on this question has opened up a quite different perspective on these issues. The most important step in this re-evaluation of the problem has been to move away from the idea of a homogeneous language and to embrace the notion of linguistic behaviour as the site of highly complex interactions between competing discourses. Sexist bias is not therefore seen as embodied in some vast monolithic scheme of categorisation but in a diverse set of heterogeneous practices with a variety of historical origins. The suggestion that there is a constant process of discourse creation, development and conflict arising out of ongoing social change conjures up a more optimistic picture of the possibilities for the expression of women's perspectives and for the contestation of existing discourses (Cameron 1985: 172–3). As we have seen, there is no shortage of linguistic resources for the expression of new meanings and perspectives. An example of the use of metaphor, for example, can be seen in the establishment of the concept of 'male chauvinism', to take just one case in point. This term neatly connects male assumptions concerning gender identity and authority to outmoded conceptions of national identity and power. It is one of many concepts to have played a part in the feminist challenge to traditional attitudes. In order for this concept to become established, it was not necessary to extend the lexical or grammatical 'capital' of the language. The mechanisms for its creation are part of very general processes constantly operating in language, processes that enable it to adapt to an ever-changing world. The real difficulty was not in the creation of the concept but in gaining general acceptance for it. This was achieved not through linguistic processes but as a result of the improved access of women to domains of public discourse. In other words, the main driving forces of change are social rather than linguistic.

It is important, nevertheless not to understate the factors operating against change in this area. Many of the concepts that articulate women's perspectives do have to be created and this is not necessarily a straightforward process.[11] Women's groups have played a crucial role here. More significantly, perhaps, established discursive and generic regularities in themselves constitute a barrier to change. As Cameron (1985: 151) points out, the emergence of women reporters, for example, did not lead to overnight change in journalistic practices. Although Whorf's ideas imposed an overly restrictive framework on early work in this area, particularly in his emphasis on the role of linguistic structure in the imposition of world-view, his general argument is still highly relevant when interpreted in the light of a rather different view of language. As soon as we move away from the notion of a relatively homogeneous language-object to a view of language as a heterogeneous set of discursive practices, it is clear that such practices can be highly effective in the construction and perpetuation of dominant ideologies. Nevertheless resources are available for challenging these dominant discourses, for the legitimation of discourses hitherto suppressed and for the development of new practices. One of the most important properties of language relevant to all these possibilities is the highly fluid nature of linguistic categories. The price that we have to pay for this is the fact that communication can never be perfect.

> The problems of expressing oneself and being understood are not exclusively women's problems. They are built into all interaction and affect all speakers. (Cameron 1985: 142)

This flexibility, however, brings with it the enormous benefit that language is infinitely adaptable to ever-changing situations. What this means is that language does not have the all-powerful role in shaping ideology attributed to it in some interpretations of Whorf's writings. As Cameron (1985: 143) succinctly notes 'where there is no determinacy, there can be no determinism'.

In the following chapter, we will take up in a more general context some of the themes indicated here, focusing in particular on the concept of texts as the site of interacting, often conflicting, discourses.

Notes

1. Following general practice I distinguish terminologically between the social category of 'gender' and the biological category of 'sex'.
2. *The Australian*, 7 November 1979, cited in Stirling 1987: 125–6.
3. *The Courier-Mail*, Brisbane, 15 October 1979, cited in Stirling 1987: 118.
4. *The Telegraph*, Brisbane, 9 October 1979 cited in Stirling 1987: 116.
5. Stanley Gerson, 'Tongue-tied by sexist language', *The Courier-Mail*, Brisbane, 4 June 1985.
6. Cited by Silveira 1980: 169.
7. Cited by Graham 1975: 62.
8. The pronoun *they* has of course long been available for use as a sex-neutral third person pronoun but its acceptability is somewhat restricted, owing to the efforts of traditional grammarians (Bodine 1975).
9. The transcriptions of the texts cited from Coates 1989 have been simplified by the omission of notational information concerning length of pauses, undecipherable utterances and so on. These transcriptions should be read rather like a musical score, each 'stave' being marked by a letter.
10. This use may be closely related to a use of the tag typical of Cockney speakers, where it seems to function as a marker of in-group solidarity. Thus (to take an example from the BBC *Minder* series), if Arthur asks Terry *Where's Dave then?* and Terry replies *He's out, i'n' he?*, the tag seems to indicate that Dave's absence is an item of shared community knowledge that Arthur might possibly have been expected to know.
11. Spender 1980 (Ch. 6), for example, deals with the male-oriented nature of certain terms and the absence of names for many experiences important to women.

7 Discursive interactions

Austen: *Emma*

This chapter focuses on the idea that texts are the product of interactive processes involving psychological, social and linguistic factors, interwoven in complex ways. Texts are typically the site of
contestation between conflicting perspectives, and linguistic processes constitute the mechanism for the resolution of these conflicts. The concept of (epistemic) modality, introduced in the
previous chapter, and the related concept of 'modalisation' will
play a major part in the discussion of the texts to be examined
here. Both of these terms refer to the process whereby speakers 'in-
trude' into and colour their speech acts (Halliday 1970: 335). We
will use the term 'modalisation' to refer to this general process of
speaker intrusion and 'modality' to refer to the very wide range of
meanings that are involved in this process. In some cases modal
meanings fuse with referential meanings in individual lexemes – a
well-known set of examples being the large number of disparaging
terms for women (Schulz 1975, Stanley 1977). In other cases
modalisation can operate through specific forms – the epistemic
modal forms discussed in the previous chapter illustrate this point.
A particularly important sub-class of modalisers are the 'modal'
verbs themselves: *may, must, can, will* and so on. Although these
elements do not express 'attitudinal' meanings such as disapproval
or anger, one of their most characteristic functions is to express
the speaker's evaluation of the evidential status of a particular
proposition and they are therefore closely bound up with matters
of speaker judgement, speaker perspective. For example, sentences
such as *John may be in Sydney now, John will be in Sydney now,
John must be in Sydney now* all express different speaker judgements concerning the evidential status of the same proposition:
John is in Sydney now. As we saw in Chapter 5, modalisation may

also operate through grammatical processes such as thematic choice, nominalisation and passivisation. In the texts under analysis in this chapter we will see a wide range of linguistic resources deployed in the process of modalisation.

The first text is the first chapter of Jane Austen's novel *Emma*. Here the focus is on the way in which two competing perspectives on the central character, Emma, are developed and finally reconciled to each other through modalisation. The novel opens with the following sentence:

> *Emma Woodhouse, handsome, clever, and rich, with a comfortable home and happy disposition, seemed to unite some of the best blessings of existence; and had lived nearly twenty-one years in the world with very little to distress or vex her.*

We have here a set of judgements that can be said to have a dual role. On the one hand they define a set of parameters against which we are apparently to judge the characters of the novel: physical appearance, intellectual ability, wealth, personality. In this sense they appear to assign to the reader a particular reading position. Already in this opening sentence, the 'rules' are laid down for the game of reading the text. The reader may not normally use wealth, for example, as a criterion in judging individuals but is placed in the position of doing so (or appears to be so placed) at the outset. The second function of the sentence is to situate Emma with respect to these parameters. She is said to possess all those qualities that appear to be the basis here of favourable judgements of character. Let me call this set of judgements on Emma 'Perspective A'.

Already in this first sentence there are indications that there may be alternatives to the judgemental criteria invoked here, suggesting the possibility of a different, less favourable perspective on Emma. The word that plays the central role here is *seem*. *Seem*, of course, is crucially concerned with perception. In some constructions in which it occurs, the perceiver is mentioned explicitly. Thus, an example such as *Emma seems to me to be rich* can be glossed as 'I perceive Emma to be rich'. However, examples such as *Emma seemed to unite some of the best blessings of existence*, in which the perceiver is not mentioned explicitly, pose problems of interpretation not dissimilar from those posed by truncated passives discussed in Chapter 5. The question is: who is to be interpreted as the perceiver, who makes the judgement in this case? Hough (1970) takes the view that the first chapter of the novel is a case of 'objective narrative', essentially defined as proffering a set of statements that are to be taken on trust by the reader. On this interpretation, we would take the unspecified perceiver as the author – 'I as narrator perceive Emma to unite some of the best blessings of existence', with the implication that the reader is expected to adopt the same perspective as the author. Clearly, however, there are problems with the concept of 'objective narrative' here. If the judgement about Emma is to be taken on trust by the reader, why does the author explicitly make reference to the process of perception? One would have expected, rather, a statement of the form *Emma united the best blessings of existence*. Reference to the process of perception has the effect of modalising the associated statement. That is, it expresses a lower degree of commitment on the part of the speaker to the truth of the associated proposition and in this sense has a similar function to the verb *may*, discussed above. To say: *I perceive that X is the case* is to imply that someone else (you the reader?) may see the situation differently. This modalising effect is even more marked in the construction where the perceiver is not explicitly mentioned. *Emma seemed to unite some of the best blessings of existence* allows for the interpretation 'someone other than me, the narrator, makes this judgement', potentially carrying the implication 'but I do not share it'. This is clearly another reason for questioning the validity of the application of the concept 'objective narrative' to this text. Instead of seeing the function of the opening sentence of the novel as being to provide information about Emma, we can see it as identifying a particular perspective on her but at the same time establishing the possibility of some sort of distance from that perspective, indicating the potential viability of a different (and by implication less favourable) perspective. I will refer to this alternative set of judgements as 'perspective B'. At this stage its existence is merely hinted at and the reader can do little more than guess at its possible basis.

It was noted above that the opening sentence here appears to have a dual role – to identify those criteria that are to operate in the judgements of character in the novel and to place Emma with respect to these criteria. As well as raising questions concerning the character of Emma herself, *seem* also casts some doubt on the wider question concerning the kind of criteria that are to be applied generally in the novel. The attributes *handsome, clever, rich* and so on are assigned to Emma without qualification. What is called into question by *seem* is whether Emma's possession of these qualities is to be taken to mean that she 'united some of the best blessings of existence'. The question, in other words, is whether these attributes are indeed the real qualities that constitute the basis of well-founded judgements of character. The whole question of the validity of such judgements that occupies so important a place in Austen's work as a whole is therefore posed at the outset here.

The opposition between the two perspectives established by *seem* is developed through the contrasting modalities associated with *distress* and *vex*. If I say *The incident distressed Emma*, Emma is perceived to have experienced the kind of emotion that normally elicits sympathy on the part of the observer. If I say *The incident vexed Emma*, her reaction is more likely to be viewed with amusement or even ironic disdain. Thus, these two terms neatly juxtapose contrasting perspectives, such that the one associated with *distress* is clearly in harmony with the favourable A-perspective, whereas that associated with *vex* is part of the less favourable B-perspective. Although *vex* does little to delineate the latter, it does enhance its viability. The ordering of terms appears to be consistent in each case. The sentence begins by characterising the A-perspective and then suggests the possible existence of a B-perspective through *seem*. This sequence is then echoed in the *distress-vex* sequence.

Further development takes place in the description of Mr Woodhouse as an *affectionate indulgent father*. However we analyse the semantics of *affectionate* and *indulgent*, it is clear that the latter contains features of disapproval not present in the former. Such disapproval applies to both participants in the expression *X was indulgent to Y*. Again we have an opposition of terms such that the first (*affectionate*) relates to the overt A-perspective, whereas the second (*indulgent*) relates to the covert B-perspective. The term *indulgent*, moreover, contributes to a much clearer delineation of the B-perspective. To this extent the latter becomes more explicit. It is at this point that we begin to glimpse the real nature of the flaws in Emma's character.

The focus now shifts for a few sentences to the governess, Miss Taylor.

> *Sixteen years had Miss Taylor been in Mr Woodhouse's family less as a governess than a friend, very fond of both daughters, but particularly of Emma. Between them it was more the intimacy of sisters. Even before Miss Taylor had ceased to hold the nominal office of governess, the mildness of her temper had hardly allowed her to impose any restraint; and the shadow of authority being now long passed away, they had been living together as friend and friend very mutually attached, and Emma doing just what she liked; highly esteeming Miss Taylor's judgment, but directed chiefly by her own.*

It is noticeable that the presentation of Miss Taylor's character and of her relationship with Emma proceeds in such a way that the perspective not only develops but shifts considerably over a sequence of three sentences. This process subtly echoes the way in which the perspective on Emma has been developed, with B gradually encroaching on A. Initially we see Miss Taylor as *an excellent woman ... who had fallen little short of a mother in affection*. This explicit judgement clearly relates to the characterisation of Mr Woodhouse as an affectionate father and belongs to the general A-perspective. Immediately, however, a re-interpretation takes place. Rather than exercising the authority associated with the office of governess, she had in fact spent sixteen years in Mr Woodhouse's family *less as a governess than as a friend*. This statement too is immediately re-evaluated: between Miss Taylor and Emma *it was more the intimacy of sisters*. The original view of the relationship between Miss Taylor and Emma as involving an unequal power relationship: governess–child has now given way to one involving an equal power relationship: sister–sister. This movement reflects the semantics of *indulgent father* ('Mr Woodhouse has power over Emma in the role of father but he fails to exercise this power responsibly'). On the surface, the comments on the relationship between Miss Taylor and Emma appear to express a favourable judgement. However, they acquire here unfavourable overtones because of the way in which they interact with perspective B. This covert interpretation is then given greater weight by a more explicit statement:

The mildness of her temper had hardly allowed her to impose any restraint.

It is perhaps significant that in syntactic terms Miss Taylor is assigned in this sentence to a patientive rather than agentive role, so that the grammatical structure of the sentence echoes its content.

The question of perspective is also taken up metaphorically in the phrase *the shadow of authority* (*the shadow of authority being now long passed away*). In this context, the expression is characterised by a certain ambiguity. One set of connotations clearly relates to the author's comments on Miss Taylor's 'mildness of temper' and on her failure to 'impose any restraint'. The office of governess which she exercised was nominal, her authority was empty – a shadow. There is, however, another set of connotations associated with what we can take to be Emma's perspective. Given what we now know, or can surmise, about her character, it is plausible to suppose that her attitude to authority might be one of resentment; on this interpretation the shadow constitutes a threat, a potential source of unhappiness. We therefore find here the fusion in a single term of author/reader perspective and character perspective. The ambiguity derives from the interplay between two different metaphors. Expressions such as *She is merely a shadow of her former self* exploit the fact that although shadows have the general shape of the objects which project them, and therefore in some ways resemble those objects, they do not have the substance of those objects. On the other hand, expressions such as *Her illness cast a shadow over the occasion* derive from the fact that shadows are dark and from the metaphor that unhappiness is dark. In this case, the notion of lack of substance is associated with the author's perspective and that of unhappiness with Emma's point of view.

By this stage in the exposition the existence of two contrasting perspectives on Emma is clear. The verb *seem* plays an important part by indicating the relevance of the process of perception in relation to the general question of value judgements. Oppositional terms such as *distress* and *vex*, *affectionate* and *indulgent* also indicate contrasting perceptual frameworks and these are echoed by ambiguities involved in the interpretation of expressions such as *shadow of authority*. The feature connecting all these elements to each other is the fact that they all involve elements of modal meaning.

Up to this point in the novel the main function of modalisation has been to develop an alternative perspective to the one explicitly presented in the opening sentence. It now acquires a rather different function. The crucial sentence is the following:

> *The real evils indeed of Emma's situation were the power of having rather too much her own way, and a disposition to think a little too well of herself; these were the disadvantages which threatened alloy to her many enjoyments.*

The sentence contains a number of modalities, interacting with each other in intricate ways. The main elements involved are *rather, too much, a little, too well* and *threaten*. By this stage perspective B has emerged strongly, having now developed to the point where it threatens to oust perspective A as the dominant term. The function of the text from here on is to fuse perspective B with perspective A, so that the perception of Emma's qualities can be reconciled with the perception of her flaws. The modalities play a crucial role in this process. Thus consider the relationships between the following:

(1) (a) *She has her own way*
     (b) *She thinks well of herself*
(2) (a) *She has too much her own way*
     (b) *She thinks too well of herself*
(3) (a) *She has rather too much her own way*
     (b) *She thinks a little too well of herself*

The examples in (1) are relatively unmodalised. It is possible to interpret either as a favourable or as an unfavourable comment. Interpretation depends in speech on intonation (obviously a major exponent of modality) and on context. The examples in (2) can be interpreted only as unfavourable judgements, with *too* (or *too much*) as the exponent of speaker disapproval. However, in (3) the modal element *too* is itself modalised by other modalities (*rather* and *a little*), whose effect is to moderate the expression of speaker disapproval. In terms of the preceding discussion the examples in (2) could be seen as belonging to perspective B whereas those in (3) – the ones actually occurring in the text – have the effect of moderating perspective B in the direction of the more favourable perspective A.

The same structure of 'modality on modality' can be discerned in *threaten* (*the disadvantages which threatened alloy to her many enjoyments*). This word combines the expression of two major kinds of meaning. In a sentence such as *Rising prices threaten to destroy the country's economy*, the word *threaten* places the associated situation (the destruction of the country's economy) in the future and simultaneously expresses speaker disapproval of this possible future situation. Thus, the narrator in *Emma* contemplates the possibility that her heroine's spoilt nature is a blemish that outweighs her good qualities (clearly part of perspective B). However, rather than identifying this as a present situation, she characterises it as a possible situation in the future, thereby distancing herself to some extent from that perspective. Thus, we could say that within the semantics of the word *threaten* the modality of disapproval is itself modalised by the modality of futurity.[1] There is a close parallel here to the way in which *rather* and *a little* are used to modalise *too much*, *too well*. In terms of the plot as a whole the reconciliation of perspective B with perspective A, which is the object of these interactive processes, is an essential preliminary to the appearance of Mr Knightley, whose judgement of Emma reconciles the perception of her flaws with the appreciation of her qualities.

As far as our present argument is concerned, what is of particular interest is the way in which the interaction between competing perspectives can be traced through a variety of linguistic processes, all involving modality. The discussion also bears on issues concerning the nature of language introduced in Chapter 4. The analysis of the processes involved in the interpretation of the first chapter of *Emma* is more compatible with the view that language is a catalyst in an interactional process which produces meaning rather than with the notion that language is a vehicle that transfers meaning from speaker to hearer (p. 79). The discussion above suggests that the reader's role is one of active engagement in the construction and evaluation of contrasting perspectives in response to rather subtle linguistic clues, rather than one of passive acceptance of authorial judgements. The catalyst metaphor also provides some explanation – in a way that the container view does not – for the fact that a novel like *Emma* can be read and re-read many times with greater pleasure at each re-reading. On the container view certain meanings should be transferred from writer (or text) to reader on each occasion, but there is no particular reason to expect that there should be any cumulative process at work here. On the other hand, if one attributes to the reader an interpretive role that is more creative than that of 'accepting' meanings, and if the nature of this process is intimately bound up with the current state of the reader's knowledge base, then there is every reason to expect the experience of re-reading to be a new and richer one on each occasion.

Discourses of power and solidarity

The second text to be discussed here is a non-literary one. It is a memorandum sent by the Head of an academic Department to members of his Department.

DEPARTMENT OF . . .

Memorandum to academic staff:

1. *STAFF FORM AB/1 TEACHING STAFF WORK LOAD*
   The annual drudgery of setting down a summary of what we
5 *do with our time needs to be undertaken again.*
   Each staff-member needs to fill in a copy of STAFF FORM
   AB/1. The purposes of the forms are
   i. *to enable the Standing Committee to see whether the*
      work-load of the Department is equitably distributed
10 ii. *to enable the Standing Committee to see whether the Department, by comparison with other departments, needs more or fewer staff*
   iii. *to enable the University to indicate to the Universities Commission how it is using its resources. It is the*
15 *Universities Commission rather than the University that needs some of the details requested.*

The form is the same as for last year. A few suggestions may, nevertheless, not be unwelcome:

   i. *Read carefully the notes on the back of the form*
20 ii. *Note especially points 9, 10, 25*
   iii. *If you take a class or classes for someone else, please make sure that only one person claims the hour(s)*
   iv. *For second semester, in a subject that contains a lecture programme as well as seminars, the course convener*

25   *should allocate the 13 (or 26 or . . .) hours of lectures*
        and inform the people involved
    v. *Do not underestimate, under D, the time needed for*
        University administration including committees. Attend-
        ance at Staff meetings probably amounts to 14 hours in
30   *the year; attendance at the Board of the Faculty perhaps*
        6–10 hours; attendance at the Improvements Committee
        and course sub-committees perhaps 30–40 hours. Con-
        sultations with colleagues and students about a current
        subject should probably appear under B: Associated
35   *Work; Other – every subject is likely to require at least*
        40 hours per semester for this
    vi. *The total of A + B + C + D should probably fall between*
        1800 and 2400
    vii. *Please let me have the completed form by 22 April –*
40   *earlier if possible.*

    2. *STAFF DUTIES: Second Semester*
        I had been hoping to defer this schedule until preliminary en-
        rolment figures were available. The need to complete STAFF
        FORM AB/1 has, however, forced me to allocate staff duties
45   *on guess-work enrolments and without the desirable range of*
        consultation. Please let me know of any problems you have
        with the allocation.

Analysis of this text will take the argument a step further. Here we
see not so much the interaction of two different perspectives but of
two distinct 'social formations'.

The concept 'social formation' designates a particular component of social structure. Each of us is a member of many different
social formations simultaneously. As a university teacher, I am a
member of the general academic community. I am also a parent,
which aligns me with a different group. My status as a taxpayer
places me in a third group. And so on. The concept of social formation is linked to the process of perception in the sense that a
particular phenomenon may have quite a different appearance for
the same individual when viewed from the standpoint of different
social formations in which she or he participates. If the government were to impose a massive cut in University funding, for
example, this might appear attractive to me as a taxpayer but dis-
astrous from my point of view as an academic (and as a parent). In
this analysis, then, we will shift the emphasis from the general no-

tion of perspective to the more specific notion of social formation. This will allow us not only to focus on some of the interactions between major social factors but also on the way in which some of the finer aspects of social structure enter into interactions of this kind.

One of the most obvious features of this text is the fact that there is a conflict between the writer's membership of two distinct social formations – a conflict which manifests itself in a range of complex linguistic interactions. On the one hand, he is a member of the university's administrative hierarchy, which places him as Head of Department in a position of authority with respect to his addressees – a position which is particularly relevant to the functions of this text.[2] On the other hand, he also stands in relation to his addressees as a colleague. This relationship derives from the similarity of their professional roles as teachers and a certain commonality of interests and duties. It is perhaps not irrelevant to note that within this institution the Head of Department is in effect elected by colleagues.

There are several features of the text that derive from the institutional context. In the first place the text owes its origins to this framework in that it was clearly triggered by a memorandum to the writer from some institutional source outside the Department. The function of the text is to act as a channel for the transmission of this externally generated message to the members of the Department. In this sense the text directly reflects the hierarchically regulated channels of communication that operate in this setting.

In the second place, the text owes much of its form to the social context in which it was generated. The fact that it has a heading (*Department of ...*), a major sub-heading (*Memorandum to academic staff*) and two numbered minor sub-headings (*1. STAFF FORM AB/1 ...*, *2. STAFF DUTIES*) with roman-numbered subsections, derives from the fact that, although this is a kind of letter, it is one that is situated within an institutional context relating to official matters, not a personal letter. Certain lexical choices can also be traced to this feature. Words such as *drudgery* (line 1) and complex nominals such as *guesswork enrolments, the desirable range of consultation* (lines 44–5) do not belong to the more informal register of Common Room conversations.

The third feature relating to the institutionally defined relationships in play here consists in the large proportion of directive utterances. Moreover, it is not only the number of directives but also their form that is relevant, in particular the high proportion of imperatives (*Read carefully* ..., *Note especially* ..., *Do not underestimate* (lines 19–27)), though we will see directly that there are complicating factors here.

A fourth relevant feature is the role of the writer as purveyor of privileged information. In his role as Head of Department the writer has access to information of the kind communicated in the first half of the text about the purposes of form AB/1. Some of this information may derive from the externally generated 'triggering' text referred to above.

It is worth making a distinction between some of the features identified above. Those features concerned with the layout of the document and with the formal register it adopts can be characterised as **generic** features, since they have to do with the 'genre' to which this text belongs – that of 'official memorandum'. The point here is that 'official memorandum' is one of a large set of text types – the concept includes other generic types such as newspaper editorial, sermon, after-dinner speech, colloquial narrative and so on. On the other hand, features such as the proportion of directives and the communication of privileged information derive from the power differential between writer and reader. The latter constitutes a separate dimension from that of genre in that the features characterising official memoranda, for example, will be found in memoranda addressed by persons out of power to those in power as well as in those moving in the opposite direction. It is therefore useful here to invoke the concept 'discourse of authority' to designate those features deriving from the power differential between writer and addressee. The text can then be seen as resulting at least in part from the interaction of the discourse of authority with the genre of official memorandum (Kress 1985: 29).

More interesting than this interaction, however, is that between the discourse of authority and a conflicting discourse – the discourse of solidarity. The wide range of features that constitute this discourse derive from the fact that the writer and reader(s) are colleagues. This discourse opens with the use of the inclusive pronoun forms *we* and *our*. With these forms, the writer identifies himself as a member of a group in which both he and his addressees are included. The semantic content of the term *drudgery* also participates in this discourse in its expression of distaste for the task in question, an attitude which the writer knows unites him with colleagues. As noted above, however, generic factors are also involved in the selection of this term – it is a site of interaction between the discourse of solidarity and the genre of official memorandum. More interesting is the function of *need* in the passive structure *The annual drudgery ... needs to be undertaken again.* In a structure such as *X needs to do Y, need* has a key role in the process of what we have referred to earlier (page 20) as the process of 'mystification'. Not only does it mystify the source of the requirement that X should do Y but it also mystifies the nature of the requirement. As far as the source is concerned, the requirement may derive from some external source ('Z requires that X do Y') or from X himself/herself ('X requires that X do Y'). This has implications for the interpretation of the nature of the requirement. If the source is external, we are dealing with an authority-based imperative; if internal, with a personal desire. It is the mystification over the source of the requirement together with the associated mystification over its nature that serves to mitigate or modalise the expression of directive meaning. The main interaction in this structure, then, is between the discourse of authority, manifesting itself in the basic, directive function of the sentence, and the discourse of solidarity manifesting itself in a number of lexical and syntactic choices.

Need occurs for a second time in the following sentence, this time as the predicate of *each staff member* (*Each staff member needs to fill in a copy of STAFF FORM AB/1*). The effect of this is to make the 'personal desire' reading even more easily available and thereby to heighten the mitigatory effect. The item occurs for a third time towards the end of the text (*The need to complete STAFF FORM AB/1 has, however, forced me to allocate ...*). By this stage the concept, still obscure in terms of its source and nature, has become reified through the grammatical process of nominalisation. As a result it can now adopt an agentive role with the writer cast in the role of patient and this serves to place the writer more firmly in the same kind of relationship as the reader to the constructed 'need'.

The mystification over the deontic source associated with *need* is concerned with directionality – does the 'need' impinge on or derive from the individual staff member? A similar mystification over directionality occurs in the clause *A few suggestions, may nevertheless, not be unwelcome.* The characterisation of directives as 'suggestions', the use of the modal verb *may* and the double negative structure all constitute part of the discourse of solidarity, but more interesting are the directionality meanings connected with the term *unwelcome.* The function of this item is to assign a certain degree of responsibility to the addressee for the genesis of the document (so that there is now some mystification over the question of its origin). The effect is that the basic directionality of the directives **from** the writer **to** the addressee is reversed.

In sum it is arguable that there are a cluster of interrelated features here involving semantic operations concerning the directionality of deontic and locutionary processes and syntactic operations (truncated passives, double negatives, nominalisations and so on). Their interrelatedness stems from the fact that they can be seen to have a unitary function – to modalise the expression of directive meaning. This function derives from the fact that there is an underlying conflict in the social context in which the text is situated between the institutionally defined hierarchical relationship of writer and addressee(s) and the egalitarian relationship defined by other aspects of their professional role.

Let me conclude this discussion by identifying a number of features that are somewhat problematic with respect to the concepts of discourse used to describe this text. Consider, for example, the tokens of *please* which occur in this text:

(4) *If you take a class or classes for someone else, please make sure that only one person claims the hour* (lines 21–2)
(5) *Please let me have the completed form by 22 April* (line 39)
(6) *Please let me know of any problems you have with the allocation* (lines 46–7)

These directives contrast with such bare imperatives as *Read carefully the notes on the back of the form, Note especially points 9, 10, 25, Do not underestimate under D the time needed for University administration.* It is tempting at first sight to assign the bare imperatives here to the discourse of authority and the *please* imperatives to the discourse of solidarity, given the fact that the function of *please* is clearly to modalise the expression of directive meaning. However, if we consider the contrast between the examples in more detail, we find that the distribution of *please* is governed by rather different factors from those operating in the discourse of solidarity. Although the function of *please* is clearly to mitigate the expression of directive meaning, the effect is not in fact to superimpose solidarity-type meanings on authoritative meanings in the way that other mitigatory elements operate. If anything, the reverse is the case. The *please* directives are in fact rather more distancing in this case than are the bare imperatives. The important factor involved in the distribution of the two imperative types here seems to have to do with the writer's perception not so much of the relationship between himself and the reader but of the relationship between the reader and the specified action. The bare imperative is used when the action is perceived as being in some sense to the benefit of the reader – where there is a danger, if the action is not performed, of readers doing themselves less than justice. The *please* directives, on the other hand, tend to be used when the opposite situation applies – when the specified action is of some cost to the reader (e.g. meeting a deadline) or when there is a danger of the reader gaining some unfair advantage (e.g. claiming to have taught a class which she or he has not in fact taken). In more general terms the distribution of *please* seems to be connected with the question of 'face' (Goffman 1967). The bare imperative is used when the specified action is concerned with positive face and the *please* imperative when it involves negative face (Brown and Levinson 1978: 66).[3]

Another illustration of this general point is provided by the distribution of the words *perhaps*, *probably* and *likely* in (indirect) directives. Examples are:

(7) *Attendance at staff meetings **probably** amounts to 14 hours in the year; attendance at the Board of the Faculty **perhaps** 6–10 hours; attendance at the Improvements Committee and course sub-committees **perhaps** 30–40 hours* (lines 28–32)

(8) *Consultations with colleagues and students about a current subject should **probably** appear under B: Associated Work;* (lines 32–5)

(9) *Other – every subject is **likely** to require at least 40 hours per semester for this* (lines 35–6)

(10) *The total of A + B + C + D should **probably** fall between 1800 and 2400* (lines 37–8)

Again, at a rather general level the function of *perhaps*, *probably* and *likely* can be said to modalise the expression of directive meaning and to that extent these items appear in this context to be candidates for classification as components of the discourse of solidarity. However, the factors which govern their distribution appear to be somewhat different from, and somewhat more specific than, those operating at the general level of discourse. It is not so much that solidarity meanings interface here with authority-related meanings. Rather, the writer appears to wish to allow for a considerable degree of variation in the way that individual readers comply with these directives, because of the nature of the actions specified.

A final illustration of the point is provided by the ambiguity of the modal *should* in the sentence *The course convener should allocate the 13 (or 26 or ...) hours of lectures and inform the people involved.* Again the modalising function of this item makes it a candidate for the discourse of solidarity. This possibility is reinforced by a certain ambiguity associated with it, since, as we have noted, ambiguity in the area of modality typically occurs as an exponent of the tension between interacting discourses. For example, if a lecturer were to say to a student *You should discuss this with the Head of Department,* there is a certain ambiguity (or mystification) over the precise nature of the requirement that the addressee see the Head of Department. Does it derive from the speaker, from the addressee or from some external factor? This kind of ambiguity mystifies the question of what kind of speech act has been produced. Is it a directive (with the requirement deriving from the speaker) or a statement? This kind of ambiguity is typically exploited in situations where the social relationship between speaker and addressee makes it desirable to obscure directive intent. The interesting point about the example here, however, is that, although it is characterised by precisely this kind of ambiguity, there is a rather different factor at work from the one just described. The sentence clearly allows both the directive reading 'I require that course conveners allocate ...' and the statement reading 'there is a general requirement/expectation that course conveners will allocate ...' and it may be that the reason for selecting an item which allows for this ambiguity derives in part from the general complexities of the speaker/addressee relationship discussed above. A far more important consideration, however, is surely the complex nature of the addressee in this case. The memorandum is addressed

to all members of the Department, some of whom are course conveners (for them the directive reading is the appropriate one), some
of whom are not (the statement reading is relevant to them). This
provides another illustration of the very complex interplay of
general and specific factors operating in the selection of a particular linguistic form.

This discussion shows that concepts such as 'the discourse of
solidarity' cannot be defined in terms of a set of linguistic forms in
abstraction from context. There may well be many situations
where the elements of epistemic modality discussed here (*please*,
perhaps, *probably*, *likely*, *should* and so on) do indeed help to express solidarity-type meanings but the 'polypragmatic' nature of
linguistic forms means that it would be an oversimplification to assume that they always do so. Their functional role (or roles) on a
particular occasion of use can only be assessed in relation to that
context. There is a clear connection here with points made in the
previous chapter concerning the interpretation of modal elements
in relation to the language-gender question. There, too, it was emphasised that some interpretations of elements of female discourse
as straightforward exponents of powerlessness involve considerable oversimplification with respect to the functional diversity of
these forms. The point supports one of the general themes of this
book – that meaning is not an intrinsic property of words but is a
product of the interaction between language and contextual
factors.

Conclusion

We have been concerned here with intra-textual tensions and their
linguistic reflexes. In the discussion of *Emma* the relationship between language and perspective is complicated by the fact that two
opposing perspectives are at work. It is not, however, a matter of
making a choice between these perspectives. The opposition is in
fact posed as a question, the answer to which is to be worked out
in the course of the novel itself. Nor is the question posed in an explicit way. It is developed through a series of textual interactions
that integrate the exponents of different exponents of perspective
into a single text in a process which reflects the larger integrative
process at work in the novel as a whole.

In the second text we find a similar interaction between contrasting perspectives, involving in this case opposing interpretations of the relationship between speaker and addressee. Here the circumstances surrounding the genesis of the text pose the essential problem. The institutional context assigns the writer to two distinct roles. He himself will need to complete the specified task but he also has the responsibility of making sure that others do so. How are these 'others' to be named? Are they 'members of his Department', a mode of reference that invokes the hierarchical aspect of the relationship, or are they 'colleagues'? As in the case of *Emma* it is not a question of making a choice between these perspectives. The function of the text is to reconcile each to the other. In both texts, this function is performed principally through the exponents of modality.

There is a danger here of presenting a general picture of textual interaction solely in terms of dualistic tensions. Certainly in many texts binary oppositions of this kind – power versus solidarity, favourable versus unfavourable perspectives, female versus male viewpoints, white versus black orientations, public versus private domains (Kress 1986), unitary versus pluralistic frameworks (Kress and Trew 1978) – are dominant. It would be misleading, however, to attempt to reduce all social and linguistic complexity to binary oppositions of this kind. The multi-dimensional character of social space is such that any text enters into a highly complex pattern of discursive and generic interactions originating in a wide variety of social and institutional structures.

Notes

1. The close association between the expression of futurity and modality is a familiar one (Lyons 1968: 310, Palmer 1977: 5).
2. The writer of this text, who has given permission for it to be used, is male – hence the use of masculine pronouns to refer to him.
3. This argument is supported by the observation that bare imperatives expressing invitations (*Have a seat!*, *Come in!*) are rather more friendly in tone than their counterparts with *please*, and that similar structures expressing wishes (*Sleep well!*, *Enjoy yourself!*) do not naturally collocate with *please*.

8 *Variety, discourse, ideology*

Post-colonial literatures

Any book concerned with the relationship between language, perspective and ideology would be incomplete without some discussion of the relationship between variation in the language code itself (what we normally think of as 'dialectal' variation in the most general sense) and questions relating to social identity and world-view. There is, however, such an enormous literature on this topic that any discussion here will inevitably need to be highly selective (for general surveys of this work see Hudson 1980, Downes 1984, Fasold 1984, Edwards 1985, Wardhaugh 1986).

Here again we will consider both a literary and a non-literary aspect of the question. In the first section of the chapter we address a number of issues in what is now usually referred to as 'post-colonial literatures' – literatures in English from various post-colonial societies such as Australia, Canada, India, the African countries, the Caribbean. We will take Australia as the main focus of interest. In the second section we will consider the role of linguistic variation in societies where there are quite different variants of the same language in general use, usually called 'diglossic' societies. From the linguist's point of view, the attraction of diglossic societies is that they illustrate with particular clarity processes that operate in a less obvious way in other societies, where linguistic contrasts are less clearly marked. As a particular case, we will focus on Switzerland, specifically on the function of linguistic variation in the genre of the television commercial.

It would be a truism to observe that the process of colonisation has made of English one of the most varied languages ever to have existed. Each of the countries that have adopted English as a major medium of communication has imprinted its own character on the language. In fact each of the countries in question has produced not one variety of the language but many. This is most obviously true of America (the first post-colonial society of the modern age) with its great variety of social and regional varieties, some of them originating in the creoles that emerged from the slave plantations. It is also true of Australia, often thought of as a linguistically homogeneous country, which in fact comprises a wide spectrum of variation from something very close to British 'Received Pronunciation' to rural varieties that are barely intelligible to speakers from the cities. Australia also has its English-based creoles in various parts of the North and West (Shnukal 1989) and, given the ethnic diversity of its population, a wide variety of accents are to be heard in the streets of its cities and towns. Perhaps the most complex post-colonial situation of all is to be found in the Caribbean, where the problem of working with the concept of a unitary entity called 'the English language' is particularly acute (Le Page and Tabouret-Keller 1985: 8).

These linguistic complexities pose major problems for any writer in a post-colonial situation trying to find an authentic language attuned to local experience. A major aspect of the problem has to do with the authority of the 'standard' language inherited from the colonising power with its alien connotations. The aura of authority can linger on long after the end of the period of colonisation as such. For some Australians even today standard British English has considerable prestige. Ashcroft *et al.* (1989: 7) make a particularly clear statement of the problem:

> One of the major features of imperial oppression is control over the language. The imperial education system installs a 'standard' version of the metropolitan language as the norm, and marginalizes all 'variants' as impurities ... Language becomes the medium through which a hierarchical structure of power is perpetuated, and the medium through which conceptions of 'truth', 'order', and 'reality' become established. Such power is rejected in the emergence of an effective post-colonial voice.[1]

A similar point is made by the Indian writer Raja Rao in the foreword to his novel *Kanthapura* (Rao 1961).

> The telling has not been easy. One has to convey in a language that is not one's own the spirit that is one's own. One has to convey the various shades and omissions of a certain thought-movement that

looks maltreated in an alien language. I use the 'alien', yet English is not really an alien language to us. It is the language of our intellectual make-up – like Sanskrit or Persian was before – but not our emotional make-up. We are all instinctively bilingual, many of us writing in our language and English. We cannot write like the English. We should not. We cannot write only as Indians.[2]

Before we consider a number of extracts illustrating how writers in various post-colonial situations have attempted to come to grips with this problem, we should devote some consideration to the processes that impinge on a language when it is transplanted to a new environment. Perhaps the first point to make is that the very nature of the colonial situation, with the marked disparities of power and wealth out of which the colonial situation is born and which it tends to perpetuate and accentuate, has a number of linguistic reflexes. The distinctions between the prestigious 'standard' variety of the wealthy colonisers and the stigmatised non-standard accents of the less wealthy is transplanted to the new environment. In the case of Australia the 'spectrum' of London English, ranging from standard middle-class English to working-class Cockney was transplanted directly to the new colony in the years following 1788, with a solid admixture of regional accents from other parts of Britain, especially from Ireland. The nature of the Australian situation inevitably led to the creation of an unfavourable image for the standard variety. It undoubtedly became at a very early stage a symbol of privilege, authority, oppression. It is of some interest to note that today standard British English has the most favourable (or perhaps least unfavourable) image in a city that never served as a penal colony – Adelaide. The accent of the Adelaide middle classes is closer to British Received Pronunciation than is that of any other Australian city.

The colonial situation, however, typically creates another parameter of variation that comes into existence alongside the inherent variation that characterises the language on its arrival. Contact with non-native speakers of English – the colonised peoples – typically gives rise to a pidgin variety. In the American slave plantations, pidgin was used not only for communication between masters and slaves but also, since slaves from many different language backgrounds were thrown together, between slaves themselves.

Because of the asymmetries inherent in the colonial situation, pidgin languages come to be based in some important respects on the language of the colonisers. Most of their vocabulary tends to be drawn from this source, though a whole range of natural phonological processes may cause many of the resulting words to be unrecognisable to speakers of the dominant language and many of the meanings expressed may be more characteristic of the indigenous 'substrate' languages than of the colonial language (Shnukal 1989: 153). Since pidgins are not the native language of any of those involved in the contact situation, they tend to have a simplified grammatical system, often quite variable from one speaker to another.

When pidgins become established, however, they can become the first language of a new generation. Conditions for this were particularly favourable in the American slave plantations, where the total disruption of African social structures militated against the use of African languages. When pidgins acquire native speakers in this way, they undergo 'creolisation'. That is, they acquire a much bigger lexicon (since they now have to serve all the functional requirements of a 'normal' language) and a more complex grammar. The lexicon typically continues to be dominated by the colonisers' language (so much so that it is often perceived as a variety of that language, though a highly 'corrupted' one). Its grammar, however, will be very different, although some influence of the dominant language is likely here too. Indigenous substrate languages usually have a major influence, as do a variety of natural processes (Todd 1974: 43). At this stage the creole is for all practical purposes not mutually intelligible with the standard language and is in effect an autonomous linguistic system.

The third stage of the cycle involves the evolution of a 'postcreole continuum'. This typically arises when a significant number of speakers become bilingual in the standard variety (or something approaching it) and in the creole. This kind of bilingualism is particularly likely to occur in those who have extensive contact with the colonisers – servants in wealthy households, locally appointed officials, those with access to education. Given the nature of the linguistic relationship between the creole and the standard, particularly the large area of shared vocabulary and grammar, a linguistic continuum comes into being with the standard language ('acrolect') at one end of the range and the creole ('basilect') at the other. Some speakers acquire the ability to 'slide' along the continuum, using speech forms close to the acrolect in formal situations and speech forms close to the basilect in informal contexts. Many, however, remain restricted to a more limited linguistic space at the lower end of the continuum.

This range of variation comes to occupy a place alongside the inherent variation that characterised the language on its first arrival in the colony. Meanwhile, of course, changes may have occurred in the colonising language itself. In Australia, the emergence of a characteristically Australian accent seems to have emerged at a very early stage in the life of the colony, probably in the first generation born in the country. The speech of many inhabitants of Sydney was clearly very close in linguistic terms to the speech of working-class London, though there were undoubtedly some early differences resulting from the special character of the 'mixing bowl' (Cochrane 1989). Local patterns of settlement seem to have produced rather different forms in other areas – the speech of the mining town of Cessnock in New South Wales, for example, shows traces of having been more strongly influenced by northern British working-class speech than other areas of Australia (Shnukal 1979: 231).

Contact between the language and the new environment produces change at various levels. At the level of word meaning, some individual words undergo semantic extension, some acquire new connotations, some begin to disappear from everyday usage in the absence of the objects which they denote in the new environment.

> There was so much difference between the 'things or objects' of Britain and those which our oecists found in Australia that familiar words either had to be given new applications or entirely new words had to be used. (Baker 1966: 3)

This applies particularly to words denoting the flora and fauna of the new environment. The Australian 'silky oak' is quite unrelated to the English oak and the great 'firs' of Canada's Pacific coast are not fir trees (New 1978: 363). John Bernard (1962: 97) makes a similar point about Australian fish:

> I compared the descriptions of some common fish in the 'Shorter Oxford' with those they have in 'Fish and Fisheries of Australia' by

T.C. Roughley (Angus and Robertson 1951). Apparently the Australian *bass, catfish, cod, garfish, mackerel, mullet, perch, sole, tailor* and *whiting* do not even belong to the genus described in the 'Oxford'. *Sprat* and *anchovy* do but are different species, while local *whitebait* is not the same as English whitebait and our *tuna* is not the kind referred to in the dictionary.

In the new environment many basic words such as *north, south, east* and *west* and the names of the months and the seasons acquire quite different connotations. For a time old perspectives may persist – witness the use in Australia of such terms as *Far East* and *Near East* to designate areas that are from an Australian perspective the 'Near North' and the 'Far West' respectively. There was a time not so long ago when many Australians, born and bred, even continued the practice of referring to Britain as 'home'. Old discourses die hard.

Some normal English words such a *woods, meadow, inn, tavern, brook, village* found no place in early Australian vocabulary. Their denotative and connotative meanings were too strongly oriented to British phenomena (Baker 1966: 21). Some phenomena give rise to the need for new words – a need which is most likely to be met by borrowings from indigenous languages. Words such as *kangaroo, kookaburra, lubra, budgeree, boomerang, bunyip, gunyah, humpy* were borrowed from Australian Aboriginal languages. In some cases words of dialectal origin acquire more widespread currency in the new situation and may then find their way back to the metropolitan centre. The word *larrikin*, for example, is attested in a *Glossary of the Cornish dialect* (1882) by a Dr Jago but in 1897 was cited in a British *Dictionary of slang, jargon and cant* by Barrère and Leland as 'imported from Australia' (Baker 1966: 9).

The new social context and new social practices add new meanings to some existing words and give rise to new terms. A *squatter* was someone who settled on unappropriated land and began to farm it. The fact that squatters became wealthy landowners spawned the term *squattocracy* as the nearest Australian equivalent to the English term 'landed gentry'. The term *new chum* came to be applied to a new immigrant and to inexperienced workers in the outback (Baker 1966: 14). The distinction between free settlers and convicts was a crucial one in the early days of the colony, receiving a number of lexical reflexes (the former being *aris-*

tocracy, sterling, pure merinos and the latter *currency, illegitimates* (Baker 1966: 26)). The term 'tramp' proved to be particularly inadequate to cope with the great variety of itinerants who became a significant phenomenon in the new society and a rich lexical field developed to match this diversity: *bagman* (travelling with his possessions in a suitcase), *waler* (camping along the big rivers), *battler, coaster, coiler, swamper, drummer, Yarra banker, dole chaser, steel jockey* (riding trains without paying), *bowerbird* (living on scraps of food), *sundowner* (dodging work by arriving at an outback station at sunset with a request for provisions) (Baker 1966: 105). The concept of 'mateship' was particularly important, as indicated by the emergence of special terms to designate those who stood out by not conforming. The term *Jimmy Woodser* was applied to a lone drinker (or to his drink) (Baker 1966: 233). A similar concept is lexicalised in current Brisbane teenage argot in the term *nigel* (a loner). Anna Wierzbicka (1986: 363–8) has pointed out the significance of various aspects of contemporary Australian English that relate to this concept – e.g. the use of idiomatic expressions such as *good on you* and 'speech act verbs' such as *dob in*, oriented to the notion of mateship.

These observations concerning the emergence of a characteristically Australian variety of English should not, however, lead us to assume that a specific, uniform, local variety appeared that captured the 'essence' of the Australian character. This view glosses over the reality of widespread variation in accent and usage, the fact that the colonial situation is typically characterised not by the emergence of a single local variety but by a complex multilingual situation, involving the co-existence of different languages as well as variation in the colonising language. It is this linguistic complexity itself that is the true marker of the new society. Central to this picture is the tension between the authority of the standard language and the range of non-standard forms – a tension that bears both a symbolic relationship to the asymmetries of power and is also involved in the exercise and perpetuation of power.

The ideological implications of the distinction between standard and non-standard varieties is particularly marked in those situations where there are both significant power differences between colonisers and colonised, accompanied by marked linguistic differences between standard and non-standard varieties. This point is illustrated with particular clarity in the following excerpt from an unpublished play *The Cord* by the Malaysian writer K.S. Maniam.[3]

> Muthiah: *What are you saying? Speaking English?*
>
> Ratnam: *The language you think is full of pride. The language that makes you a stiffwhite corpse, like this!*
>
> Muthiah: *But you're nothing. I'm the boss here.*
>
> Ratnam: *Everything happens naturally. Now the language is spoke like I can speak it ... I can speak real life English now.*
>
> Muthiah: *You can do that all day to avoid work!*
>
> Ratnam: *You nothing but stick. You nothing but stink. Look all clean, inside all thing dirty. Outside everything, Inside nothing. Taking-making. Walking-talking. Why you insulting all the time? Why you sit on me like monkey with wet backside?*

In this passage we see operating in a very explicit way the kind of discursive interactions explored in the previous chapter. What makes them explicit here is the fact that the different discourses operate through discrete varieties, the discourse of power through standard English, the discourse of challenge through non-standard forms. The varietal difference is also imbricated with different ways of speaking. Ratnam's attack on the fundamental colourlessness and emptiness of Muthiah's character (and indirectly on the alien irrelevance of the colonial power) is expressed through a rich expressive range, not commanded (or at least not employed) by Muthiah. His use of metaphor (*The language that makes you a stiffwhite corpse, You nothing but stick*), simile (*Why you sit on me like monkey with wet backside?*), original coinings (*stiffwhite*) and word plays (*taking-making, walking-talking*) mount a powerful attack on the cold, exploitive presence of the colonial regime. Ratnam's verbal skills, his delight in playing with the patterns of language (*You nothing but stick, you nothing but stink; Outside everything, inside nothing*) in order to produce new and striking meanings, is highly reminiscent of the skills that have been commented on by sociolinguists working on other vernacular cultures (for a particularly well-known example, see Labov 1969). In other words, there is independent evidence that the verbal skills demonstrated here in Ratnam's speech are not a mere literary flight of fancy but constitute a genuine component of the local sociolinguistic situation. Ratnam's assertion of power over 'real life English' in opposition to the deadness of standard discourses is a crucial element in the means of challenging colonial power and its associated ideology.

The same kind of discursive contrasts are found in a great variety of texts. Here is an Australian example from Joseph Furphy's novel *Such is life*:

> '*Now Mosey,' said Willoughby, courteously but tenaciously, 'will you permit me to enumerate a few gentlemen – gentlemen, remember – who have exhibited in a marked degree the qualities of the pioneer. Let us begin with those men of whom you Victorians are so justly proud, – Burke and Wills. Then you have –* '
>
> '*Hold on, hold on,' interrupted Mosey, 'Don't go no furder, for Gossake. Yer knockin' yerself bad, an' you don't know it. Wills was a pore harmless weed, so he kin pass; but look 'ere – there ain't a drover, nor yet a bullock driver, nor yet a stock-keeper, from 'ere to 'ell that couldn't 'a' bossed that expegition straight through to the Gulf, an' back agen an' never turned a hair – with sich a season as Burke had. Don't sicken a man with yer Burke. He burked that expegition, right enough'* (Furphy 1944: 32–3).[4]

Here again we see the imbrication of varietal contrasts in ideological conflict. The nexus of colonialist and class-based ideology – specifically the claim that 'gentlemen' are to be accorded special status in the opening up of the new country – is challenged quite explicitly. The debunking of this particular myth symbolises a more general exposure of the deceit and hypocrisy that lie at the heart of the colonialist enterprise. Here too the frank assertion of an egalitarian ideology operates through the colourful, creative use of language – note the novelty of the construction *bossed through to the Gulf* in comparison with the stilted style of Willoughby (*Will you permit me to enumerate, exhibited in a marked degree*) and the witty play with Burke's name (*He burked that expegition right enough*). Like Larry Hawthorne, the speaker of Black English who figures so prominently in Labov 1969, Mosey makes his point logically, succinctly but with considerable force.

The same novel presents a broad picture of the linguistic diversity of the Australian linguistic scene at this time. Here are just two further examples from a rich patchwork – the speech of the Irishman Rory O'Halloran and the creolised English of the Chinese boundary rider:

Blessin's on ye, Tammas! Would it be faysible at all at all fur ye till stap to the morrow mornin', an' ride out wi' me the day? (p. 98)

Me tellee Misa Smyte you lescue ... All li; you name Collin; you b'long-a Gullamen Clown; all li; you killee me bimeby; all li. (p. 191)[5]

Some writers seek to capture the linguistic intricacies of the colonial situation not through explicit contrast in dialogue but by weaving local speech patterns into the fabric of standard English in narrative. Below are three examples from different regions and different times. The first is from Mark Twain's *Huckleberry Finn*, the second from a short story by Henry Lawson, the third from a story set in Papua New Guinea by John Kasaipwalova.

MARK TWAIN
We slept most of the day, and started out at night, a little ways behind a monstrous long raft that was as long going by as a procession. She had four long sweeps at each end so we judged she carried as many as thirty men, likely. She had five big wigwams aboard, wide apart, and an open camp fire in the middle, and a tall flag-pole at each end, There was a power of style about her. It amounted to something being a raftsman on such a craft as that. (Twain 1967: 86)

HENRY LAWSON
Maoriland scenery is grand mostly and the rivers are beautiful – They are clear and run all summer. The scenery don't seem to brood and haunt you like our bush. It's a different sort of loneliness altogether – sort of sociable new-mate kind of loneliness – and not that exactly. I can't describe it. But there was something wanting and I soon fixed on it. You see, they don't understand travelling and mateship round there – they're not used to it. A swagman is a tramp with them – same as in the old coastal district of NSW ... But that was on another track, after where they were all Scotch and Scandies (Norwegians). And I had a pound or two and a programme then. (Kiernan 1982: 167)

JOHN KASAIPWALOVA
The afternoon passed very quickly and soon four o'clock brought more people into the bar until it was full with men, beers, smoke

and happiness. My head was already starting to turn and turn, but I didn't care as I was feeling very happy and wanted to sing. The waiters by now had become like Uni Transport trucks speeding everywhere to take away our empty bottles and bring new ones to our table. They liked our group very much because each time they came we gave them each one bottle also, but because their boss might angry them for nothing, they would bend their bodies to the floor pretending to pick up rubbish and while our legs hid them from sight they quickly emptied the beers into their open throats. By five o'clock our waiter friends couldn't walk straight, and their smart speeding started to appear like they were dancing to our singing.

*That was when their boss saw them. He gave a very loud yell and followed with bloody swearings. But our waiter friends didn't take any notice. Our beer presents had already full up their heads and our happy singings had grabbed their hearts ... **Man, man, em gutpela pasin moa ya!** Everybody was having a good time, and the only thing that spoiled the happiness was that there was not the woman in the bar to make it more happier.* (Beier 1980: 69–70)

One feature common to the first two texts is the high frequency of coordinate structures, so typical of speech. But it is clearly the presence of non-standard forms and other expressions from spoken discourses that give these passages their colloquial flavour. Lawson succeeds in evoking not only the sounds of Australian speech but also something of white Australian mythology – the special status of the tramp, the importance of mateship. These themes emphasise the sense of an independent Australian identity by explicit contrast with New Zealand attitudes, which are more closely aligned with the those of the 'mother country'.

The extract from Kasaipwalova is a particularly good example of the way in which local speech patterns have engaged in a kind of chemical interaction with those of standard English to produce a unique text, full of local flavour. The violation of the grammatical categories of the standard language (*The boss might angry them for nothing, Our beer presents had already full up their heads*), the non-standard plurals (*bloody swearings, happy singings*) and creative juxtapositions (*smart speeding, beer presents*) evoke the forms and processes of creoles. Again the general theme is one of local solidarity (*our waiter friends*) opposed to an alien authority, the creativity of the language of the text itself challenging the conventional, prosaic discourses of power (*bloody swearings*).

There is one issue arising from the examples cited above that connects with certain general concerns in sociolinguistics. This has to do with the relationship between variety and discursive style. The central question is whether the differences between linguistic varieties – specifically between standard and non-standard varieties – is simply a matter of superficial formal contrasts, or whether there are more important differences having to do with the kinds of meanings expressible in different varieties. It is, of course, a commonplace that there are marked ideological differences associated with the use of a standard or non-standard variety – a point which is amply illustrated in the texts cited above. The question at issue, however, does not have to do with the general ideological meanings that are signalled by the use of a particular code but whether the codes themselves are oriented towards different meaning potentials.

As a specific illustration of this issue, let me consider two questions addressed by William Labov in his classic (1969) study of the speech of black adolescents in New York City. On the one hand, Labov argued that the differences between standard English and non-standard varieties are of a purely superficial kind, that the latter are no less well adapted than the former to the expression of logical thought. On the other hand, he suggested that speakers of standard English tend to adopt discursive styles that involve a much greater degree of verbosity than those typically used by speakers of non-standard varieties. Although these arguments are not necessarily incompatible with each other, the implications of each do tend to run in rather different directions.

It is useful to consider these issues in the light of arguments put forward by the British sociolinguist Basil Bernstein over a number of years. Essentially Bernstein has suggested that there are differences between the ways in which middle-class and working-class children tend to use language in certain contexts – that middle-class children orient themselves more easily to the expression of 'universalistic meanings' (meanings concerned with general principles of behaviour and organisation), whereas working- class children turn more naturally to 'particularistic meanings' (those related to specific contexts).[6] He has applied the term 'code' to distinctions of this kind, identifying ways of speaking that involve universalistic meanings as 'elaborated code' and those involving particularistic meanings as 'restricted code'.

Labov (1969: 12) rejects Bernstein's concept of code, arguing that the contrasts between the ways in which speakers from different social groups use language involve nothing more than differences of surface form. He maintains that standard and non-standard varieties simply provide different ways of saying 'the same thing', that it is possible to translate from one system into the other, that there is a level of semantic representation common to both. In particular, he argues that non-standard speakers use exactly the same type of logic that speakers of standard varieties employ and thus that there are no 'deep' differences between the meanings produced by the two groups of speakers of the kind implied by the concept of code.

Nobody is likely to disagree with this conclusion as far as the specific question of the relationship between language and logic is concerned. However, Labov's later argument (1969: 11–19) concerning the possible relationship between standard English and verbosity and, more particularly, his work on the vernacular culture of New York adolescents, suggests that there are in fact quite significant discursive differences between speakers of standard and non-standard varieties, though these have nothing to do with logic and they do not support Bernstein's claims concerning the nature of the differences between the linguistic practices of middle- and working-class speakers. In particular, Labov and others have identified a whole range of discursive styles that are an integral part of the vernacular culture but are more or less unknown to speakers of standard English. Many of these are so salient to vernacular speakers that they have names in the culture itself: 'toasts', 'sounds', 'the dozens', 'riffing', 'capping' (Labov 1972b: 208). It is important, therefore, to reconcile the two strands of Labov's argument to each other. The claim that the differences between standard and non-standard varieties are merely superficial should be interpreted cautiously, in the context of a quite specific question. The area of post-colonial literature seems to provide another source of evidence in support of the view that different varieties may be associated with different ways of speaking, different meaning orientations, different discourses. It is extremely difficult to imagine, for example, how the meanings expressed by Ratnam in the extract from *The Cord*, cited above, could be expressed in standard English. They are inextricably enmeshed in the formal patterns and discursive practices of non-standard speech. The study of post-colonial literatures confirms Labov's general claims that verbal skills are highly developed and highly prized in vernacular cultures. We will pursue the question of the complex relationship between variety and discourse in the following section.

Switzerland

LANGUAGE, VARIETY AND IDEOLOGY IN SWITZERLAND

There are a number of similarities between the linguistic situation in Switzerland (specifically in German-speaking Switzerland) and the kind of situations that we have considered in the previous section. The common features have to do with the fact that the varieties of German that are the carriers of Swiss identity are all local non-standard varieties, whereas the standard language (High German) is in many respects an alien tongue, associated with a foreign nation. The Swiss would understand perfectly the feelings expressed by Raja Rao in the passage quoted on page 155 above. On the other hand, Switzerland has of course never been a German colony, though it has not entirely escaped some of the attitudinal postures of post-colonial societies. The prestige of German culture gives it the same kind of metropolitan status in the eyes of the Swiss that Britain enjoys in relation to her former colonies (Steinberg 1976: 38).

The nature of the sociolinguistic situation in Switzerland is such that the relationship between the concepts of variety, discourse and ideology shows up in a particularly clear way. We will attempt to demonstrate this by considering in some detail the interaction between High German and localised Swiss varieties in television commercials. The analysis has quite general implications for other societies and other genres.

German-speaking Switzerland is a 'diglossic' society. This term comes from Ferguson's classic (1959) study. Diglossic societies are those in which there is functional separation between two distinct varieties of the same language, such that the 'High' variety is used in formal contexts (the school classroom, university lectures, sermons, political speeches, broadcasting), whereas the 'Low' variety is used in informal settings (home, shops, cafes and so on). The High variety is also the one used in the written language.

Although Switzerland is usually cited as one of the classic cases of a diglossic society, there are a number of ways in which it diverges from the ideal model. In the first place there is not one 'Low' or localised variety but many. Watts (1988: 317) notes that 'the mother tongue of virtually every German-speaking Swiss is one of over thirty mutually intelligible Alemannic dialects of German'. The considerable variation in Swiss German from place to place means that each variety has a strong local flavour. This point applies to the urban centres as much as to the country areas – there are noticeable differences between the speech of the main German-speaking Swiss cities, Basle, Zürich, Berne, Lucerne and there is even some class-related differentiation within the dialects of these cities (Weinreich 1952: 151, Christ 1965).

A second way in which contemporary Switzerland diverges from the classic diglossic situation has to do with the fact that the localised varieties are coming to be used more and more frequently in domains where the ideal diglossic model would predict the use of the High variety only. For example, there is a growing tendency for Swiss German to be used in certain parliamentary debates (in cantonal parliaments), in an ever wider range of radio and television programmes and in many lessons at high-school level (Watts 1988: 317, Pap 1990: 131). The one domain where High German retains a strong foothold is in the written language and in certain genres in broadcasting such as television news programmes. One factor working in favour of the continued use of High German in Switzerland is the fact that it is this variety that is learned by Swiss in the French and Italian-speaking areas. The spread of Swiss German is causing major problems for them (Schläpfer 1985, Watts 1988).

The differentiation between High German and Swiss varieties has important implications for the question of ideology. In the first place Swiss German identity is partly constructed in opposition to that of the Federal Republic of Germany. Weinreich (1952: 136) notes that 'one of the most important ideological supports of *Schwyzertütsch* (Swiss German) is the anti-German sentiment which has, in varying degrees, been a part of Swiss cultural life' and Watts (1988: 330) also remarks that 'the German-speaking Swiss are almost unique in regarding their dialects as precious guarantors of national independence and self-sufficiency and in cultivating them actively and consciously as a bulwark ... against other forms of German beyond their national boundaries, in particular those of the Federal Republic'.

At a lower level Swiss German identity is also constructed in strongly localised terms. This is connected with the heavily decentralised system of Swiss administration, within which many affairs are decided at a cantonal level. Local stereotypes affect attitudes towards local varieties. Steinberg (1976: 100) suggests that the Zürich dialect has a reputation for harshness (stemming from the historical 'aggressiveness' of the city), that the Berne variety has a more homely, folksy flavour, that the Basler's reputation for the witty use of words and the Lucerner's reputation for 'liveliness and emotionalism' colour attitudes towards the dialects of those cities. It is pertinent to note here that observations of this kind confirm the points made above concerning the links between code (or dialect in this context) and discourse. There are indications here that the differences between the speech of the Züricher and the Luzerner extend beyond the domain of variety, conceived in the narrow sense in which linguists tend to use this term, to encompass more general discursive practices.

Of particular importance for our purposes is the fact that Swiss German is 'the language of childhood, family, the heart' (Steinberg 1976: 101). The Bernese writer Friedrich Dürrenmatt made this point neatly and succinctly in describing Swiss German as his 'mother tongue', High German as his 'father tongue' (cited in Brändle 1989: 59). The warm affection that all Swiss have for their dialects manifests itself strongly whenever they speak or write about them (Christ 1965). Unlike the situation in many other parts of the world, use of the dialect carries no social stigma whatsoever.

We have noted above that, when we consider the language(s) of a particular community as a complex web of interacting discourses, then it is clear that access to and command of these discourses will be differentially distributed across the members of the community. Given the connections between the domain of discourse and that of variety, the same point applies to the distribution of the varieties found in a diglossic community. In this respect Switzerland is no exception. Although many German Swiss speak and write High German with complete fluency, this is by no means a universal phenomenon. Swiss educators frequently express concern over falling levels of proficiency in the standard language.

Even those with good command of High German do not always

feel entirely comfortable in it. Brändle (1989: 61) notes that 'even the well-educated are not at ease with spoken [High] German; they speak it like a foreign language' and Steinberg (1976: 102) makes the same point in the following colourful terms:

> The average Swiss speaks German woodenly. His prose is stilted, heavy and lifeless. He never makes a joke and by comparison with a witty German or Austrian seems about as lively as the grumpy dwarf in 'Snow White'. The same man using dialect in his 'local', chatting away and laughing, is simply another human being, easy, often very funny and spontaneous.

In other words, there are constraints on the use of High German even for the most educated Swiss, deriving from the fact that certain discursive practices tend to operate in Switzerland solely through the medium of the local varieties.

Yet in many respects, High German is clearly not an alien tongue. Brändle (1989: 61) describes it as a 'vibrant and living language in Switzerland'. Watts (1988: 327) argues strongly against the view that young children do not come into contact with the standard language until they go to school, noting that they experience extensive exposure to High German in the media and that they often reproduce this variety with considerable accuracy in playing games. I have had the personal experience of communicating quite easily with a four-year-old Swiss child who spoke only Swiss German by using standard German myself. Of course, the standard language derives a considerable amount of prestige from the fact that there is a long tradition of use in such formal contexts as parliamentary proceedings, the mass media, education, the law courts and for written communication (Watts 1988: 317).

VARIETY, DISCOURSE, IDEOLOGY IN SWISS TELEVISION COMMERCIALS

We will consider now some of the ways in which the ideological aspects of code-related variation in Switzerland show up in a particular genre – that of the television commercial. As well as shedding some light on the connections between variety, discourse and ideology, these texts also illustrate from a slightly different perspective the kind of interactional processes involved in the production of text discussed in the previous chapter. Of particular interest is the interplay here between High German (henceforth 'H') and localised varieties of Swiss German (henceforth 'S'). The discussion is based on a corpus of 108 commercials, broadcast on the Swiss-German channel *DRS* in Berne in August and September 1989.

According to Bakhtin (1981) one of the primary distinguishing features of the novel as a genre is that it is characterised by what he calls 'heteroglossia'. The same can be said of the television commercial. Like the novel, the commercial is the meeting place of many different ways of speaking, many discourses. It constitutes a genre in its own right but it also incorporates a multitude of other genres – conversations in the café, the shop and the pub, political speeches, lovers' talk, office talk, teacher talk, scolding, banter, joking and so on. In this sense commercials mirror the discursive practices of the society in which they operate.

The most important factor in the selection of code in these texts has to do with the format of the genre. Of particular relevance is the distinction between the 'Comment' component and the 'Action' component (Sussex 1989). The Comment component is the voice of an unseen speaker, whose typical function is to name the product and provide some general information about it. The following represent typical Comment statements:

Ambiance – das neue Geschmackserlebnis von Nescafé Gold.

*[Ambiance – the new taste experience of **Nescafé Gold**.]*

Barilla – die köstliche Teigwarenkollektion aus Italien.

[Barilla – the exquisite pasta collection from Italy.]

Dedicace – das neue Betönungskrem von Loréal.

[Dedicace – the new hair toner from Loréal.]

The Comment component is present in nearly all tokens and it is primarily, (though not exclusively) a High German voice. In the total corpus of 108 commercials, there are 98 tokens of the Comment voice and 'H' is used in 67 cases (68.4 per cent). This component is also predominantly a male voice. Eighty-six commercials use a male commentator, seven use a female commentator and two use one male and one female commentator. The figures by gender and variety are:

	Male	*Female*
High German	61	6
Swiss German	27	3

The Action component is present in all commercials but it does not always contain speech. In this corpus there is a spoken Action component in just 38 items. These consist primarily of conversations between two participants. In one advertisement for a skin cream, two women in an aircraft discuss the problems of dry skin in air travel. In another commercial, two workmen discuss the merits of a particular brand of mattress. The Action component is dominated here by Swiss varieties. 'S' is used in 28 out of the 38 tokens of the speaking actor component (73.7 per cent).

We should note parenthetically that Sussex (1989: 165) observed a similar correlation between the components of the genre and the selection of linguistic variety in a study of Australian television commercials. In particular the Comment tended to be spoken by an 'educated' rather than by a 'broad' Australian voice and, perhaps more surprisingly, North American voices were found in the Action component more frequently than in the Comment. He too found a predominance of male voices in the Comment (p. 166). Similar results were reported for a corpus of British television commercials (but at a less significant level). These observations confirm the claim made above that the characteristics of the Swiss corpus constitute a particular manifestation of more general patterns.

A third component identified by Sussex in which the distinction between 'H' and 'S' can show up is the Chorus or Song. In this corpus this component was found in only thirteen commercials. Not only do we find both 'H' and 'S' in these items but English also makes its presence felt, occurring in three items. We will return to this point briefly later.

The bias of the Comment component to 'H' and that of the Action component to 'S' in Switzerland derives from the general nature of the relationship between discourse and variety. The (predominantly male) Comment voice articulates with general discourses of power and authority, within which 'H' constitutes the normal or 'unmarked' choice in diglossic societies. The function of this component is to act as purveyor of privileged information (one of the major functions of the discourse of power identified in the previous chapter). In some cases, this information purports to derive from the results of technological advantages. For example, one advertisement for *Mobil* oil highlights its resistance to low temperatures by showing how a banana can be used to drive home a nail at 35 degrees below and how the viscosity of less 'advanced' oils increases dramatically at such temperatures. As for *Mobil*:

(1) *Das vollsynthetische Mobil Eins aber bleibt auch bei fünfund-dreissig Minusgraden flüssig and schützt den Motor Ihres Wagens vom Start weg. Mobil Eins, klar die erste Wahl.*

[But fully synthetic **Mobil One** stays liquid even at thirty-five degrees below and protects the engine of your car right from the start. **Mobil One**, clearly the first choice].

Similarly, many advertisements for detergents and shampoos attempt to indicate the research effort that has been devoted to the product in order to enhance its technical qualities.

(2) *Das neue Shampoo Aquavital gibt Ihrem Haar neue Vitalität ... Aquavital der laboratoires Garnier, die einmalige Formel mit Meeresextrakten.*

[New **Aquavital** shampoo gives your hair new vitality ... **Aquavital** from the Garnier laboratories, the unique formula with marine extracts.]

In these cases the voice becomes that of the technical 'expert' – a function imbued with authority and power.

The dominance of the Action component by Swiss varieties, on the other hand, derives from the fact that this component articulates with discourses of everyday informal interaction. Whereas the Comment voice is monologic, the Action component normally comprises dialogic interaction. Whereas the Comment voice is decontextualised (usually accompanying a shot of the product), the voices of the Action component are those of specific individuals speaking in well-defined contexts using local varieties. For example, a Zürich housewife talks about the merits of *Ariel* in the garden of her home, two office workers comment on the untidy state of their desks, a couple of factory hands discuss the qualities of the mattress on which they are working. In these cases, unlike that of the Comment voice, the viewer is able to construct some notion of the speaker's social identity on the basis of perceived attributes of gender, dress, age and so on. The fact that there is no social stigma attached to the use of 'S' in Switzerland is reflected in the fact that the speakers appearing in these items represent a wide social spectrum. The garden setting for the *Ariel* commercial is clearly that of a prosperous middle class Zürich family. The speaker is well-dressed and she speaks clearly and confidently. The women who appear in the Oil of Olaz item are seasoned air travellers and are also clearly middle class. The setting for one item is an elegant restaurant in which a gourmet businessman addresses the viewer in 'S'. There are just two examples in the corpus in which working-class people appear, one featuring a Security Guard, the other the two workers in the bedding factory. 'S' is used in both.

Although the Comment voice is predominantly 'H', the presence of 'S' in this component is by no means insignificant. This may be due in part to the way in which 'S' has infiltrated in recent times into domains that have traditionally been the preserve of standard German. It would be a mistake, however, to see this as providing a full explanation for the phenomenon. One danger associated with using terms such as 'the Comment voice' or 'the Comment component' is that these expressions tend to construct the idea of a homogeneous entity. That this is an oversimplification is demonstrated not merely by the presence of 'S' in this voice but by the fact that the use of local varieties signals a somewhat different range of discourses from those associated with the 'H' comment. The text below provides some illustration of this point. It accompanies a visual text in which a man is seen struggling with the unsatisfactory results of having his film processed by a firm other than Kodak.

(3)   *Das hät me devo wenn me sin Film in irgend en Sack steckt ... D'rum git's jetzt de Showbox Fotiservice ... i de Showbox sind Ihri Fotene gschützt, glatt zum aluege, immer schön versorget ... und schöni Bilder git's dank* **Kodakfarbfilm.** *Zum Showbox Fotiservice chömed Ihri Film i dem Sicherheitsbütel ... Besser gaht's nüme.*[7]

[*That's what you get when you put your film into any old bag. That's why we now have the Showbox Photoservice ... in* *the Showbox. Your photos are protected, easy to look at, always kept nicely ... and you get nice pictures thanks to **Kodak** colour film. With the Showbox Photoservice your film comes in a safety packet ... Couldn't be better.]*

One of the most striking features of this spoken text is that it is characterised by a variety of rhythmic cadences that are quite different from those associated with the 'H' voice. The first phrase, for example, is produced with a quite distinctive intonation pattern, with a Low Fall on the first word immediately followed by a High Rise to the second word, followed by a Mid Fall. The effect is lively, arresting, amusing. A similar effect is produced by the cadences in the three tone groups */sind Ihri Fotene gschützt/*, */glatt zum aluege/*, */immer schön versorget/*, where a sequence of Low Rise patterns leads to a closing High Fall in the phrase */und schöni Bilder git's dank **Kodakfarbfilm**/.* There is also considerable play with syncopation between the intonational rhythms and a variety of curious beeping background noises. There is a sense of wittiness, liveliness and sheer fun here that is quite different from the measured tones of the 'H' Comment. This is not the voice of the serious commentator, more that of a friend experiencing a certain amount of ironic – even gloating – pleasure at the fact that one's photos have not turned out too well and who has discovered a much better way of doing it.

A similar point is illustrated by the following advertisement for a skin cleanser. The voice quality is infused with gently mocking laughter, echoing the visual text in which Rick and Carola are seen making fun of John, whose skin problems are so bad that he doesn't dare to go out except in a helmet.

(4) *OK, das isch de John ... de wäscht sich gründlich mit Seife. De Rick nimmt Wäschlotion ... das gaht tüüf bis i d'Poore und stoppt d'Bakterie, wil em Rick syni Wäschlotion heisst **Topexan**. De John hät unreini Huut – de Rick hät e keini. De John gaht nu no mit Helm, de Rik gaht mit de Carola. **Topexan** ... by Mitässer u' Bibeli besser als Wasser und Seife.*

*[OK, this is John. He washes his face thoroughly – with soap. Rick uses wash lotion. It goes deep into the pores and stops bacteria. Rick's wash lotion is called **Topexan**. John has bad skin – Rick doesn't. John always goes out with his*

> *helmet on, Rick goes out with Carola.* **Topexan** ... *for spots and pimples better than soap and water.]*

In conjunction with the use of 'S', the voice quality and colloquial rhythms of this passage create a mood of animated involvement that would be quite inconceivable (at least in Switzerland) in High German. These examples recall Steinberg's (1976: 102) comments concerning the stilted quality of 'H' discourses in Switzerland as opposed to the witty spontaneity of many discourses in 'S', thereby confirming the more general point that code and discourse are related parameters.

The variation between 'H' and 'S' in the Comment indicates the presence of heterogeneity within this component. This leads us to a further point – that there is discursive differentiation at the lower level within the 'H' and the 'S' commentary voices themselves. In an advertisement for *Impulse* the sensual voice quality of the Commentator is borrowed from discourses of seduction:

(5)   *Wenn Ihnen ein völlig Unbekannter plötzlich Blumen schenkt, das ist* **Impulse** ... *neu* ... **Incognito** *von Impulse, das Parfum-Deodorant mit dem unwiderstehlicher Duft.*

[When a complete stranger suddenly gives you flowers, that's **Impulse** ... *new* ... **Incognito** *from* **Impulse** ..., *the perfume-deodorant with the irresistible fragrance.]*

On the other hand the tenser articulatory setting used in a commercial for an oil company (accompanying visuals of an aircraft, a locomotive and a truck converging on a roadside service station) is somewhat reminiscent of the strident, insistent tones of newsreel commentaries.

The 'S' voice is characterised by a particularly wide discursive range: mockery, scolding, banter, obsequiousness, complaint, reproach, intimate confidence. In general these texts shed a good deal of light on the complex relationships between linguistic variety, discursive practices and generic form.

The bias of the Comment component to 'H' and that of the Action component to 'S' means that there are a number of commercials that combine the use of 'H' in the Comment with the use of 'S' in the Action. These items are of particular interest in that they exploit to the full the discursive potential of the diglossic situation. There are several possible formats. In one typical structure the 'H' commentary voice is used to 'sandwich' the 'S' Action component. An advertisement for *Ariel*, for example, is introduced by the following general statement by a male commentator in 'H':

(6) C: *Ariel flüssig wäscht nicht nur sauber, sondern rein. Das entdecken Frauen in ganz Europa.*

[Ariel liquid washes not only clean but pure. As women throughout Europe are beginning to discover.]

This comment accompanies visuals of the product itself followed by a montage of still photographs of women's faces superimposed on a map of Europe. Then follows the Action component, which consists in this case of a conversation in 'S' between a Zürich housewife and an unseen interviewer. (This item is somewhat unusual in that the only speaker in the 'conversation' is the housewife.)

(7) F: De *Ariel flüssig isch für mich absolut es guets, perfekts Produkt* ... *Ich bin mit em Mäx go laufe* ... *er isch natürlich au im Gras g'sy, dänn hät's eso richtigi Strieme gäh. Ich han vorher immer nume Pulverwöschmittel brucht gha, und irgendwie hät's mi eifach tunkt es seg nöd so suber worde. Ich han dänn s' Ariel flüssig diräkt uf d'Hose taa, d'Arielette gfüllt mit dem 'Ariel' und au wider die chly Wöschmaschine i die gross ine taa* ... *und bi vierzig Grad gwäschet* ... *und s'isch tatsächlich suber woorde. Also ich find s' Ariel flüssig wirklich es super Produkt* ... *s'hät* ... *wys, rein, suber gwäsche.*

[For me Ariel liquid is a really good ... perfect product ... I took Max [the dog] out for a run ... of course he went into the grass ... then I got these marks [on my clothes] ... I've tried various other detergents ... and somehow it seemed to me they didn't make my things really clean ... so I put some Ariel liquid directly onto the slacks, filled the Arielette with Ariel, placed this little gadget in the big washing machine ... and put on a wash at forty degrees ... and it came out really clean. So I think Ariel liquid is a really super product – it washes really white, pure, clean.]

This 'conversation' takes place in the garden of the speaker's home, with flashbacks to scenes of the dog running in the fields, jumping at the speaker's legs, the speaker pouring *Ariel* on the stains, placing it in the washing machine, examining the results. At the end of the sequence the visual text focuses in on the product itself, which is standing on a garden table near the speaker. This shot is accompanied by a final summarising comment in 'H':

(8)   C: **Ariel flüssig** ... *wäscht nicht nur sauber sondern rein.*

Ariel liquid ... *washes not only clean but pure.*

A slightly different format is used in a similar advertisement for *dato*. The item features women who are twin sisters and begins with the Action component in 'S'.

(9) F^1:   *Hoi!*
      F^2:   *Myni Zwillingschwöster hät genau die glyche Vorhäng wien ich. Uf jede Fall han ich das gmeint.*
      F^1:   *Oh, wo isch dänn das Wiess blibe? Ich nimm doch äxtra es Fiinwöschmittel.*
      F^2:   *Das gnüegt ebe nid. Du hettsch sölle* **dato** *neh ... Mit Wyssschutz.*

      [F^1:   (To F^2) *Hi!*
      F^2:   (To viewer) *My twin sister has exactly the same curtains as I do. At least, that's what I thought.*
      F^1:   *Oh, where's all the whiteness gone? Yet I put in extra fine detergent.*
      F^2:   *But that's not enough. You should have used* **dato** ... *with White Protection.]*

The visual text then shifts to a shot of the product, accompanied by a (male voice) comment in 'H':

(10) C: *Ja, mit einem gewöhnlichen Feinwaschmittel kann Weisses mit der Zeit grau werden. Der Weissschutz in* **dato** *aber erhält die Vorhänge strahlend weiss – wie neu.*
      [That's right, with ordinary detergents white can become grey in time. But the White Protection in **dato** *keeps curtains gleaming white – like new.]*

The scene then shifts back to the Action component, concluding with a brief exchange between the two sisters in 'S':

(11) F^1: *Jetzt han ich neui Vorhäng gchauft und die werdet wie neu blybe mit **dato**.*

F^2: *Gnau wie myni.*

[F^1: *Now, I've bought new curtains and they'll stay as new with **dato**.*

F^2: *Just like mine!*]

In this case, then, it is the 'H' component that is sandwiched between two sections of the 'S' component.

Perhaps the most striking feature of these items is the way in which the contrast between 'H' and 'S' is used to create a 'contrapuntal' effect, operating in tandem with a number of related processes: the transition from female actor voice to male comment, from a local scene to a decontextualised shot of the product, from the particularistic, local meanings of Bernstein's restricted code (p. 165), to the generalised, universalistic meanings of elaborated code.

One of the main advantages of this format is that it allows the designer of the commercial to appeal simultaneously to two different types of value. The 'H' discourses articulate with formal discourses in general, incorporating connotations of authority and prestige into the message. The 'S' discourses carry more intimate associations. In other words, the co-presence of 'H' and 'S' invokes contrasting values of the kind identified by Trudgill (1972) as 'overt prestige' and 'covert prestige', the former oriented to status, the latter to solidarity. This functional duality is directly related to the twofold nature of the goals of the commercial. The initial aim is to promote acceptance through the process of consumer identification with the Actor or Actors who 'represent' the product. The positive connotations of 'S' clearly have a crucial role to play here along with the other carefully selected features oriented to this end. The contexts in which this process purports to take place may be domestic or exotic but in most cases they tend to be removed from the shopping situation. The commercial would not, however, achieve its goals unless the process of consumer acceptance culminated in the actual act of purchase. An important prerequisite here is that the consumer should easily recognise the product when next in the shopping situation. Those sections of the visual text that focus on the product itself, usually situated at the close of the item, are clearly oriented to this end. The 'H' discourse that typically accompanies this section can perhaps be interpreted as providing the rational sanctioning authority for the action of purchase.

We noted above that the generic form of the commercial interacts with other factors in the production of language variety – that the Comment voice is not a homogeneous entity for example, although there is a tendency for it to articulate with discourses of authority and expertise. One factor participating in the general processes of interaction involved here in the production of text is that of product 'image'. In a study of Australian television commercials, Lee (1984) showed that this was certainly a factor impinging on phonological variation, in that advertisements seeking to associate with their product images of status, elegance, sophistication (including technological sophistication) tended to use the phonological variants of 'Cultivated' Australian English, whereas those aiming to invoke images of friendliness, toughness, reliability, humour tended to use the 'Broader' variants. The same point is illustrated in the Swiss corpus. The 'H' variety is almost invariably used in commercials that attempt to associate with their product images of elegance and the exotic. For example, the advertisement for *Impulse* cited at (5) above (p. 176) features a masked woman in flowing robes walking through the streets of Venice.

The question of image is to some extent independent of the nature of the product. Commercials for pet food contrast sharply in this respect. An advertisement for *Whiskas*, using 'S' in the Chorus, adopts a homely image with a group of playful tabby cats in a domestic garden setting. Similarly a dog food item shows a young woman talking to her pet in warm, affectionate tones – also in 'S' – as she feeds him in the kitchen. On the other hand, another cat food commercial, featuring a stately white Persian cat in a highly idealised setting aims for quite a different image. The only salient element in this context is an antique clock around which the cat moves carefully and gracefully – to the accompaniment of Mozart. The commentary voice is male, rich, deep and, of course, High German.

There is a similar contrast between two commercials for pasta recipes. One from *Findus* emphasises the high quality of the ingredients in the serious tones of a commentary in 'H', with a relatively abstract visual text. In complete contrast, an advertisement for a similar product from *Dolmio* emphasises the theme of enjoyment with a much more animated commentary in 'S' and a specifically contextualised visual text (a lively, engaging Italian family feast).

Since the question of image is largely independent of the nature of the product, it is not surprising to find that, with one exception, the latter does not appear to play an important role in the selection of language variety. In a number of cases where there appears at first sight to be such a correlation, closer analysis shows that the relevant factor is in fact genre. For example, there is an apparent tendency for items of personal toilet (shampoos, skin lotions, etc.) to be associated with 'H' but this is almost certainly due to the fact that most of these items use the commentary-only format. The few which contain an Actor component all use 'S'. The same applies to the category of domestic products. 'H' is employed in all but one of the items using the commentary-only genre, whereas all those containing an action component are dominated by 'S'.

The one case in which there is a relationship between type of product and language variety is found within the food category. Overall, the two varieties are relatively evenly balanced here. There is, however, one subset showing a marked bias towards 'S'. This consists of fifteen commercials advertising confectionery items – chocolate bars, mint sweets and so on. Within this set 11 commercials use 'S' whereas 'H' accounts for only three items (and English one). However, this bias does not derive, as it normally does, from the presence of an Actor component involving speech, since there are only four such instances in this set. The preference here in fact is for a Chorus, with a brief concluding Comment. Out of the 13 items in the corpus as a whole containing a Chorus, seven are found in this category. Three of these use 'S', one 'H' and three English. Clearly the most important factor in the general favouring of 'S' here (eight out of the 12 tokens of the commentary voice) is the fact that these items are addressed primarily towards a teenage audience. This derives directly from the type of product and is also relevant to the question of product image, which accounts for the use of English pop songs.

The main point to emerge from the discussion is that, although the structure of the commercial in terms of the components of Comment and Action plays an important part in the selection of language variety, this does not derive from a straightforward relationship between language and generic form. Certainly there are tendencies for the components of the commercial to articulate with certain kinds of discourse, for the Comment to invoke discourses of authority and expertise and to express generalised meanings whereas the Action invokes the discourses of everyday informal interaction. A variety of other factors also enter into the equation, however – factors relating to the various functions of the genre, product image, audience, tone (seriousness *vs* humour) and so on. There are also interactions between linguistic features, with the use of a particular variety tending to be associated with certain rhythmic and intonational characteristics. Again we see here something of the complexity of the interactional processes involved in the construction of text.

Conclusion

In this chapter we have pursued the theme of discursive interaction by focusing on the interplay between different linguistic varieties in the production of text. In the literary texts cited here these interactions mediate the ideological conflicts that operate in colonial and post-colonial situations. The interactional processes work themselves out in a number of different ways. In some cases, conflict operates through the literary concept of 'character', particularly through dialogue. In this format the interaction between individual speakers functions both as a site and a symbol of ideological tensions. In other cases the colonial assertion of power (including the assertion of power over language) is challenged by the infiltration of non-standard forms into the standard-oriented language of narrative.

These linguistic interactions function at a number of different levels. The use of non-standard forms is in itself an ideological statement, a crucial marker of local affiliation and local identity. This is not merely a construct of the literary text – the observation is amply supported by a vast range of research in recent sociolinguistics. There are, however, other ways in which non-standard speech enacts the challenge to the colonialist ideology. We see in a number of these texts the exercise of discursive practices that are so closely integrated into the vernacular culture and vernacular speech as to be inaccessible to speakers of standard English. The exercise of the consummate verbal skills constitutes in itself a refutation of the imperial ideology that non-standard speech is corrupt and impoverished. The creativity of the linguistic processes itself functions as a direct statement of the vitality and energy of the ver-

nacular culture in opposition to the impoverished, moribund ideology of the dominant class.

There are certain similarities between the interactive processes
documented above and those operating in the Swiss context,
though the underlying ideological tensions are muted in the Swiss
situation by the absence of the colonial factor. The parallels between the orientation of the Swiss to High German and that of the
post-colonial societies to standard British English are nevertheless
quite striking. In both situations the standard variety derives considerable prestige from its role in intellectual life but it is not the
language of the heart and the emotions. The long-standing political independence and economic strength of Switzerland has, however, given the Swiss dialects a security that non-standard varieties
in post-colonial societies find much more difficult to achieve. Paradoxically this derives in part from the traditional willingness of the
Swiss to accept High German as the appropriate language for certain formal contexts, an acceptance that leads to widespread bidialectalism at the level of the individual speaker. The bitterness that
is so often a legacy of the colonial situation, however, tends to
militate against bidialectalism. The emergence of an autonomous
local standard variety may be the long-term solution to this problem but this is a difficult process, partly because of the international importance of the imperial standard language. Even the
solid Swiss are having to face up to difficulties of this kind as a result of the spread of local varieties into domains traditionally occupied by High German.

Notes

1. There are echoes here of the claim in some of the early literature on
   language and gender that the structure of language is oriented to male
   imperialism and power.
2. The texts cited in the first section of this chapter are taken from Ashcroft et al. 1989, a work which has strongly influenced this section as
   a whole. The extract from *Kanthapura* is cited on p. 61 of that work.
   I am particularly indebted to one of the authors – my colleague,
   Helen Tiffin – for stimulating discussion of some of the issues raised
   here.
3. Cited in Ashcroft et al. 1989: 54 from Ooi Boo Eng 1984: 95.
4. In 1860 Robert O'Hara Burke and William John Wills led an ill-fated
   expedition from Melbourne through the interior of the Australian

continent to the Gulf of Carpentaria. Both men died (with Charles
Gray) on the return journey from famine and exposure.

5. Cited in Ashcroft et al. 1989: 74.

6. There are of course considerable oversimplifications here in the
presentation of Bernstein's views. For more extensive discussion and
references to the extensive literature on the topic see Lee 1986:
199–209.

7. I am most grateful to Daniel Stotz, Beatrice Curran and Richard
Watts for help and advice with the transcription of the Swiss German
materials in this chapter.

9 Conclusion and Overview

Introduction

In the course of this book we have developed an argument against a traditional view of language that is firmly entrenched in almost all the ways in which we think and talk about the phenomenon. This final chapter draws together the various elements of the book by analysing at a general level the way in which they relate to each other and thus illuminate the central theme.

The traditional view of language

The most important characteristic of the traditional view is that a human language is essentially a homogeneous 'object' – a formal system that is to a large extent independent of its users and its context of use. From this follow a number of corollaries. Since a language is an object, it is 'acquired' by its native speakers during the course of language development. Since it is characterised primarily in terms of a certain inventory of phonological, lexical and grammatical features, most of which can be identified in the speech of the child at a relatively early stage, the process of 'acquisition' can be said to take place very rapidly. The most important aspect of this process is that the child learns to 'segment' reality in a particular language-specific way. In other words, the child constructs a certain set of conceptual units, each of which is paired with a particular lexical or grammatical unit in the system. These cognitive constructs are relatively discrete entities. Observed phenomena in the world fall relatively clearly into one or other of the lexicogrammatical pigeon-holes provided by the linguistic system because of certain shared objective properties. The classificatory scheme which this system 'imposes' on the child learner constitutes a particular world-view that she or he shares with other speakers of the language. Metaphorical processes are peripheral to the system and belong to 'special' areas such as 'literary language'. The latter constitutes the domain of the literary critic rather than the linguist. The concerns of the linguist are with 'ordinary' language usage, a domain that can be distinguished quite clearly from the domain of literature.

In this framework the native speakers of a particular language are thought to share essentially the same cognitive system, so that communication between them is seen as a relatively straightforward process. 'Meaning' originates as a particular cognitive structure in the mind of the speaker, a structure that is composed of the basic conceptual units acquired during the course of language development. This meaning is then 'encoded' via the lexicogrammatical system into the appropriate linguistic elements. Since the cognitive processes of the addressee operate in terms of essentially the same set of cognitive units as those of the speaker and since both share the same grammar – i.e. the same set of conventions for pairing conceptual units with forms – the addressee, on hearing a particular utterance, is normally able to produce a conceptual structure that is for all practical purposes identical to the originating structure in the mind of the speaker. Thus, meaning can be said to be 'conveyed' from the speaker to the addressee, with language operating as the vehicle of transmission.

At a more specific level the traditional view attributes to many individual words a number of different senses. The word *man*, for example, can mean either 'male human being' or 'human being in general'. The word *leave* can mean either 'to move away from' or 'to abandon'. Each of these meanings associated with a particular word is seen as being relatively independent of the others. Since meaning is placed into texts by speakers, the meaning that a particular word has in a particular context is determined by the intention of the speaker when the utterance is produced. If addressees construct a different meaning from the one that was intended, then they have misunderstood the utterance – they have produced a meaning that does not correspond with the 'real' meaning of the text.

On this view phenomena in the real world normally fall unproblematically into the discrete categories provided by the linguistic system and it is therefore clear in most cases whether a sentence is true or false. The objective properties of a particular event define it either as 'a demonstration' or as 'a riot', for example. Thus, in the case of a sentence such as *A riot took place in Johannesburg yesterday*, the main question arising, if we wish to test for the truth or falsehood of the proposition, has to do with whether 'a riot' did or did not take place. Speakers may of course misclassify happenings of this kind for particular purposes, calling some event 'a riot' when it was in fact simply a demonstration. If they do, however, they are guilty of misrepresentation. The question of whether the process of naming this event is in itself problematic does not easily arise in this framework. Nor does the more basic question of whether 'the event' can in fact legitimately be constructed as a single phenomenon.

One minor qualification to the view of a language as a single, homogeneous object within the traditional framework is that individual languages clearly present themselves in different guises. English appears in such guises as standard British English, Cockney, Geordie, New York English, Australian English, to mention but a few. German appears in the form of High German, Plattdeutsch, the various varieties of Swiss German and so on. However, this is not a real problem because each of these varieties is a relatively homogeneous entity, each defined in terms of a particular set of phonological, lexical and grammatical features.

The view of language outlined above is one that has dominated linguistics until quite recently. Following Saussure linguists have tended to conceptualise linguistic systems as closed, static phenomena and to see the main task of the linguist as being to specify the nature of the relationship of the various elements to each other within such a closed system. In generative grammar the notion of the individual's internal mental grammar (or 'competence') as a homogeneous system has reinforced this perspective. The initial preoccupation of generative grammarians with the formal properties of linguistic systems meant that the crucial problem of meaning was initially defined as being outside the scope of the subject (Chomsky 1957: ch. 2). When the problem of semantics eventually came to be addressed in the 1970s, it was approached through the syntactic model. Thus the problem of meaning was defined (quite counter-intuitively) as one which involved the task of grafting a semantic component onto a model that was essentially syntactically-based (Moore and Carling 1982: 8). It is very clear how such an approach reinforces the notion that a language is a system external to its speakers, that texts 'contain' meaning, that the 'truth-value' of a sentence can be evaluated by relating its semantic representation to the state of some actual or possible world – all without reference to the role of the human interpreter in the production of meaning. There is also a sense in which the concept of 'grammaticality' tends to reinforce the authoritative status of the code. In spite of the claims of the subject to be a descriptive science, there are certain features of the model that articulate with the prescriptive orientation of traditional approaches. One such feature is the heavy emphasis on standard English – which is after all in many respects an artificial object, constructed by the collaborative efforts of lexicographers, grammarians and educators over the centuries. Moreover, in spite of the lip service paid to the primacy of speech, most grammatical description and theory has been oriented to the written language. One reflex of this orientation is that linguists still tend to take the sentence as the basic unit of analysis, even though it is well-known that the sentence is not a satisfactory unit for the analysis of speech (for a very clear illustration of this point see Crystal 1980). The concrete nature of the written sentence confirms the notion of language as an object.

This approach has also produced a quite impoverished account of the nature of creativity in language. Chomsky, for example, sought to locate creativity in such technical characteristics of the system as recursive rules instead of in the much more flexible, open-ended processes of metaphor and metonymy. (For a discussion of the relationship between creativity and recursion in Chomskyan linguistics, see Moore and Carling 1982: 94–9.) The major source of new meanings and new kinds of meaning surely stems from semantic processes rather than syntactic ones. Thus when I read in today's newspaper that the Australian economy is 'on a sombre tack', this is for me a novel juxtaposition of terms (though the general message is all too familiar). Yet I have no difficulty in constructing a meaning for this expression. It is an entirely straightforward matter to combine the metaphorical meanings of darkness with the metaphorical construction of the Australian economy as a ship at sea. Few traditional models of language, however, shed a great deal of light on such commonplace (but crucial) examples of creativity.

The epiphenomenalist view of language

Let me now attempt to survey the major phenomena in this book that have led to an alternative perspective. The argument started out from observations concerning the problematic nature of categories. There are two rather separate points here (though the boundary between them is somewhat indeterminate). The first point is that linguistic categories themselves may not be particularly clear-cut. Saussure and Whorf both argued that a particular language 'segments' reality into language-specific units but in fact these are often much less discrete than the traditional view suggests. The most basic items in the language – words such as *leave*, *give*, *take*, *go* and many others – are the most problematic in this respect. Words of this kind show considerable semantic flexibility (Moore and Carling 1982: ch. 5). In different contexts they make different contributions to the meaning of the utterance as a whole. Dictionaries attempt to deal with this problem by identifying a certain number of meanings for an item but the problematic nature of this process is highlighted by the fact that different dictionaries rarely identify precisely the same number of meanings for a particular word. The general practice is, in fact, to give their readers one or two examples of contexts in which the word occurs and leave it to them to construct a hypothesis about its semantic range. The consequence of this indeterminacy is that the meaning of a particular utterance is often open to negotiation and may be subject to 'mystification'. We have discussed many instances in the course of the book. Of particular interest are those cases where the different perspectives or reading positions of the speaker and addressee can produce quite different interpretations of a text.

The second point is that, even when linguistic categories do have relatively well-defined boundaries, phenomena in the real world are such that mapping of perceptions onto language may be quite problematic. For example, most speakers of English would agree on the nature of the distinction between a 'demonstration' and a 'riot'. One is essentially a peaceful happening, the other involves violence. However, actual events in the real world often do not divide themselves up quite so neatly. It would clearly be impossible to define a cut-off point relating to the degree and kind of violence involved, according to which a particular event is to be assigned to one or the other category. This indeterminacy in the world with respect to language also bears on some of the cross-language relationships noted in the first chapter. Phenomena such as storms, lightning and waves have both object-like and event-like properties, so that they are problematic with respect to the universal distinction in human languages between nouns and verbs. Hence their appearance in different languages in different grammatical categories.

In certain cases the problematic nature of the fit between world and language derives from both factors (the indeterminate nature of linguistic and real-world categories). Consider, for example, the question of whether the kind of Aboriginal incursions mentioned by Blainey in the first text discussed in Chapter 1 (page 15) constitute tokens of the category of 'invasions' or not. Does this linguistic category include the kind of natural (often temporary) migrations of peoples from one area to another – migrations which may not involve significant aggression towards the traditional occupiers? Or does the category include only those migrations which comprise hostile actions with the intention of establishing permanent occupation and ownership? As a native speaker of English, I do not have any firm intuitions on this question, though I incline towards the latter view. But even if I do make a clear distinction, such that 'invasions' are necessarily characterised by hostility and the intention to establish permanent occupation and ownership, there will clearly be many events in the world that remain problematic with respect to this scheme of categorisation.

In all these situations where either linguistic categories or real-world phenomena pose classificatory problems, language proves to be an ideal tool for focusing on certain aspects of a phenomenon and backgrounding others, for imposing certain classificatory schemas, leading in turn to the construction of certain explanatory schemas. In some cases, these possibilities undoubtedly lead to the use of language as an instrument of ideological manipulation. More insidiously, however, the speaker's selection of a particular term, or a particular way of structuring an experience, may be a much less conscious process than the notion of manipulation suggests. It seems much more likely that the construction of meaning operates in terms of a whole range of presuppositions and acquired practices that lie below the level of our conscious awareness. For example, how many speakers were aware until relatively recently of the existence of sexist discourse and of its ideological sources? It is only by making some of these processes explicit that we can develop an awareness of the relationship between language and ideology.

This view of the nature of the relationship between language and 'reality' also has important implications for our understanding of the nature of meaning. If language is as indeterminate as the preceding discussion suggests, the question arises as to how communication normally succeeds as well as it does. On the epiphenomenalist view, the problematic nature of the process derives from the fact that language is only one of the ingredients involved in the production of meaning. The contribution of the knowledge base of the addressee (and of the speaker) is crucial. Language does not 'convey' meaning, it simply helps the understander to produce it. This point is illustrated in a particularly clear way in reading *The Inheritors*. One of the intriguing features of this novel is the fact that the reader does succeed (though not without some difficulty) in understanding the text, even though the language is in many respects quite alien. Consider, in particular the following extract from the passage discussed in Chapter 3.

> *A stick rose upright. It began to grow shorter at both ends, then it shot out to full length again. The tree by Lok's ear acquired a voice. "Clop!" By his face there had grown a twig – a twig that smelt of other and of the bitter berries that Lok's stomach told him he must not eat.*

It is an interesting exercise to present this passage to a class of students who are unfamiliar with the novel, in order to discover how much background information is needed for the reader to make sense of it. As the text unfolds, one person comments – 'it's silly', another asks 'is it a plant?' while a third suggests 'it's a dream'. In the absence of any contextual information, people either give up the attempt to make sense of it or try various hypotheses in order to make the text fit into their conceptual framework. Sticks do not normally perform movements on their own but may do so if they are parts of plants, or if the normal laws of physics are suspended, as in a dream. Gradually informants move to more specific interpretations. The sentences involving the twig produce the interpretation that 'something has hit the tree' ('is it a bird?'). In order to make progress beyond this, however, further information concerning the context usually needs to be provided. When informants are told that they should imagine the narrator as a Neanderthaler, who knows that there is someone else across the river in the trees, where he can see the stick behaving in a peculiar way, interpretation begins to close in. One tentatively suggests a gun and finally arrives at the bow and arrow explanation. The exercise shows quite clearly that the construction of meaning involves an ongoing process of hypothesis formation, involving interaction between language and the understander's mental store. The richness and success of a particular hypothesis at a particular moment depends on the relevance of that area of the store to which the understander has access at that moment.

That this process is not an artefact of the literary text is shown by an experimental study conducted by Bransford and Johnson (1972). They investigated the reactions of informants when presented with such texts as the one below.

> The procedure is actually quite simple. First you arrange things into different groups. Of course, one pile may be sufficient depending on how much there is to do. If you have to go somewhere else due to lack of facilities that is the next step otherwise you are pretty well set. It is important not to overdo things. That is, it is better to do too few things at once than too many. In the short run this may not seem important but complications can easily arise. A mistake can be expensive as well. At first the whole procedure will seem complicated. Soon, however, it will become just another facet of life. It is difficult to foresee any end to the necessity for this task in the immediate future, but then one never can tell. After the procedure is completed one arranges the materials into different groups again. Then they can be put into their appropriate places. Eventually they will be used once more and the whole cycle will then have to be repeated. However, that is part of life.

Not surprisingly, they discovered that most informants find it difficult to make a great deal of sense of this text in isolation but that the passage becomes much more meaningful when it is brought into interaction with specific areas of a listener's knowledge base (in this case the washing of clothes). The same is true even of individual sentences. Examples such as *The journey was not delayed because the bottle shattered* and *The haystack was important because the cloth ripped* seem quite anomalous at first sight but much less so when they interact with specific contextual information (our knowledge of what is involved in the naming of a ship in the first case or a parachute jump in the second). It is important to note that these texts do not become meaningful simply because they reproduce items of information contained in the knowledge base but that they produce new and quite specific meanings, once the very general information present in the hearer's knowledge base is applied to the process of interpretation.

The nature of categories is intimately connected with the nature of meaning and with the process of metaphor in a number of ways. Once we abandon the Objectivist view that our native language organises the world into clear-cut, discrete, homogeneous categories, we also have to abandon the idea that communication involves the transmission of a clearly structured object-like meaning from speaker to listener. However, in order to make sense of the world, we clearly do have to make connections between different areas of experience and many of these connections are shared by other speakers of our language. This is due to the existence of certain conceptual units in our language – units which constitute the building blocks of our experience – and because of the existence of certain ways of talking about events that are prevalent in our speech community.

Metaphor plays a crucial role in the process of understanding in two ways. First, it provides us with a way of connecting various domains of experience to each other in that it allows us to construct relatively abstract domains of experience in terms of the more concrete domains of physical activity and physical space. Secondly, it provides us with alternative ways of conceptualising particular areas of experience, for example by talking about argument in terms of war, in terms of a game, in terms of a commercial operation (*I don't want to buy into that one*), in terms of a dance or in other ways that have not been generally exploited as yet. The crucial property of metaphor is that the process is entirely open. There are relatively few constraints on the construction of 'likeness' and the complexity of our social and conceptual world, the fact that it is constantly changing and developing, means that there is no upper bound on the innovative capacity of the process.

Variety, discourse, genre

VARIETY

We have devoted a good deal of attention in this book to the classificatory role of language in the mediation of 'reality'. We have, however, tended to take for granted the classificatory terms that we apply to language itself – terms such as 'variety', 'discourse' and 'genre'. Like many of the other classificatory concepts discussed here, these terms are far from unproblematic.

Let us take first the notion of variety, since this is in some ways the most sharply defined of these concepts. In principle a linguistic variety (or 'dialect') is characterisable in terms of a particular cluster of phonological, lexical and grammatical features. One might approach the task of describing Cockney, for example, by identifying particular pronunciations which differentiate Cockney from other varieties of English and then go on to specify certain grammatical and lexical usages that are also peculiar to this variety. The important point to note here is that the variety is not defined by a single feature (the use of a glottal stop in words like *bottle*, *water*, *city*, for example) but by a whole range of such features. A similar approach might be adopted to the description of Broad Australian English, Platt-Deutsch and other linguistic varieties. The Objectivist view of language takes such constructs to be 'real' entities which have some kind of objective existence in the world.

However, one of the most important findings of work in sociolinguistics in the last twenty years or so is that the concept of variety, although undoubtedly a useful one for certain purposes, involves a considerable degree of abstraction away from patterns of actual language use on the ground. Findings in sociolinguistic research have undermined the assumption that speakers can be unambiguously assigned to specific varieties of language on the basis of fixed correlational patterns in their speech. It has been shown, for example, that individual speakers tend to modify their speech as they move from one kind of context to another but that it would be a gross oversimplification to describe this in terms of switching from one variety to another. The phenomenon of style shifting is a gradient phenomenon involving relative frequencies of pronunciations rather than a wholesale switch from one pattern to a quite different one (Trudgill 1974: 45). Patterns can be complex in that pronunciations of a particular set of words may undergo much greater change than others that are related to it by the dialect model. Even within a single 'style' there may be a considerable amount of somewhat unpatterned variation – an observation that does not sit comfortably either with the idea that speakers are using a particular 'dialect' or that they are switching between dialects. The problematic nature of the assumptions built into the notion of variety is discussed at length by Le Page and Tabouret-Keller 1985 (ch. 1).

There is one situation in which the concept of a homogeneous linguistic variety is viable – the case of a national standard language. The fact that so much linguistic research focuses on standard languages, for all kinds of (non-linguistic) reasons, should not however be allowed to obscure the fact that standard languages are in many respects artificial entities, superimposed on an underlying stratum characterised by extensive variation. It would run counter to the nature of the argument being put forward here to attempt to count the number of 'languages' in the world today but those who are prepared to accept the degree of idealisation and abstraction required by this exercise usually estimate the number to be in the region of five thousand. Yet less than one hundred of these are national standard languages. There is therefore an important sense in which these national standard languages do not accurately represent the phenomenon of language. Moreover, even in a country such as Britain with a well-established educational system, less than 20 per cent of the population are speakers of standard English, according to an estimate of Peter Trudgill (personal communication).

The basic point then is that, when the forms of language are themselves subject to categorisation, the varietal categories employed are as problematic as are other category notions discussed in this book. The usefulness of the concept of variety stems from the fact that there are close similarities in the speech of particular groups of speakers occupying a particular area of regional and/or social space. These similarities can be characterised as a cluster of features that constitute the core of the category. This does not however, imply that all speakers will exhibit all the relevant features in all situations. Rather, their speech will approximate more or less closely to the central area in terms of their position in the complex structures of social space. There are clear parallels here with Lakoff's notion of categories as radial structures – the concept appears to be as applicable to the categories we apply to language itself as it does to those that we apply to other areas of experience.

DISCOURSE

Within the field of contemporary sociolinguistics, there are two rather different research traditions. The kind of research indicated in the preceding discussion of the concept of variety has concerned itself primarily with variation involving the formal elements of language, particularly with variation in phonological and grammatical systems. The second strand of research, associated with linguists such as Dell Hymes and John Gumperz, is concerned with variation in what ethnographers of communication call 'different ways of speaking' within a particular culture (for a useful review of this field see Saville-Troike 1982). We have used the term 'discourse' informally in this book to indicate this notion. The concept is intuitively quite clear – particularly as many of these 'ways of speaking' have informal names in our culture – banter, scolding, hectoring, pleading, joking, pontificating and so on. There is some relationship between discourse and variety, since both dimensions of variation are related to variation in the social context. If we were giving a speech at a funeral, for example, it is unlikely that we would use the vernacular end of our accent range and it is equally unlikely that we would adopt a jocular speech style. The texts discussed in the previous chapter provide ample illustration of the way in which certain areas of the dialect spectrum may be closely associated with certain ways of speaking.

There are nevertheless important differences between the two dimensions of variation. In the first place, it is often extremely difficult not only to define a particular discourse but even to know what **kind** of features might characterise it. Although we would normally recognise banter, for example, it is far from obvious precisely what cues trigger our recognition of the fact that someone is teasing us (and we do, of course, occasionally fail to recognise this). Secondly, the ways of speaking found in a particular culture do not constitute a particular 'set' in the way that varieties do. Subject to the kind of qualifications expressed in the preceding section, it is possible to suggest quite plausibly that there are, for example, thirty varieties of Swiss German (Watts 1988: 317) or (rather less plausibly) that there are four varieties of Australian

English (Bernard 1985: 18). But no linguist has yet been so bold as to attempt to identify the number of different ways of speaking within a particular culture. A third difficulty is that discourses interact with each other in complex ways in the production of text, as we have seen in the course of this book. The fact that a single word or phrase can evoke a specific way of speaking (the evocation of religious discourses in the 'nukespeak text' simply through the use of a word such as *awesome*) makes possible significant discursive complexities. The ubiquity of metaphor is also a factor in these interactions.

These difficulties are no doubt part of the reason for the uncomfortable fact that the term 'discourse' is used to cover a wide range of phenomena – phenomena that will almost certainly need to be recategorised as we come to understand better the nature of discursive practices. In this book I have undoubtedly been guilty of inconsistencies in this respect, using the term to cover a wide range of practices from such relatively well-documented phenomena as sexist discourse to ways of speaking that are easy to recognise in particular texts but difficult to describe in general terms (competitive discourse, discourse of solidarity etc.). The kind of textual analysis that is currently being undertaken by those working in the field is an essential preliminary to the development of a more adequate theory of discourse than we have at present.

GENRE

The distinction between genre and discourse, although again intuitively clear, is even more difficult to make than that between discourse and variety. The intuitive distinction rests on the fact that not only do we recognise particular ways of speaking but we also recognise particular categories of text. Again these text types have well-established names such as sermon, lecture, after-dinner speech, conversation, official memorandum, interview. This notion is, of course, derived from the concept of genre in literary criticism, where it is also associated with particular types of text such as epic, drama, novel, sonnet.

Perhaps the major difference between the concept of genre and that of discourse has to do with the fact that genre is much more oriented to the nature of the formal character of a text than is that of discourse. Whereas discourses may involve the expression of certain kinds of meaning often deriving from particular perspectives (for example male-oriented meanings), genres are concerned with particular forms. In the case of the second text discussed in Chapter 7 (pages 144–5), there is a range of formal properties that identify it as an official memorandum. Similarly there are very specific formal features that characterise the television commercials discussed in the previous chapter. Context also plays a particularly important part in the identification of genres. Although there might be little difference of content between an archbishop's address to the congregation in Westminster Abbey and a radio talk given by the same speaker, the former constitutes a much better example of a sermon than the latter.

Lakoff's theory of categories also has a good deal of light to throw on the nature of generic categories. One of the difficulties with the concept of 'novel', for example, is that it covers an enormous range of texts, some of which appear to have very little in common with others. The same is true of non-literary genres. Although the concept of official memorandum is a reasonably familiar one, it would be extremely difficult to draw up a list of characteristics that every official memorandum must possess, though it might be possible to identify a cluster of features that constitute the central core, with individual members of the category connecting to the core in a variety of dimensions. Related to this point is the fact that genres may change and develop. Although we think of the television commercial as a fairly stable genre, for example, early examples of this genre bear very little relationship to contemporary commercials. Early commercials were usually much more closely integrated into the surrounding programmes, with the compère of a show simply taking a few minutes out to advertise the sponsoring product. Today commercials are much more like mini-movies and are quite clearly demarcated from the surrounding programmes.[1] These developments have allowed quite new structures to emerge – the distinction between the Comment and the Actor component, for example, that now plays an important role in the genre. Lakoff's concept of chaining provides a clear explanation of how quite disparate texts can nevertheless be thought of as members of the same genre and in general of how genres – which we think of as relatively stable structures – can change and develop.

Conclusion

Perhaps the main reason why the distinctions between such concepts as variety, discourse and genre are so difficult to draw (although they are intuitively reasonably clear) have to do with the fact that there are so many different dimensions of variation in language, each enjoying a certain amount of autonomy with respect to the others but also cutting across each other in complex ways. The dimensions involve phonological structure, grammatical structure, semantics, cultural processes, contexts, textual forms and many others. Since we observe that features within these various dimensions cluster together in certain patterns, we apply our categorial frameworks to these structures. However, the complex connections across the dimensions mean that these concepts also cut across each other in intricate ways. Certain areas are somewhat more autonomous than others – the formal aspects of language structure enjoy a good deal of independence with respect to the other components, so that the concept of variety is relatively distinct. However, linguists have perhaps tended to exaggerate the degree of autonomy of these various elements, particularly in their attempts to single out the formal aspects of language for special attention. Even in recent sociolinguistics there has been a tendency for the two strands of research mentioned above – variation theory and the ethnography of communication – to operate as independent traditions. It has been part of our aim here to subvert that distinction. This boundary, like others we have attempted to cross – between spoken and written forms, between 'high' and 'low' genres, between literary and non-literary texts – is itself a product of the compulsive tendency of the human mind to divide the phenomena of experience into neatly differentiated compartments. The attempt to move across it follows from our general concerns with the problematic nature of classificatory processes and with the heterogeneous nature of language itself.

Note

1. I owe this point to Graeme Turner.

References

Ashcroft B, Griffiths G, Tiffin H 1989 *The Empire writes back: theory and practice in post-colonial literatures*. Routledge, London.

Austin J L 1962 *How to do things with words*. Oxford University Press, Oxford.

Baker S 1966 *The Australian language*. Currawong, Sydney.

Bakhtin M M 1981 Discourse in the novel. In Holquist M (ed) *The dialogic imagination*. University of Texas Press, Austin, pp 259–422.

Beedham C 1983 Language, indoctrination and nuclear arms. *University of East Anglia Papers in Linguistics* 19: 15–31.

Beier U 1980 *Voices of independence: new Black writing from Papua New Guinea*. University of Queensland Press, Brisbane.

Bernard J R L 1962 The need for a dictionary of Australian English. *Southerly* 22: 92–100.

Bernard J R L 1985 Australian Pronunciation. In *The Macquarie Dictionary* (revised edn). The Macquarie Library, Dee Why pp 18–27.

Blainey G 1980 *A land half-won*. Macmillan, Melbourne.

Bodine A 1975 Androcentrism in prescriptive grammar. *Language in Society* 4: 129–46.

Brändle M 1989 Revelations of Swiss Pluralism. *Institute of Modern Languages Occasional Papers* (University of Queensland) 3: 38–68.

Bransford J D, Johnson M K 1972 Contextual prerequisites for understanding. *Journal of Verbal Learning and Verbal Behavior* 11: 717–26.

Brown G 1977 *Listening to spoken English*. Longman, London.

Brown P, Levinson S 1978 Universals in language usage. In Goody E N (ed) *Questions and politeness: strategies in social interaction*. Cambridge University Press pp 56–289.

Brugman C 1983 The use of body part terms as locatives in Chalcatongo Mixtec. In *Survey of California and Other Languages* (Report no. 4). University of California, Berkeley, pp 235–90.

Brugman C 1984 Metaphor in the elaboration of grammatical categories in Mixtec. Linguistics Department, University of California, Berkeley.

Cameron D 1985 *Feminism and linguistic theory*. St Martin's Press, New York.

Cameron D, McAlinden F, O'Leary K 1989 Lakoff in context: the social and linguistic function of tag questions. In Coates, Cameron (eds) pp 74–93.

Carroll J B (ed) 1971 *Language, thought and reality: selected writings of Benjamin Lee Whorf* (first published 1956). MIT Press, Cambridge, Mass.

Carroll J B, Casagrande J B 1958 The functions of language classifications in behaviour. In Maccoby E E, Newcombe T M, Hartley E M (eds) *Readings in social psychology*. Holt, New York pp 18–31.

Cheshire J 1978 Present tense verbs in Reading English. In Trudgill P (ed) *Sociolinguistic patterns in British English*. Edward Arnold, London pp 52–68.

Cheshire J 1982 *Variation in an English dialect*. Cambridge University Press, Cambridge.

Cheshire J 1984 The relationship between language and sex in English. In Trudgill P (ed) *Applied sociolinguistics*. Academic Press, London pp 33–49.

Chilton P 1985 *Language and the nuclear arms debate: nukespeak today*. Francis Pinter, London.

Chomsky N A 1957 *Syntactic structures*. Mouton, The Hague.

Chomsky N A 1965 *Aspects of the theory of syntax*. MIT Press, Cambridge, Mass.

Chomsky N A 1986 *Knowledge of language: its nature, origin and use*. Praeger, New York.

Christ R B (ed) 1965 *Schweizer dialekte*. Birkhäuser, Basel.

Clark H H, Clark E V 1977 *Psychology and language*. Harcourt, Brace, Jovanovich, New York.

Coates J 1987 Epistemic modality and spoken discourse. *Transactions of the Philological Society*. 110–31.

Coates J 1989 Gossip revisited: language in all-female groups. In Coates, Cameron (eds) pp 94–122.

Coates J, Cameron D 1989 (eds) *Women in their speech communities*. Longman, London.

Cochrane G R 1989 Origins and development of the Australian accent. In Collins, Blair (eds) pp 176–86.

Coffey C 1984 Language: a transformative key. *Language in Society* 13: 511–13.

Collins P, Blair D (eds) 1989 *Australian English: the language of a new society*. University of Queensland Press, Brisbane.

Crosby F, Nyquist L 1977 The female register: an empirical study of Lakoff's hypothesis. *Language in Society* 6: 289–94.

Crystal D 1980 Neglected grammatical factors in conversational English. In Greenbaum S, Leech G, Svartvik, J *Studies in English Linguistics*. Longman, London pp 153–166.

Derrida J 1982 *Margins of philosophy*. University of Chicago Press, Chicago.

Dijk T van (ed) 1985 *Handbook of discourse analysis* (vol 4). Academic Press, London.

Dixon R M W 1972 *The Dyirbal language of North Queensland*. Cambridge University Press, London.

Downes W 1984 *Language and society*. Fontana, London.

Edwards J 1985 *Language, society and identity*. Blackwell, Oxford.

Fasold R 1984 *The sociolinguistics of society*. Blackwell, Oxford.

Faulkner W 1964 *The sound and the fury* (first published 1931). Penguin, Harmondsworth.

Ferguson C 1959 Diglossia. *Word* 15: 325–40.

Fishman P M 1983 Interaction: the work women do. In Thorne, Kramarae, Henley (eds) pp 89–101.

Forster E M 1936 *A passage to India* (first published 1921). Penguin, Harmondsworth.

Foucault M 1971 Orders of discourse. *Social Science Information* 102: 7–30.

Foucault M 1972 *The archaeology of knowledge*. Tavistock, London.

Fowler R, Hodge R V, Kress G R, Trew A (eds) 1979 *Language and control*. Routledge & Kegan Paul, London.

Fowler R, Kress G 1979a Rules and regulations. In Fowler *et al.* (eds) pp 26–45.

Fowler R, Kress G 1979b Critical linguistics. In Fowler *et al.* (eds) pp 185–213.

Furphy T C 1944 *Such is life* (first published 1903). Angus & Robertson, Sydney.

Geertz C 1960 *The religion of Java*. The Free Press, New York.

Goffman E 1967 *Interaction rituals: essays in face to face behaviour*. Doubleday, New York.

Golding W 1961 *The Inheritors*. Faber & Faber, London.

Goldman L R 1987 Ethnographic interpretations of parent–child discourse in Huli. *Journal of Child Language* 14: 447–66.

Graham A 1975 The making of a non-sexist dictionary. In Thorne, Henley (eds) pp 57–63.

Haas A 1979 The acquisition of genderlect. In Orasanu J, Slater M, Adler L *Language, sex and gender: does la différence make a difference? Annals of the New York Academy of Sciences* 327: 101–13.

Halliday M A K 1970 Functional diversity in language as seen from a consideration of modality and mood in English. *Foundations of Language* 6: 322–61.

Halliday M A K 1971 Linguistic function and literary style: an inquiry into the language of William Golding's *The Inheritors*. In Chatman, S (ed) *Literary style: a symposium*. Oxford University Press, London and New York pp 330–68.

Heider E (E Rosch) 1971 'Focal' color areas and the development of color names. *Developmental Psychology* 4: 447–55.

Hodge R V, Kress G R, Jones G 1979 The ideology of middle management. In Fowler *et al.* (eds) pp 81–93.

Holmes J 1984 Hedging your bets and sitting on the fence. *Te Reo* 27: 47–62.

Hough G 1970 Narrative and dialogue in Jane Austen. *The Critical Quarterly* 12: 201–29.

Huddleston R D 1984 *Introduction to the grammar of English.* Cambridge University Press, Cambridge.

Hudson R A 1980 *Sociolinguistics.* Cambridge University Press, Cambridge.

Joos M 1966 *Readings in linguistics* (4th edn). University of Chicago Press, Chicago.

Katz J J, Fodor J A 1964 The structure of a semantic theory. In Fodor J A, Katz J J (eds) *The structure of language.* Prentice-Hall, Englewood Cliffs pp 479–518.

Kiernan B (ed) 1982 *The essential Henry Lawson.* Currey O'Neill, Melbourne.

Knapp S, Michaels W B 1987 Against Theory 2: hermeneutics and deconstruction. *Critical Inquiry* 14: 49–68.

Kress G R 1976 *Halliday: system and function in language.* Oxford University Press, London.

Kress G R 1985 Ideological structures in discourse. In van Dijk (ed) pp 27–42.

Kress G R 1986 Language in the media: the construction of public and private. *Media Culture and Society* 8: 395–419.

Kress G R 1989 Towards a social account of linguistic change. *Journal of Pragmatics* 13: 455–66.

Kress G R, Fowler R 1979 *Interviews.* In Fowler *et al.* (eds).

Kress G R, Hodge R V 1979 *Language as ideology.* Routledge & Kegan Paul, London.

Kress G R, Trew A 1978 Ideological transformation of discourse: or how *The Sunday Times* got *its* message across. *Journal of Pragmatics* 2: 311–29.

Labov W 1969 The logic of non-standard English. *Monograph series on language and linguistics* (Georgetown) 22: 1–43.

Labov W 1972a *Sociolinguistic patterns.* Blackwell, Oxford.

Labov W 1972b *Language in the inner city.* Blackwell, Oxford.

Lakoff G 1987 *Women, fire and dangerous things: what categories reveal about the mind.* University of Chicago Press, Chicago.

Lakoff G, Johnson M 1980 *Metaphors we live by.* University of Chicago Press, Chicago.

Lakoff R 1975 *Language and woman's place.* Harper & Row, New York.

Langacker R W 1987 *Foundations of cognitive grammar.* Stanford University Press, Stanford.

Lavandera B 1978 Where does the sociolinguistic variable stop? *Language in Society* 7: 171–82.

Le Page R B, Tabouret-Keller A 1985 *Acts of identity.* Cambridge University Press, Cambridge.

Lee D A 1984 Image and speech style in the Australian television commercial. *AUMLA* (Journal of the Australasian Universities Language and Literature Association) 61: 52–68.

Lee D A 1986 *Language, children and society.* Harvester, Brighton.

Lee D A 1987 The semantics of *just. Journal of Pragmatics* 11: 377–98.

Lee D A 1989a Discourse: does it hang together? *Journal of Cultural Studies* 31: 58–72.

Lee D A 1989b Sociolinguistic variation in the speech of Brisbane adolescents. *Australian Journal of Linguistics* 9: 51–72 .

Lee D A 1990 Text, meaning and author intention: a linguist's perspective on 'Against Theory 2'. *Journal of Literary Semantics* 19: 166–86.

Lyons J 1968 *Introduction to theoretical linguistics.* Cambridge University Press, Cambridge.

Maltz D N, Borker R A 1982 A cultural approach to male–female miscommunication. In Gumperz J J (ed) *Language and Social Identity.* Cambridge University Press, Cambridge (England) and New York pp 196–216.

Meditch A 1975 The development of sex-specific speech patterns in young children. *Anthropological Linguistics* 17: 421–33.

Moore T, Carling C 1982 *Understanding language: towards a post-Chomskyan linguistics.* Macmillan, London.

New W H 1978 New Language, New World. In Narasimhaiah C D (ed) *Awakened conscience.* Sterling, New Delhi pp 361–77.

Ooi Boo Eng 1984 Malaysia and Singapore. *Journal of Commonwealth Literature* 19: 93–9.

Owen M 1983 *Apologies and remedial exchanges.* Mouton, Berlin.

Palmer F R 1977 Modals and actuality. *Journal of Linguistics* 13: 1–23.

Pap L 1990 The language situation in Switzerland. *Lingua* 80: 109–48.

Rao R 1961 *Kanthapura.* New Directions, New York.

Reddy M J 1979 The conduit metaphor – a case frame conflict in our language about language. In Ortony A (ed) *Metaphor and thought.* Cambridge University Press, Cambridge pp 284–324.

Rosch E 1973 Natural Categories. *Cognitive Psychology* 4: 328–50.

Sanders N (nd) Selling Woomera: weapons testing and civil defence. *Intervention* 18: 8–32.

Saussure F de 1974 *Course in general linguistics* (first published 1916). Fontana, London.

Saville-Troike M 1982 *The ethnography of communication: an introduction*. Blackwell, Oxford.

Schläpfer R (ed) 1985 *La Suisse aux quatres langues*. Editions Zoë, Geneva.

Schmidt A 1985 *Young people's Dyirbal*. Cambridge University Press, Cambridge.

Schulz M 1975 The semantic derogation of woman. In Thorne, Henley (eds) pp 64–75.

Shnukal A 1979 *A sociolinguistic study of Australian English*. PhD dissertation, University of Georgetown, University Microfilms International, Ann Arbor.

Shnukal A 1989 Pidgins and creoles. In Jupp J (ed) *The Australian People: an encyclopedia of the nation, its people and their origins*. Angus & Robertson, Sydney pp 153–9.

Silveira J 1980 Generic masculine words and thinking. *Women's International Quarterly* 32: 165–78.

Slobin D I 1982 Universal and particular in the acquisition of language. In Wanner E, Gleitman L R (eds) *Language acquisition: the state of the art*. Cambridge University Press, Cambridge.

Spender D 1980 *Man-made language*. Routledge & Kegan Paul, London.

Stanley J P 1977 Paradigmatic woman: the prostitute. In Shores D L, Himnes C P (eds) *Papers on language variation*. University of Alabama Press, Birmingham, Alabama pp 303–21.

Steinberg J 1976 *Why Switzerland?* Cambridge University Press, Cambridge.

Stirling L 1987 Language and gender in Australian newspapers. In Pauwels A (ed) *Language and gender in Australian and New Zealand society*. Australian Professional Publications, Sydney pp 108–28.

Sussex R 1989 The Americanisation of Australian English. In Collins, Blair (eds) pp 158–68.

Sykes M 1985 Discrimination in discourse. In van Dijk (ed) 83–101.

Thomson J R, Chapman R S 1977 "Who is Daddy?" revisited: the status of two-year-olds' over-extended words in use and comprehension. *Journal of Child Language* 4: 359–75.

Thorne B, Henley N (eds) 1975 *Language and sex: difference and dominance*. Newbury House, Rowley MA.

Thorne B, Kramarae C, Henley N (eds) 1983 *Language, gender and society*. Newbury House, Rowley MA.

Todd L 1974 *Pidgins and creoles*. Routledge and Kegan Paul, London.

Trew A 1979 Theory and ideology at work. In Fowler *et al.* (eds) 94–116.

Trudgill P 1972 Sex, covert prestige and linguistic change in the urban British English of Norwich. *Language in Society* 1: 179–95.

Trudgill P 1974 *Sociolinguistics*. Penguin, Harmondsworth.

Twain M 1967 *The adventures of Huckleberry Finn* (first published 1885). Holt, Rinehart & Winston, New York & London.

Ward J 1984 Check out your sexism. *Women and Language* 7: 41–3.

Wardhaugh R 1986 *The sociolinguistics of society*. Blackwell, Oxford.

Wardhaugh R 1987 *Languages in competition*. Blackwell, Oxford.

Watts R 1988 Language, dialect and national identity in Switzerland. *Multilingua* 7: 313–34.

Wax M L and Wax R H 1971 Cultural deprivation as an educational ideology. In Leacock E B (ed) *The culture of poverty: a critique*. Simon & Schuster, New York.

Weinreich U 1952 *Research problems in bilingualism with special reference to Switzerland*. PhD thesis, Columbia University.

West C, Zimmermann D 1977 Women's place in everyday talk: reflections on parent–child interaction. *Social Problems* 24: 521–9.

Whorf B L 1971a Discussion of Hopi linguistics. In Carroll (ed) pp 102–111.

Whorf B L 1971b Grammatical categories. In Carroll (ed) pp 87–101.

Whorf B L 1971c Languages and logic. In Carroll (ed) pp 233–45.

Whorf B L 1971d Science and linguistics. In Carroll (ed) pp 207–19.

Whorf B L 1971e A linguistic consideration of thinking in primitive communities. In Carroll (ed) pp 65–86.

Wierzbicka A 1986 Does language reflect culture?: some evidence from Australian English. *Language in Society* 15: 349–74.

Zimmermann D, West C 1975 Sex roles, interruptions and silences in conversation. In Thorne, Henley (eds) pp 105–129.

Index